SUBSIDIA MEDIAEVALIA

6

Cantaria be marie in ecclia sancte marie magdalene de Toneworth·

Quartodecimo die mensis novembr. Anno dni ... suprascripto idem Reverendus pater apud Westenham Wygorniensis dioc. ad primam Cantariam be marie virginis in ecclia proch. sancte marie magdalene de Toneworth dci dioc. nunc primo fundatam dmi Johem Blakenhale pbrm ad presentacionem nobilis mulieris Rosie alias dicte Rose mountfort admisit et capellanum perpetuum iuxta formam fundacoe predce ac ordinacois ... patris proprii in ea parte faciende de fideliter deserviendo eidem cantarie e de observando contenta in fundacoe e ordinacoe ... ad sancta dei evangelia p eundem corporaliter tacta iuramentum instituit canonice in eadem cum suis iuribz omnibz e ptin universis et sunt idem Johannes lras institucionis sub forma que sequit· Ricardus pmissione divina Wygorniensis Epus dilco filio Johi Blakenhale pbro salutem gram e ben. Ad primam cantariam beate marie virginis in ecclia prochiali sancte marie magdalene de Toneworth nre dioc. iam primo fundatam ad quam p nobilem mulierem Rosiam alias dictam Rosam mountfort nobis presentatus existis. te isto quarto decimo die mensis novembr. Anno dni milimo quadringentesimo quarto in forma iuris ... te dicte cantarie capellanum perpetuum iuxta formam fundacois predce ac ordinacois iuxta p nos in hac parte faciende de fideliter deserviendo cantarie eidem e de observando contenta in fundacoe e ordinacoe predce ad sancta dei evangelia p te corporaliter tacta iuramentum instituimus canonice in eadem cum suis iuribz, oneribz e ptinentiis universis specialibz iuribz e consuetudinibz ac iure Wygorniensis ecclie dignitate in omnibz semp salvis In quor testimonium sigillum nrm fecimus hiis apponi· Dat apud Westenham die e anno dni supradscripto Et nre translacois anno quarto Quibz pdce Johes miserunt etiam dno tunc ibidem et sunt mandatum ad inducend directum·

Secunda Cantaria beate marie virginis in eadem ecclia de Toneworth

Eisdem die mense anno dni e loco quibz ... supra pfatus Reverendus pater ad secundam Cantariam be marie virginis in ecclia prochiali sancte marie magdalene de Toneworth sue dioc. nunc primo fundatam Ricardum Wyre pbrm ad presentacionem nobilis mulieris Rosie alias dicte Rose mountfort admisit et capellanum perpetuum iuxta formam fundacoe predce ac ordinacois ipius patris p ipm in ea parte faciende de fideliter deserviendo eidem cantarie e de observando contenta in fundacoe e ordinacoe pdce ad sancta dei evangelia p eundem Ricm corporaliter tacta iuramentum instituit canonice in eadem cum suis iuribz oliibz e ptin universis Quibz die e loco ... Ricardus miserunt etiam dno et sunt lras institucionis sub forma px supra annotata mutatis mutandis ac ad inducend directum

Ecclia sancte Wereburge Bristoll

Decimo die mensis Decembr·. Anno dni milimo cccc quarto dns Reverendus pater in ... sua london Vacationem prochi sancte Wereburge Bristoll sue dioc. p mortem dni Johis ... ultimi Rectoris eiusdem vacantem Willm Longeshurr clicum ad ... Religiosos viros· Abbe e conventus monasterij de Kenesham in psenti

THE REGISTER
OF RICHARD CLIFFORD
BISHOP OF WORCESTER,
1401-1407

A CALENDAR

BY

WALDO E. L. SMITH
M.A. (Toronto), Ph.D. (Edinburgh), D.D. (St. Andrews)
Emeritus Professor of Church History
Queen's Theological College
Kingston, Ontario

PONTIFICAL INSTITUTE OF MEDIAEVAL STUDIES
TORONTO, CANADA
1976

ACKNOWLEDGMENT

This book has been published with the help of a grant from the Humanities Research Council of Canada, using funds provided by the Canada Council.

CANADIAN CATALOGUING IN PUBLICATION DATA

SMITH, Waldo E.L., 1901-
   The register of Richard Clifford, Bishop of Worcester, 1401-1407, a calendar

(Subsidia mediaevalia ; 6 ISSN 0316-0769)

Bibliography: p.
Includes index.
ISBN 0-88844-355-2 pa.

1. Worcester, Eng. (Diocese) — History — Sources.
I. Worcester, Eng. (Diocese) Bishop, 1401-1407 (Richard Clifford). Register of Richard Clifford.
II. Pontifical Institute of Mediaeval Studies.
III. Title. IV. Series.

CD1068.W7S55   282'.424'4   C76-017090-8

PRINTED BY UNIVERSA PRESS, WETTEREN, BELGIUM

CONTENTS

BIBLIOGRAPHICAL REFERENCES

BL, Add. MSS	British Library, Additional Manuscripts
C.C.R.	*Calendar of the Close Rolls.* Public Record Office. London, 1902-.
C.F.R.	*Calendar of the Fine Rolls.* Public Record Office. London, 1911-.
C.I.C.	*Corpus Iuris Canonici,* ed. A. Friedberg. Leipzig, 1879-1881, 2 vols.
C.P.L.	*Calendar of Entries in the Papal Registers referring to Great Britain and Ireland. Papal Letters.* Public Record Office. London, 1893-.
C. Pat. R.	*Calendar of Patent Rolls.* Public Record Office. London, 1901-.
Emden, *Cambridge*	A. B. Emden, *A Biographical Register of the University of Cambridge to 1500.* Cambridge, 1963.
Emden, *Oxford*	A. B. Emden, *A Biographical Register of the University of Oxford to A. D. 1500.* Oxford, 1957-59.
Foedera	T. Rymer, *Foedera, conventiones, literae,* etc. (ed. Thomas Rymer, London, 1740).
Liber Albus	Liber Albus. Worcester Cathedral Library. MS A5.
Lyndwood	William Lyndwood, *Provinciale (seu constitutiones Angliae),* ed. H. Hall. Oxford, 1679.
P.R.O.	Public Record Office, London.
Reg.	Bishop's register followed by the name of the bishop.
Rot. Parl.	*Rotuli Parliamentorum,* Public Record Office, London, undated. 6 vols.
Sext.	*Liber Sextus Decretalium Bonifacii VIII,* cited by book, title and chapter, e.g., *Sext.* 1.14.6.
V.C.H.	*The Victoria History of the Counties of England.*
X	*Decretales* or *Extravagantes Gregorii IX* cited by book, title and chapter, e.g., *X* 1.14.9.

LIST OF ABBREVIATIONS

a. & c.	abbot and convent
abp.	archbishop
abt.	abbot
acol.	acolyte
archdcn.	archdeacon
Aug.	Augustinian
b.ll.	bachelor of laws
B.V.M.	Blessed Virgin Mary
Ben.	Benedictine
bp.	bishop
br.	brother
can.	canon
Cant.	Canterbury
Carm.	Carmelite
cath.	cathedral
ch.	church
chap.	chapter
Chich.	Chichester
chpl.	chapel
chpln.	chaplain
chty.	chantry
Cist.	Cistercian
clk.	clerk
Clun.	Cluniac
coll.	collegiate
conv.	convent
convl.	conventual
ct.	court
d.(etc.)	dimissus, dimissi (etc.)
d. & c.	dean and chapter
dcn.	deacon
d.h.	dimissus ad hunc [ordinem]
d.h.d.	dimissus ad hunc et diaconatus ordines
d.h.p.	dimissus ad hunc et presbyteratus ordines
d.h.s.	dimissus ad hunc et subdiaconatus ordines
d.h.t.	dimissus ad hunc tantum
dioc.	diocese
dn.	dean
dns.	dominus, Sir
d.o.	dimissus ad omnes [ordines]

d.o.s.	dimissus ad omnes sacros ordines
d.s.	dimissus ad subdiaconatus ordines
d.t.	dimissus ad titulum
exch.	exchange
Glouc.	Gloucester
hosp.	hospital
inst.	institution
kt.	knight
l.d.	litterae dimissoriae
l.d.o.	litterae dimissoriae ad omnes ordines
l.d.o.s.	litterae dimissoriae ad omnes sacros ordines
ld.	lord
lic.	licence
m.a.	master of arts
mand.	mandate
mk.	monk
monast.	monastery
Mr.	magister, Master
ny.	nunnery, convent of nuns
O. Carm.	Order of Carmelites
O. Cist.	Order of Cistercians
OESA	Order of Hermits of St. Augustine
OFM	Order of Friars Minor
O. Gilb.	Order of Gilbertines
OP	Order of Friars Preachers
OSA	Order of St. Augustine
OSB	Order of St. Benedict
offl.	official
p.	priest
p. & c.	prior and convent
par.	parish
pat.	patron
p.c.	parish church
p.d.	per [litteras] dimissorias
perp.	perpetual
pr.	prior
preb.	prebend
preby.	prebendary
pry.	priory
r.p.c.	rector of the parish church
rec.	rector
recy.	rectory
Roch.	Rochester
s.d.	sufficienter dimissus
s.d.h.p.	sufficienter dimissus in hac parte
subdcn.	subdeacon
t.b.s.	[dimissus] ad titulum beneficii sui
t.e.s.	[dimissus] ad titulum ecclesiae suae

t.p.s.	[dimissus] ad titulum patrimonii sui
t.s.s.	[dimissus] ad titulum stalli sui
tit.	[ad] titulum
vic.	vicar
vicge.	vicarage
Winch.	Winchester
Worc.	Worcester

If no diocese is given with the name of a church, that church belongs to Worcester diocese. The county is given in the Index of Persons and Places, if this can be determined.

Names in the Index of Ordinations do not appear in the Index of Persons and Places unless the same names are mentioned outside the Ordinations lists. For cross-references, note that the Ordination Lists are sections 108 to 133.

Names in the foot-notes are not indexed when the same names have been indexed in the corresponding text.

INTRODUCTION

I

RICHARD CLIFFORD AS SERVANT OF THE CROWN

Richard Clifford is an example of the mediaeval clerk who rose to high office in the Church through service in the secular government, and his career illustrates the close relationship between Church and State in the Middle Ages. For twenty-one years, 1380 to 1401, the duties he discharged were secular, and even after promotion to be Bishop of Worcester it would seem that concerns other than diocesan received most of his attention. After a six year episcopate he was transferred from Worcester to London where his participation in the life of the Church was more in evidence and included attendance at the Council of Constance during its last sessions.[1] Clifford's career after becoming Bishop of London can be treated in conjunction with his London register.[2] The present introductory essay deals only with his known activities to the end of his tenure of the see of Worcester.

There appears to be no certainty as to his family background. It has been conjectured that he was one of the northern Cliffords prominent in the affairs of Cumberland and Westmoreland, but no clues have appeared that definitely point that way.[3] It is equally permissible to guess that he was of

---

[1] H. Finke, *Acta Concilii Constanciensis* (Münster in W., 1923), 2: 77, 79, *et passim*; J. Lenfant, *Histoire du Concile de Constance* (Amsterdam, 1714), vol. 1, 423.

[2] Guildhall Library, London, MS 9531/4, a cumulative register that includes the registers of Walden, Bubwith, Clifford, Kemp, Grey and Fitzhugh and covers the period 1404-1434/5; Hermann Junghanns, *Zur Geschichte der englischen Kirchenpolitik von 1399 bis 1433* (Freiburg in B., 1915), 35, 68; Historical Manuscripts Commission, 9th Report. Report on the MSS of the Dean and Chapter of St. Paul's (London, 1883), App., pp. 52, 57, 58; E. F. Jacob, *The Register of Henry Chichele, Archbishop of Canterbury*, 1414-1443 (Oxford, 1938-47).

[3] Ibid., 2: 647; T. F. Tout, *Chapters in the Administrative History of Mediaeval England* (Manchester, 1920-33), 5: 54. Some significance may possibly belong to an order of 12 July 1388, to the escheator in Northumberland to deliver to Richard Clifford or his attorney money and other goods that had been seized (*C.C.R. 1385-89*, 518). Gervase Mat-

the Clifford family living on the borders of the diocese of Worcester and
Hereford. He is believed to have attended university at Oxford, but again
there is an uncertainty: what did he study and what degree did he take?[4]
His Latin is good in the mediaeval manner, for his letters, assuming he
composed them, show ample vocabulary and on occasion a forthright style.[5]
One infers that he did not specialize in theology, for on his elevation to his
first see he wrote urgently to a Dominican, John Montagu, master in
theology, to join him as colleague and adviser in theological matters.[6]

Clifford's first benefice would appear to have been the king's free chapel
at Jesmond, Northumberland, received in July 1380.[7] His earliest employ-
ment of which we have knowledge was in the following up of the poll tax in
1381. There was much falsification of returns and Clifford was one of a
team of seven in the county of Cambridge to investigate and levy what was
owing.[8] Ecclesiastical emolument came rapidly to this clerk of the King and
in due course an indulgent pope allowed him to hold two benefices with
cure along with other dignities or offices and to exchange them as often as
he might wish for two other incompatible benefices.[9] A grant of tenements
made to him by the King in 1386, tenements described as "occupied by
Thomas Orgrave while living" and "adjacent to the palace of Westminster," suggests that he stood high in the royal favour.[10] In the following
year King Richard sent a letter to the court of Rome by way of his ambassador Henry Bowet, *pro caro clerico nostro R<icardo> C<lifford>*,
asking an official there to use his influence to get a grace for his clerk in the
matter of pluralism. The unnamed official could look for a favour in return,

---

thew believed he was of the northern baronage and a cousin of the Nevilles and Percys, (*The
Court of Richard II*, (London, 1968), 152, 166). J. L. Grassi does not mention Clifford,
'Royal Clerks from the Archdiocese of York in the Fourteenth Century,' *Northern History*, 5
(1970), 12-33.

[4] Emden, *Oxford*.

[5] BL, Royal MS 10B IX, fol. 196ᵛ; BL, Harleian MS 431, fols. 108ᵛ, 109, his reprimand
of a newly elected prior of the Dominican house in London for cupidity and mendacity; MS
Oxford, Bodleian Library, Bodley 859, fols. 9 *et passim*.

[6] Ibid., fol. 32. The name does not appear in Emden's *Oxford* or *Cambridge*.

[7] Not to be confused with his kinsman, Richard Clifford, Jr., who received it in 1399 (*C.
Pat. R.* 1396-99, 536) and appears from time to time in *Rotuli Scotiae* (Record Commission, London, 1831), vol. 2, pp. 15, 19, 113, 128.

[8] *C.F.R., 1377-1383*, 249.

[9] *C.P.L., 1396-1404*, 90. For the extensive list of his benefices see Emden. For Clifford's
seal as archdeacon of Canterbury see BL, Add. MSS 33, 926, fol. 25.

[10] *C. Pat. R. 1385-89*, 234. Orgave had been Chamberlain of the Exchequer (Ibid. 236).

in tangentibus vestri status augmentum uberiorem a nobis graciam expectantes.[11]

The close association of Clifford with the King ensured that he was among the royal servants who were proscribed by the Lords Appellant and the Merciless Parliament in 1388. He was imprisoned in the Tower for several months but as Richard began to recover his position he freed his servant and later made him Keeper of the Great Wardrobe, which post he was to hold for seven years, 1390-1397.[12] The Great Wardrobe had passed its time of expansion as major war treasury or personal treasury of the King that threatened to rival or supersede the Exchequer of the realm, and it had little importance now in the administration of the country. It did continue to have significance, however, as a personal treasury of the King from which he paid the expenses of diplomacy and various military undertakings.[13] The Keeper had full knowledge of the King's financial affairs and by his nearness to his master was in a position of influence. Through the fluctuations of royal moods and policies from 1390 to the end of the reign, Clifford was in the inner circle of the curial party. In November 1397, he was promoted to be Keeper of the Privy Seal by which move he became one of the three great officers of the state and a permanent member of the King's Council.[14]

At this time the Statute of Provisors that restrained papal appointments in England, and the Statute of Praemunire that restrained appeals to the papal court were being reviewed. In their operation they had brought inconvenience to English parties and Parliament authorized the King to take counsel with wise persons for moderating their application. Richard con-

---

[11] Edouard Perroy, *Diplomatic Correspondence of Richard II*, Camden Society, 3rd Series, vol. 48 (London, 1938), 77. The King could use means other than church benefices to maintain his servants, for example, the gift of vills and hamlets to Clifford and his clerks (P.R.O. Exchequer, Council and Privy Seal, File 4, ♯ 80). Cf. the comment by Tout on Clifford, 'who had won the king's favour as a clerk of his chapel in the evil days before 1388,' *Chaps. in Adm. Hist.*, 5: 53.

[12] *C. Pat. R. 1388-1392*, 334. James Wylie referred to Clifford as 'King Richard's boon companion' (*History of England under Henry IV*, (Reprint, 1969, of London, 1884-1898 edition)), 3: 132. Tout judged him to be the first man of strong personality to be in charge of the Great Wardrobe during Richard's reign, *Chaps. in Adm. Hist.*, 4: 50. Cf. E. F. Jacob, *Essays in the Conciliar Epoch* (2nd ed. Manchester, 1953), 72. Junghanns considered Clifford to have been the personality nearest to Henry IV, *Zur Geschichte*, p. 68.

[13] Cf. Tout, *Chaps. in Adm. Hist.*, 4: 349ff. Tout commented that Clifford was the only Wardrobe functionary of the time to become a bishop, ibid., 4: 188.

[14] *C.C.R., 1396-1399*, 259.

sulted his judges as to his legal rights and then sent Richard Clifford to meet the clergy of the northern province about the matter.[15]

The office of Privy Seal was the recognized clearing house for royal instructions to Chancery and Exchequer. It was also an office from which royal writs were sent out directly to a wide range of persons and institutions on a variety of matters. As Keeper of the Privy Seal and a member of the King's Council, Clifford examined petitions that came up to this body from many quarters,[16] and as the Council became an instrument of royal despotism in King Richard's last eighteen months he was involved in his arbitrary and capricious measures.[17]

When the country turned against King Richard in the summer months of 1399, Henry of Lancaster founded his kingship on its discontents. The administrators forsook the King who had promoted them, Clifford among them. What does it suggest as to his character? Had he been a willing agent in Richard's despotic acts or had he tried to moderate and restrain? If a churchman as royal servant had opposed Richard, what price would he have had to pay? Clifford was not yet a bishop, and indeed was only in minor orders.[18] The King had become suspicious, vindictive and ruthless and the Keeper of his Privy Seal knew the whole tale of misgovernment. He was much beholden to his master for past favours and in the reversal of royal fortunes eleven years before had shared Richard's misfortune. Did loyalty to him now require him to resign the seal of office? The procedure in dethroning Richard was crude and even cruel. As there was little spirit of chivalry at the end of the fourteenth century among the nobility, little was to be expected from others. Thomas Merke, who had been a royal chaplain, was the only churchman in the hierarchy who was the forthright friend of his King and spoke up; he was a bishop and lost his see, for his protest was a challenge to the supplanter.[19] Clifford may have supposed as he watched

---

[15] N. Nicolas, *Proceedings and Ordinances of the Privy Council of England* (Record Commission (1834-37)), 1:80.

[16] The following is an example of this procedure. Canons of the chapel royal at Windsor and the prior and convent of Hull, in dispute over the patronage of the church of North Molton in Devonshire, were ordered to appear before the council and put all the facts before the Bishop of Worcester, Keeper of the Privy Seal (P.R.O. Privy Seal Warrants, P.S.O., Series 1, File 1, 27A).

[17] Cf. Tout, *Chaps. in Adm. Hist.*, 4:48; 5:57-60; Caroline Barron, 'The Tyranny of Richard II', *Bull. Inst. Hist. Research*, 41 (1968), 8.

[18] Worcester Cathedral Library, Liber Albus, fol. ccccxxx^v.

[19] Merke had been a trusted servant of Richard. Two years previously he had been his

the position of his royal master deteriorate that abdication or rebellion would sooner or later put an end to the reign and, knowing his contemporaries, he was prepared for harsh events. Administration of the realm had to go on; might it not be as well to stay in office until discharged?[20]

He who wins a throne by arms is usually willing enough to continue with an obedient adminstrative staff of his predecessor but he may want to put his own proven followers into the senior posts. Archbishop Arundel, returning with Henry of Lancaster, resumed the chancellorship that he had lost in 1396 but resigned it in a matter of weeks. Another companion, John Norbury, received the office of Treasurer made vacant by the death of the Earl of Wiltshire. With two new men in these two posts of first importance it could well have been important to Henry that Clifford, with his long experience of government, should continue to keep the Privy Seal, the administrative link between the King and the two great departments of state. A spirit of violence was abroad in the land, there had been much disorder, financial irregularity and lawlessness; the country needed good government and it may have seemed to Clifford that since there was little prospect of this under the king he had served, he ought to stay on and serve a king who promised to give it now.

So through the first nineteen months of the new reign Richard Clifford held office, through the brief revolt by nobles in the winter of 1399-1400, through the abortive expedition to Scotland in August and through the beginning of the formidable Welsh rising.

In Scotland and in France Henry Bolingbroke was held to be a usurper and the truces made with his predecessor were no longer considered to be in force. An insecure king needs to negotiate for recognition and support abroad which in this case will have meant for Henry's secretary, the Keeper of the Privy Seal, considerable attention to diplomacy. Marriage treaties were the subject of exchanges with the courts of France, the Empire and

---

proctor to request and receive 100,000 gold francs owed by Charles VI as part of Queen Isabella's dowry. See Pierre Chaplais, 'English Diplomatic Documents, 1377-99', in *The Reign of Richard II: Essays in Honour of May McKisack*, ed. F. R. DuBoulay and Caroline Barron (London, 1971), 29, 43-45. Merke was at first imprisoned in the Tower but was later put into the custody of the abbot of Westminster (*C.C.R., 1399-1402*, 167). He had been a monk there (Tout, *Chaps. in Adm. Hist.*, 4:64). He was pardoned, 5 Nov. 1401, and allowed to receive benefices (*C. Pat. R. 1401-1405*, 6). Cf. Calendar, # 240. For his later advancement in the church see Junghanns, *Zur Geschichte*, p. 30.

[20] As Keeper of the Privy Seal Clifford was among the witnesses at the confirmation of the charters (J. L. Kirby, *Henry IV of England* (London, 1970), 73).

Denmark. From France the answer was a rebuff. In the Empire, where two princes contended for the imperial crown, a royal betrothal was achieved between the Emperor's heir, Lewis, and Henry's eldest daughter Blanche.[21] After some time, a royal marriage was arranged between King Eric of Denmark and Henry's second daughter, Philippa. Foreign diplomacy was carried on at home in London as the Greek Emperor, Manuel Palaeologos, visited that capital in an endeavour to get financial and military help against the Turks from England's newly established king who had once campaigned with the Teutonic Knights against heathen Slavs.[22]

The presumption that Clifford was informed in diplomatic affairs is supported by an order of Henry in April 1401, addressed to him as *guardien de notre prive seel*. He was told to repair to the royal castle at Leeds with his fellow clerk, John Prophet, bringing all the documents relative to the treaties made between the late King Richard and the Duke of Guelders.[23] Again, the protracted negotiations for the return of the widowed Isabella to her native France were discussed and the decisions were made in the Council of which Clifford was a member.[24] The direct negotiators of the marriage of Princess Blanche were three laymen who brought back a treaty that was ratified under the Great Seal by writ of Privy Seal, 1 August 1401.[25]

As it had been customary for churchmen holding the highest offices of state to be given episcopal rank, Clifford with his long service and seniority could be regarded as a candidate for such. He had held appointments well up the ecclesiastical ladder of promotion, notably as archdeacon of Canterbury and as dean of York, both held simultaneously with canonries in three cathedral churches. It is not clear at what date Henry decided upon those changes of staff that were to relieve Clifford of the Privy Seal in the summer of 1401, but in the event it was to be clear enough that no discredit to that royal servant was intended by the change.

The see of Bath and Wells fell vacant with the death of Ralph Ergum at the end of March 1401. The dean and chapter of Wells reported this to the

---

[21] For a detailed study of this betrothal and marriage see Walter Holtzmann, 'Die englische Heirat Pfalzgraf Ludwigs III', *Zeitschrift für die Geschichte des Oberrheins*, Neue Folge, 43 (1929-30), 1-18.

[22] Collections made to help him are reported in P.R.O. Exchequer, Ecclesiastical Documents, E 135, 25/13, 14. Later returns from Worcester are in 25/18. Clifford as bishop took the matter seriously under the urging of the Pope.

[23] Nicolas, *Proceedings and Ordinances*, 1:129. Prophet was clerk of the King's Council.

[24] BL, MS Cotton Cleopatra, F III, fol. 14ᵛ.

[25] *Foedera*, 4:11.

King as their petition for licence to elect a new bishop was carried to Westminster by two of the clergy, one from each cathedral church. The letter was
dated 2 April, and stated that two other clergy had been made proctors to
make the election. Later in the month a second letter from the prior of Bath,
dated the 23rd, informed the King that the two bearers of the first letter had
now been made proctors in addition to the other two and that the dean and
chapter promised to accept whatever they decided.[26] The result was the election of Richard Clifford.

Before the bishop-elect was consecrated, however, a new vacancy appeared, this time at Worcester, in June. The royal licence having been
sought and granted, the monks of the cathedral church there chose Richard
Clifford as their bishop by way of postulation, *voluntate unanimi et consensu*, and asked for the royal assent.[27] In church affairs an appointment by
postulation implies a possible deficiency in qualifications or a contingent
authorization and in this case the cathedral clergy could not be sure that
they would not be overridden.[28] The end of it was that Pope Boniface translated Clifford to the see of Worcester as bishop-elect of Bath and Wells, and
Henry Bowet, who had served on diplomatic missions to the court of Rome,
received that vacated see by papal provision.[29]

Both these men were career civil servants, one might say, and undoubt-
edly the King had a hand in their promotion to bishoprics. One may ask
why Clifford was given Worcester which might as easily have fallen to
Bowet. One is inclined to conjecture that considerations of military defence
had something to do with it and the type of usefulness that each king's clerk

---

[26] P.R.O. Ecclesiastical Petitions, C 84/38/13, 14.

[27] P.R.O. Ibid., C 84/38/24. Dated 28 June, 'as if by inspiration of the Holy Spirit.' Cf.
J. W. Willis-Bund, *Register of the Diocese of Worcester During Vacancy of the See* (Oxford,
1893-97), 373. Clifford is here referred to as 'Master' and a bachelor of both laws. As early
as 2 July the King granted him custody of the temporalities of the bishopric during the
vacancy, for which he later made payment of £100 to the treasurer of the household (*C. Pat.
R. 1394-1401*, 529, 448). E. F. Jacob considered him to have lacked wide legal knowledge
(*Reg. Chichele*, 1:xxxii).

[28] *Sext*. 1. 5. (C.I.C. 2:945a) *De Postulatione*. Cf. *X* 1. 6, 20 (C.I.C. 2:61a): the error
of the prior and chapter of Worcester, 1199, in electing a clerk of illegitimate birth instead of
seeking a postulation.

[29] There would appear to have been opposition to Clifford's appointment to Worcester. In
the Bodleian is a copy of a letter of his to the Pope humbly urging him to persevere in the
matter of providing him away from Bath and Wells. People were persistently attacking the
appointment *in detrimentum status mei subtiliter*. He reminded the Pope that he represented
the firm rock on which the Church was founded whose power could not be broken (MS
Bodley 859, fol. 7).

could provide. Worcester was the firm base for military action in South
Wales and the church was the largest landholder in that county. If Clifford
belonged to a family established near the Welsh border — and this is only
hypothetical — he could be considered to have some special knowledge of
the people and conditions there. Such could make him a more effective
leader in both church and community. Or we may look at the appointment
in terms of logistics: Worcester as a supply and administrative base and
Clifford as the experienced public administrator.[30] Bowet, on the other
hand, had spent most of his years in the diplomatic service of the Crown.
His special training was in law and since Henry was still using him on
diplomatic business, if he was to be absent from his diocese, less inconvenience might result if the diocese was Bath and Wells.[31]

The bishops of Worcester had for some time had a London house and a
manor in Hillingdon close by. Whatever responsibilities Clifford might have
in or toward his diocese, he continued to have a base near the centre of
government. After his translation he did not visit his diocese for sixteen
months and on different occasions he wrote to his clergy that business affairs — sometimes as matters of state — prevented him from dealing with
diocesan concerns or from coming in person. Of these detaining causes
the most noteworthy was his participation in the marriage of Princess
Blanche.[32]

He was one of four negotiators who worked out the arrangements for this
wedding and accompanying treaty,[33] details of which can be followed in
Rymer's *Foedera*.[34] The King appointed him to go overseas with his young
daughter in the summer of 1402 as she went to meet her future husband.[35]

---

[30] Cf. *C. Pat. R. 1401-1405*, 296, orders of King Henry to the bishops of Worcester and
Exeter and various officers of the counties of Worcester, Gloucester, Devon and the town of
Bristol to provision his troops in South Wales. Worcester had been the mustering centre for
Edward's feudal host in his Welsh wars of 1277 and 1294 (Sir Maurice Powicke, *The Thir-
teenth Century* (Oxford, 1953), 408, 441). For a summary of the feudal position of the
bishops of Worcester and their military resources, see J. W. Willis-Bund, *The Register of
Bishop Godfrey Giffard* (Oxford, 1902), xiiff. See also Calendar # 7, for a report of feudal
aids due from episcopal manors.

[31] See Calendar # 333. He had been a papal chaplain and Auditor-General of Causes in
the Camera (*C.P.L. 1396-1404*, 628).

[32] See Calendar, # 52.

[33] BL, Harleian MS 431, 55, fols. 26, 122b.

[34] 4:8, 11, 20-26, 106.

[35] Ibid., 16. Blanche was probably not more than ten years old (Holtzmann, 'Die
englische Heirat', p. 19).

The marriage negotiations had been carried out at Dordrecht and there the company from England now met the bridegroom and his train.[36] The arrival of these notables from England gave to certain citizens of Dordrecht an opportunity to lay a complaint about having been despoiled by subjects of the English King, a complaint which Clifford and the Earl of Somerset promptly reported with the recommendation that they be given satisfaction.[37] In due course all arrived at Cologne where, on 6 July, the bishop of Worcester married Lewis and Blanche.[38]

This event, one surmises, was a gratifying recognition of long service and evidence of royal favour. In point of diplomatic success it was the most important in the reign of Henry, dramatically consummated in a royal wedding. One is tempted to see in the choice of Clifford to celebrate the nuptials some acknowledgment of his participation in the carefully prepared approach. With this stately occasion his public participation in diplomacy ceased for quite some years, to be renewed later on the larger stage of the Council of Constance.[39]

II

RICHARD CLIFFORD AS BISHOP

As this servant of the Crown took up his episcopal office the general mediaeval pattern of church-state relationships still obtained. This meant in England recognition of the right of the church courts to deal with all misdemeanours of clergy, and the authority of the Church over the laity within its

[36] For Clifford's expenses in accompanying Princess Blanche to Cologne, see P.R.O., Lists and Indexes, No. XI, Foreign Accounts, p. 79: Nuncii, F 3 Henry IV, A.

[37] *Royal and Historical Letters during the Reign of Henry the Fourth*, Rolls Series, 18 (Ed. F. C. Hingeston, London, 1860), 1:103.

[38] *Continuatio Eulogii*, Rolls Series, 9 (Ed. F. S. Haydon, London, 1863), 3:403. E. F. Jacob was mistaken in supposing that this marriage took place in Castile (*Reg. Chichele* 1:xxxii; 2:647). Clifford and Somerset had been given instructions to respect the current marriage treaty as a continuation of the earlier treaty between Richard II and the King of the Romans and Bohemia. They were directed not to discuss policy concerning the Pope (Holtzmann, 'Die englische Heirat', pp. 13, 32; cf. BL, MS Cott. Galba, B I fol. 138 (old 157)).

[39] Henry V wanted the Schism ended and as Clifford was sent to Constance to join the English delegation it is reasonable to suppose that he had instructions to that end. That delegation's decision to support Martin V may have reflected an influence by Clifford but this has not been clearly established. However, see the assumption by David Knowles, *The Religious Orders in England* (Cambridge, 1955), 2:180.

spiritual jurisdiction.[40] Behind this attitude was the conservatism that discountenanced innovation in doctrine or insubordination to constituted authority. The secular government acted when clerics were accused of civil offences, and while acknowledging the right of the Church to try them, it instructed sheriffs to bring them into the lay court first.[41]

For twenty years Clifford had looked at church-state relations from within the King's service. No certain evidence meets one that he had made a special study of any discipline that qualified a clerk for high position in the Church or gave his mind an ecclesiastical orientation. Some royal servants had special qualifications in canon law and an occasional one was qualified in theology. Thomas Becket by special legal training had been at least conversant with the theological assumptions that were the underlying principles of canon law and on elevation to the Primacy was equipped to give right of way to the interests of the Church. There is nothing in Clifford's background to suggest a preparation for such a change in his thinking on his advancement to episcopal office. As bishop he continued to spend far more time in or near London than in his diocese and what survives of his register lacks the references to various aspects of diocesan supervision that one finds, for example, in the register of an earlier predecessor at Worcester, Wolfstan Bransford, who was a bishop first and last.

Clifford himself was aware of a lack. He was only in minor orders when chosen for a bishopric and he wrote, as we have seen, to John Montagu, a Dominican theologian, to come and help him. He had just been raised to pontifical dignity, *noviter consecratus*, and now had the responsibility of the

---

[40] The secular government might call clerics to order, however. Dominicans at Oxford were commanded to keep their own rules (*C.C.R. 1399-1402*, 523). In support of clerical discipline sheriffs were ordered to round up runaway Carmelites who were trying to escape the discipline of their Prior Provincial (*C.C.R. 1399-1402*, 17). As Keeper of the Privy Seal Clifford directed a letter to the sheriff of Carnarvon. Hugh Conewey, chaplain, was contumacious to the authority of the bishop of Bangor and the sheriff was ordered to produce him before the bishop for his offences and contempt, Westminster, 15 June 1398 (P.R.O. Exchequer, 28, File 4/71). Yet there was a certain ambivalence in the actions of the secular government. It repeatedly inhibited the bishops from giving effect to their excommunications when the subjects appealed to the Archbishops of Canterbury or papal see, and bishops were told to answer in Chancery to show cause why there should be no stay. Clifford sent a second letter to the sheriff to say that Hugh had appealed to the Apostolic See in correct legal form. In order that he, the sheriff, should be correct according to the law of England, he was now instructed to facilitate Hugh's appeal (ibid., 4/72).

[41] The Rolls of the King's Bench show on most membranes clerks summoned for transgression of property or theft usually with such notations as *non inventus est, non venit, nihil habuit*.

cure of souls. With so large a flock this was an insupportable burden and he urged Montagu to join him as colleague and adviser.[42]

It can be said that the most notable aspect of Clifford's Worcester episcopate was his absence from his diocese. His first appearance there was in January 1403, for his enthronement and by mid-May he was back at his manor of Hillingdon near London. He was in his diocese again for three months that summer, which period coincided with military operations in the West and the Battle of Shrewsbury on 21 July. King Henry was at Worcester in the first week of September and then returned to London. The bishop was again at his Hillingdon manor by 24 September and did not appear in his diocese again until the end of August next year, 1404. Then in December following he went back to London, not to reappear in Worcestershire, so far as one can tell, until March, 1407. From then until 14 July the date of the latest entry in the *memoranda*, we find him in his diocese.[43] One concludes that at most Clifford spent no more than seventeen months in his diocese during his six years of tenure. Two long absences may be explained in part by duties connected with Parliament. At the Parliament called for Hilary, 1404, Clifford was named among the twenty-two — six bishops and sixteen laymen — to be a continuing council to advise the King on petitions, and for the March Parliament, 1406, he was one of the triers of petitions.[44]

To conduct the routine affairs of his diocese during his absence the bishop had his staff. William Forster, bachelor of laws, was his Commissary and principal executive officer until his death. Gilbert Stone, a canon of Hereford, was his vicar in spirituals. Duties of bishop's ordinary for claiming criminous clerks were divided according to the three counties

---

[42] 'Idcirco dilectissime odor bonus nominis vestri et honeste conversacionis vestre redolens sanctitas immo eminentissime facultatis theologice profunda maturitas et medulla quibus personam vestram honorabilem a multis retroactis temporibus ex parte nominis insignita merito nos excitat' (MS Bodley 859, fol. 32). Montagu was elected prior of the Dominicans' London house, 1407, but did not accept the office. See *The Victoria History of London*, vol. 1, ed. Wm. Page (London, 1909), 502.

[43] He was in his diocese in September for ordinations in Blockley parish church. The absence of entries after 14 July and the pattern of Clifford's coming and going point to this as a brief visit. On 26 September he authorized a signification at his manor there (P.R.O. C 85/165/f. 4). See Calendar # 18n. His translation to London would appear to have overlapped his final activities in Worcester diocese. Le Neve gives 22 June 1407, as the date of translation (*Fasti Ecclesiae Anglicanae 1300-1541*, vol. 5, St. Paul's, London, comp. Joyce M. Horn (London, 1963) 5:3). The authority cited is Reg. Arundel 1, fol. 39ᵛ.

[44] *Rot. Parl.* 3:530, 567.

represented in the diocese, i.e. Worcester, Gloucester east of Severn and part of Warwick, in each of which, and in the town of Bristol clergy were named to claim clerks who were charged in the lay courts.[45] His sequestrator was John Chewe. Nothing appears in the register to tell when Forster or Chewe were appointed. The appointment of Stone to be vicar in spirituals was in May 1402, and would seem to have been occasioned by Clifford's impending journey overseas that summer for the marriage of Princess Blanche.[46]

The senior churchman in the diocese next to the Bishop was the prior of the cathedral chapter at Worcester. Frequent absences of earlier bishops had provided opportunities for priors to increase their influence. During vacancy of the see they assumed some of the bishop's functions and between Bishop Tideman's death and the consecration of Clifford Prior John Malvern conducted an energetic visitation.[47] Rights of prior and cathedral chapter within the cathedral and the city and over numerous church manors were well established and jealously watched.[48]

Clifford's long delay in appearing in his diocese may well have retarded some diocesan business but institutions and exchanges appear to have gone on in normal volume. Whatever may have been done in hearing ecclesiastical causes or in the probate of wills leaves no record in the register. In the matter of ordinations, it is detailed.

Bishop Clifford celebrated ordinations twenty-four times during his Worcester episcopate, according to his register.[49] The first six occasions were in London or its vicinity when he conferred orders on numbers of men from various dioceses and on twelve from his own.[50] Appearing in his diocese in

---

[45] See sections 12-15 of the Calendar.

[46] For a comprehensive description of the administration of the diocese, see R. M. Haines, *The Administration of the Diocese of Worcester in the First Half of the Fourteenth Century* (London, 1965).

[47] John Malvern, a doctor of laws, was one of two who were commissioned by Archbishop Arundel to investigate the bishop of Salisbury's refusal to admit to a particular vicarage (London, Lambeth Palace Library, Reg. Arundel 1, fol. 104^v). For details of his activities when the see was vacant, see J. W. Willis-Bund, *Register Sede Vacante*, 381 ff. He was prior, 1395-1423.

[48] King Henry sent John Oldcastle, sheriff of Hereford, and John Brygge, escheator, during the summer of 1406 to discover what rights and franchises were in the hands of the cathedral chapter (Liber Albus, fol. ccccxxix^v).

[49] Clifford did not adhere strictly to the traditional observance of Ember Days for his ordinations. See App. 9.

[50] Five of the twelve appeared twice. See App. 9.

January 1403, for his enthronement and diocesan business, he held ordinations in the conventual church of Llanthony on 3 March where he received fifty-five candidates from his own people, nineteen of whom were for the first tonsure. He followed up with further ordinations in his own chapel at Hartlebury on 31 March and in the cathedral on 14 April, adding forty more from the diocese of Worcester. He was in London for a few weeks in May and June during which time he celebrated orders in St. Stephens's chapel in the palace at Westminster when three of the nine ordinands were from his own bishopric. Later, in December, at his manor at Hillingdon, he held a special ordination for the rector of Burton, Worcester diocese, advancing him to the diaconate. Among his ordinations at his London house and Hillingdon in the months of February, March and May 1404, approximately one quarter of the candidates were of his own diocese. In September of that year the bishop was again at Llanthony where he admitted twenty-six men of his diocese to their first tonsure and conferred further orders on a substantial number.

Forseeing that he might not be available in his own diocese in 1405 he commissioned the Bishop of Dunkeld, who had left his own country which was adhering to the Antipope, to conduct the September ordinations there.[51] The entries in the register continue to show Bishop Clifford still in or close to London through the year 1406[52] and again the Bishop of Dunkeld was used for Worcester ordinations, this time in December of that year.[53]

As just noted, the summer of 1403 found Clifford in his diocese for a second period. The alliance of Glendower and Hotspur had brought a military crisis that must have compelled the bishop to be in his episcopal

[51] Boniface IX gave to Nicholas <Duffield>, bishop of Dunkeld, indult to grant to twenty-four persons of the realm of England, at his choice, the indulgence of the jubilee year of 1390, the indult to hold good for three months after his arrival in the said realm, dated 11 June 1401 (*C.P.L. 1362-1404*, 379). The bishop of Dunkeld celebrated ordinations in the cathedral church of Worcester, 24 Sept., 1401 (Willis-Bund, *Register*, p. 374). He was commissioned to act as suffragan in the diocese of Hereford during the vacancy between the death of Bishop Trevenant and the consecration of Robert Mascall, 1404 (*Reg. Mascall*, 2, 8, 15, 125, 130; P.R.O. Ecclesiastical Documents, E. 135, 4/46). His seal, in excellent condition, is appended to a certificate of dedication of the baptistry in the chapel of Knowles, Hampton-in-Arden, Warw., Coventry and Lichfield diocese, in the following year (E. 135/9/68).

[52] Clifford was at the Convocation in St. Paul's, which met 2 May 1406: '... missa ibidem de sancto spiritu per venerabilem patrem dominum Ricardum Dei gratia Wigorniensem episcopum ad summum altare ipsius cathedralis ecclesiae ... primitus ut moris est solempniter celebrata ...' (Reg. Arundel 1, f. 65).

[53] See tables of ordinations and notes in Appendix 9.

charge. Approximately two thirds of Worcestershire was church land and at that juncture when the Earl of Warwick was a youth, the bishop's responsibility as a magnate could have been more than usually significant.[54] In the beginning of the preceding year he had transmitted to his clergy an order from the Primate for a season of humiliation to invoke divine blessings upon King and realm. The national martyrs Alphage and Thomas were to be especially appealed to and Clifford added the local patron saints Oswald and Wolfstan.[55] Now on 1 July 1403, from his manor at Alvechurch, he wrote to his clergy on behalf of the royal cause. The country was suffering from wars and tumult, the rebellion of the Welsh and the invasion by the Scots. He ordered prayers and processions for the King and realm and, for the Church, prayers against the heresies of the Lollards. All these matters were to be explained to the people in the vulgar tongue.[56]

Whatever visitation may have taken place in the diocese has left little trace in the register as we have it. Bishop Clifford wrote from Hillingdon, 20 August 1404, to the prior and chapter of the cathedral church that he would personally hold a visitation there in the first week of September, that every monk should be present and that nothing must be permitted to prejudice the visit.[57] The Benedictine monks of the cathedral were to have another visitation the following May, it turned out, this time from William, abbot of Winchcombe, whom the last general chapter, held at Northampton, had made visitor for their Order in the diocese of Worcester.[58] A document in the cathedral library leads one to wonder whether the papal curia had confidence in the absentee Clifford as a disciplinarian. The abbot of Pershore received a special papal commission to cite certain clergy of the city of Worcester, *contradictores et rebelles*, dated 18 August 1406. They were the rectors of St. Helen's, St. Swithun's, All Saints', the vicar of St. Peter's Great, together with their holy water clerks.[59]

---

[54] Clifford did not go to his diocese in the summer of 1402 after his return from Germany. The threat from the Welsh was then serious enough to keep Prior John Malvern from attending the chapter of his order. He sent a proxy with the message that they had killed or captured the flower of the Herefordshire miltia and the people were fearful (W. A. Pantin, *Documents Illustrating the Activities of the General and Provincial Chapters of English Black Monks*, Camden Society, 3rd series, vol. 54 (London, 1937), 209, 212).

[55] See Calendar # 11.

[56] Liber Albus, fol. ccccxv[v].

[57] Ibid., fol. ccccxxii[v]. He was moving about the diocese from the end of August to the beginning of December. See Calendar ## 241-257.

[58] Ibid., fol. ccccxxiii.

[59] MS B 957. The office of holy water clerk, *aquaebaiulus*, was an ecclesiastical benefice

A bishop's supervising authority was considerably hampered in the diocese by the numerous exemptions of religious houses and areas under their jurisdiction. The monastery of Evesham was almost an ecclesiastical palatinate with complete rule over an enclave of some twenty-five square miles.[60] Great Malvern, on the west side of the county, was a cell of the royal abbey of Westminster and continually claimed special privileges and exemptions. The abbot of St Peter's, Gloucester, had the privilege from Boniface IX to reconcile churches and cemeteries and to confer minor orders on monks and other persons of the monastery and its priories and churches.[61] Certain houses acknowledged the supervisory authority of the prior of Worcester cathedral to the exclusion of the bishop. It was a complex pattern that would have required careful study by a bishop who was resident; there is little to suggest that Clifford made any serious effort to assert episcopal authority in this context.[62]

In relation to the civil power, however, the situation may have been somewhat different. A mediaeval bishop had to be watchful for the privileges of his clergy vis à vis the lay authority. Within the first four months of his office Clifford was to remind his clergy of their right to be tried in a church court.[63] The bishop of Worcester had his own liberty, that is, his

---

to which rectors and vicars of parishes made appointment. He carried the holy water in processions and ritual (E. G. C. F. Atchley and E. G. P. Wyatt, *The Churchman's Glossary of Ecclesiastical Terms* (London, 1923), 13).

[60] Evesham was known as a royal foundation directly subject to Rome. Its mitred abbots had power to try and to correct all persons secular or ecclesiastical who were charged under canon law. A new abbot could be blessed by any bishop and the bishop of Worcester was never chosen (*V.C.H., Worcester*, eds. J. W. Willis-Bund and W. Page (London, 1906) 2:124; Wm. Dugdale, *Monasticon Anglicanum* (London, 1819), 2:11).

[61] *C.P.L. 1362-1404*, 433. For exemptions of religious houses see E. F. Jacob, *Henry Chichele and the Ecclesiastical Politics of his Age* (London, 1952), 9-12.

[62] Although Bishop Clifford had a deputy for the confirmation of elections he might be superseded. The prior of Worcester was appointed by the papal curia to preside at the election of a new prioress by the nuns of Westwood and to confirm (Liber Albus, fol. ccccxxiiii[v]).

[63] See Calendar # 12. 'Si malefactor captus a Judice Laico dicit se Clericum: hujus rei cognitio ad Judicem Ecclesiasticum spectat' (*Sext.* 5. 11. 12 (C.I.C. 2: 1101 b)). Gaol Delivery Rolls and King's Bench Rolls make it fairly clear that it was not left to the church courts alone to determine guilt or innocence of clerks under charge. Inquisition was made in the lay court with a lay jury to find out how — *pro qualiter* — a clerk should be delivered to the bishop's Ordinary. Whatever the clergy may have thought about their theoretical right to trial by the church court, many put themselves on jury for better or worse. The formula recurs, 'se posuit de bono et malo super patriam'. They were often acquitted and the Church had at least the advantage of not being blamed for it. If a man claimed to be of the clergy and was found to be married or a bigamist he lost his rights (P.R.O., Gaol Delivery Rolls, J. I. 3/189, membr. 26[v]).

own area of jurisdiction within the city which his own men policed. In this connection he had his own seneschal, bailiff and, of course, his prison. Gaol Delivery Rolls give an account of an inquiry by royal justices into the actions of these officers when they had arrested a suspect on a larceny charge and were supposed to have delivered him out of the bishop's prison into the hands of the sheriff.[64] When taxes were to be met there were laity who claimed that the cathedral clergy should contribute from their tenements to what the city had to raise. In the Michaelmas Parliament, 1402, the Commons petitioned that as the laity of cities, boroughs and landed estates had paid the King fifteenths and tenths ever since the twentieth year of Edward son of Henry, churchmen who had acquired such tenements since then should contribute from their rents because these were temporals.[65] When the citizens of Worcester put it to the cathedral clergy that they ought to contribute from their city tenements to what the city was expected to pay, they replied that their tenements had been annexed as spirituals by the King 'twenty years before Edward son of Henry' and were 'extra libertatem civitatis predicte et non parcella eiusdem'.[66]

Clifford, like other clerks who received high promotion from the papal court, had costly expenses to meet there. He made some agreement with a Florentine financier, Gerard de Alberese, who was to pay expenses of his earlier appointment to Bath and Wells. Eleven months after his translation to Worcester a letter from the court of Rome to the English archbishops directed them to compel Clifford to pay up, using ecclesiastical censures, adding, perhaps rhetorically, that personal excommunication and an interdict on his church were to be applied, with the help of the secular arm if necessary.[67] This bill was to dog the bishop for years. In September 1406,

---

[64] P.R.O. Gaol Delivery Rolls, J. I. 3/189, m. 14. Bishop Clifford's seneschal, bailiff and gaoler were Thomas Delve, Thomas Cade and Thomas Alder respectively. Robert Braybrook, Bishop of London, was heavily fined for the escape of fourteen convicted clerks from his London prison (C. Pat. R., 1401-1405, 409, 418). He had been pardoned for the earlier escape of ten convicted clerks from his castle at Stortford, Herts (C. Pat. R., 1399-1401, 501). There is much evidence of an erosion of the Church's position in the last decade of the fourteenth century and in the early years of the fifteenth. Lay authorities were increasingly of a mind to examine and criticize the conduct of its affairs. The archdeacon of Bucks. was brought into the court of King's Bench on charges of extortion in probating wills, illegal seizures of chattels and taking bribes. The judge found him guilty (P.R.O. KB 27/518, membr. 26). Outlawry was not infrequently declared against clerics who failed to appear in this court (KB 27/519, Rex membrs. 2-18ᵛ).

[65] Rot. Parl. 3:503.

[66] Liber Albus, fol. ccccxxiii.

[67] C.P.L. 1362-1404, 351.

we find him protesting that the sum of 8,000 florins that the partners and heirs of Gerard were now demanding was quite insupportable and he took over the issues of the parish church of Cleeve to help towards payments on it, getting the consent of the prior and chapter.[68] On appointment to Worcester Clifford had promised to pay the 2,000 florins due from that diocese *pro suo communi servicio* and had recognized that he must pay one hundred florins still owing from his predecessor, Bishop Tideman.[69] In August 1402, he was credited with a payment of 1,000 florins[70] but during the rest of his Worcester episcopate his payments of the *communia servicia* were in sums varying from twenty-seven to eighty-four florins, made twice a year.

The register has entries concerning clerical grants of money and their collection. In the twenty year period from 1388 to 1408 twenty levies on the Church in England were demanded by pope or king. In these efforts the schismatics and the schism were especially mentioned by the papacy as causes of financial need. The royal formula emphasized the defence of the king and realm. Sometimes it was the archbishops who were told to cause the churchmen in Convocation to vote the money; at other times special collectors were sent.[71] King Henry was to add to the pope's difficulties by forbidding the sending of gold overseas.[72]

The King expected subsidies from the Church and by this time the Convocation of Canterbury met in London when Parliament was summoned there. Each time it was made clear to the clergy what King and Parliament expected of them.[73] Each bishop was told to see that collectors were ap-

[68] Liber Albus, fol. ccccxxx^v.

[69] Before his translation to Worcester he had paid *communia servicia* from Bath and Wells to the amount of 1,000 florins (Archivio Segreto Vaticano, *Obligationes et Solutiones*, vol. 55, fol. 152). The common services expected by the papal camera from the see of Worcester were 2,000 florins, and from Bath and Wells 4,300. These were the amounts assessed on the annual value of the two sees. 'Predicto loco indictione predicta die xxiii mensis Augusti Reverendus in Christo pater dominus Ricardus Episcopus Wygorniensis per venerabilem virum magistrum Baroncum de Pistorio procuratorem suum ad hoc legatum constitutum promisit Camerae pro suo communi servicio duo milia florenorum auri de Camera' (*Obligationes et Solutiones*, vol. 57, fol. 66). Cf. *X* 3. 23 (C.I.C. 2:531a): 'Successor in beneficio tenetur solvere debita praedecessoris pro necessitate ecclesiae contracta.'

[70] *Obligationes et Solutiones*, vol. 55, fol. 248.

[71] There was no doubt about it that the revenues of the court of Rome were greatly reduced as the Schism went on. The accounts of the papal Camera, *Introitus et Exitus*, under Boniface IX and Clement VII show the rival popes receiving more or less equal revenues, each from approximately half the divided Church.

[72] *C.C.R. 1405-1409*, 324.

[73] Cf. D. B. Weske, *Convocation of Clergy* (London, 1937), Appendices A, B, C. For files

pointed for each archdeaconry, that their names were sent to the Exchequer by a set date and that in due course they sent in what they had collected. Collecting was a strenuous and expensive business and it was not unusual for individuals or religious houses to ask to be excused from undertaking it.[74] The King and his officials of the Exchequer could crack the whip over the unhappy ecclesiastical collectors, ordering them to cease every excuse and under penalty of heavy fine to be before the King with the money.[75]

In the diocese of Worcester this duty was passed around. Particular houses might be ordered to collect specified instalments, as in the case of the tenth and half tenth granted by Convocation in January 1401. No secular clergy were used to collect moneys intended for the government. During the years of Clifford's tenure of the see of Worcester the Convocation of Canterbury was called together five times — twice in 1404 — and never met without a subsidy being demanded for the King.[76] On every occasion it made a grant but when called in November 1404, obviously for no other reason but to vote money for the government, it was stubborn and only on the fourth day agreed, doing so with stipulations that were written into the record and agreed to by the King.[77] Prior to the grant of April, 1404, Bishop Clifford made a valuation of the religious houses in his diocese which became the basis for the subsidy.[78] Of course bishops them-

---

of letters from heads of religious houses concerning tenths see P.R.O. Ecclesiastical Documents, Exchequer, E. 135, 10/20, 10/21. See Calendar ## 137-139. There was pressure also from the papal camera as Boniface threatened with deprivation clergy who defaulted in their payments required for it (*C.P.L. 1362-1404*, 312).

[74] The abbot of Revesby sought and obtained relief from this duty (*C.C.R. 1405-1409*, 170; see also Calendar 222).

[75] *C.F.R., 1399-1405*, 225.

[76] Reg. Arundel 1, fols. 54, 57, 62^v, 65.

[77] Ibid., 1, fol. 62^v. One stipulation was that they were not to be harried about payment. The clergy's unwillingness to make this grant may have derived in part from the use made of money agreed to in April. Of that grant, £3,000 had been made over to Joan, 'the king's consort,' to pay arrears of an annuity of 10,000 marks granted to her in dower (*C. Pat. R., 1401-1405*, 418). Of more interest to bishops was the use of clerical subsidies to reimburse them for their expenses in attending Parliament (P.R.O. Privy Seal Warrants, P.S.O., Series I, File 2). For observations on these subsidies see E. F. Jacob, 'The Canterbury Convocation of 1406,' in *Essays in Medieval History Presented to Bertie Wilkinson* (eds. T. A. Sandquist and M. R. Powicke (Toronto, 1969)), pp. 343-353 and F. D. Logan, *Excommunication and the Secular Arm in Mediaeval England* (Toronto, 1968), pp. 53-61. See Calendar ## 222-224.

[78] P.R.O. Exchequer K.R., Ecclesiastical Documents, E 179/58/23, 24. Details of these various levies are found in this series and in Ecclesiastical Documents, E 135, 10/20, 21.

selves were frequently asked for loans by the King and it is possible to believe that they were given a personal interest in the successful collection of clerical subsidies as he promised them repayment out of these.[79] For clerical collectors who were having difficulties the government provided secular assistance under writs of aid.[80]

It remains to consider any clues there are to Bishop Clifford's character and interests.

He was a man of standard orthodoxy as illustrated by his injunctions for prayers for the King and realm, invoking Mary and the saints. To the abbot and convent of St. Augustine, Bristol, he sent a message, making his own the instructions by the bishops in Convocation that prayers for the dead be offered, 'foedus amicitiae spiritualis ad animarum salutem effecacius inire volentes ... qui pro aliis orat, pro se laborat'.[81] The bishop particularly asked that his late neighbour, John Trevenant, bishop of Hereford, be prayed for.[82]

Clifford appears to have had some scruples in churchmanship even though he was absent so much. When parishes were being taken over by religious houses he showed concern that charitable trusts be respected and that vicars have rights that were safeguarded. In the appropriation of the parish churches of Cleeve and Himbleton by the prior and cathedral chapter of Worcester he made such provision. In this policy he had the reinforcement and authority of Parliament which had decided to take a hand in the ordering of such church matters. In the Parliament of 15 Richard II the Commons had petitioned that appropriating houses be made to do what was right,[83] with the result that a statute was enacted that the diocesan must see to it that a suitable sum of money be set aside, proportionate to the value of

---

[79] *C. Pat. R., 1405-1408*, 413, 422, 472.

[80] *Ibid.*, 13, 90, 92.

[81] D. Wilkins, *Concilia Magnae Britanniae et Hiberniae* (London, 1737), 3:278.

[82] From his manor at Hillingdon, 7 April 1404, Clifford wrote to all the religious of his diocese to pray for the soul of Bishop John Trevenant (MS Bodley 859, fol. 37ᵛ), also a letter of sympathy to an unnamed relative of the late bishop (MS Oxford, Corpus Christi Coll. 72, fol. 65ᵛ). He was concerned for the obsequies of his colleague, John Prophet (Calendar # 160).

[83] Two notable cases of such appropriation had occurred at this time with papal approval. The alien priory of Lewes was allowed to take three churches and a chapel. The bishop of London appropriated three churches to his *mensa* because the yearly influx of notables into London when Parliament met put him to great expenses in hospitality (*C.P.L. 1362-1404*, 396, 410).

the benefice, to be given annually to the poor of the parish.[84] In 4 Henry IV Parliament reaffirmed this statute, disallowing any appropriation made since the earlier one that had not fulfilled its terms.[85] Clifford dealt firmly and in detail with the cases in his diocese.[86] He showed concern for parish churches in another way when, in granting permission for oratories in private houses, he required that they be not to the prejudice of such. Clerks who got dispensation to be absent from their parishes for study had time limits set to the privilege and must ensure that spiritual offices continue.

The human side shows occasionally. When appealed to by a widow who was being slandered about her husband's death his response was forthright.[87] His promotion of Gilbert Stone to be his vicar in spirituals was made in spite of a recent rivalry with him over a benefice when Clifford held the Privy Seal.[88] Stone had written to him then frankly that he should not compromise his reputation for justice for any benefice however fat and reminded him of Ahab's coveting of Naboth's vineyard.[89] Later we find Stone being sent as Clifford's special messenger to the dean and chapter of Wells bearing letters which he would explain to them more fully by word of mouth. Certain dangerous matters were on foot and he was proposing collaboration.[90] We get a glimpse of the bishop in the role of patron as he asks a certain abbot for a benefice for a deserving clerk who has never had one. 'Affectuose rogamus quatinus presentacione vestra ad aliquod beneficium ... pro aliquo nostrorum commensalium ... concedere dignemini graciose'.[91] Similarly he wrote to the abbot of Evesham on behalf of a monk of

---

[84] *Rot. Parl.* 3: 293-94.

[85] Ibid., 468, 499.

[86] See Calendar, ## 225-233. The vicarages sanctioned by Clifford were not liable for maintaining the fabric of the chancel. Cf. R.A.R. Hartridge, *A History of Vicarages in the Middle Ages* (Cambridge, 1930), 146.

For the actual ritual of appropriation see the account of the appropriation of Pucklechurch, Gloucestershire, by the canons of Wells, 1397, Historical Manuscripts Commission. *A Calendar of the MSS of the Dean and Chapter of Wells* (ed. W. H. B. Bird, London, 1907), 1:357. The constitution of the legate Ottobon in 1268 to restrain appropriations was not stringent: see F. M. Powicke and C. R. Cheney, eds. *Councils and Synods with Other Documents Relating to The English Church* (Oxford, 1964), pp. 314, 389 n. 1, 399, 492, 537, 709, 713 n. 1, 770, 771.

[87] See Calendar # 161.

[88] BL, Royal MSS 10B IX, fol. 196ᵛ.

[89] MS Bodley 859, fol. 9. Stone later thanked Clifford for his part in getting him promotion in the churches of Bath and Wells (ibid., fol. 23).

[90] Ibid., fol. 34ᵛ.

[91] Ibid., fol. 34.

Worcester, John Fordham, inceptor in theology, who did well at Oxford and was competent in business.[92]

As bishop and pastor Clifford on occasion dealt with concubinage. To the provost of Westbury he wrote regarding continence, having heard — 'ut narratur' — that he kept a woman of his parish. If this was true he was being foolish and sacriligious and he warned him against the corrupting influence of womankind.[93] He wrote to the rector of Wick that it was reported that he was keeping a girl who was in spiritual relationship with him in adulterous and incestuous connection. He knew how rumours are taken up and did not lightly give them credence. A sense of shame deterred him from making matters public but some were saying that he was shutting his eyes. Although he did not accuse, there was an opinion that where there is smoke there must be fire.[94] From his castle at Hartlebury he sent a letter to a lay notable, a married man, that his present infirmity was a divine visitation and he must send away the concubine whom he had kept for fifteen years to the great peril of his soul and the souls of his ancestors.[95]

Friendships were of concern to him. To an unnamed friend whom he had not seen for a long time he wrote urging him to come to London for a talk.[96] On the other hand he wrote testily to John de Maydenhith, dean of Chicester, who omitted to come to see him when he was in London. He reminded the dean that they were old friends, that he had helped him get benefices and, when he had been feloniously indicted, he had given him shelter in his house.[97] Clifford wrote tartly to Simon Sydenham, an advocate at the papal court for whom he had solicited favours and who was supposed to be attending to his interests there. He reprimanded Simon for not reporting and asked whether he was exhausted from labour or just ungrateful and inconstant.[98]

---

[92] On another occasion Clifford wrote to the bishop of Chichester asking for an exchange of canonries 'inter Gilbertum Stone ab antiquo socium predilectum ecclesie Wellensis et dominum Johannem Gonnel' (ibid., fol. 34).

[93] Ibid., fol. 28. De tenore presencium amicabiliter praemunimus ac in visceribus Iesus Christi cuius preciosissimi corporis et sanguinis sacramentum conficiendo tangis in altari monemus et ortamur quatinus nullo immo tangas de cetero picem illam sed visis presentibus cum omni celeritate possibili illa feminini generis massa carnea corruptibilis et putrida omni pice deterior coinquinans quicquid tangit a tua comitate dimoveatur omnino.

[94] Ibid., fol. 28ᵛ: Tamen opinatur aliquis quod ubi ignis abest fumositas non ascendit.

[95] Ibid., fol. 34. He wrote this admonition in French. In a case of contumacy he could call on the lay power to coerce: see Calendar # 155, # 156.

[96] MS Bodley 859, fol. 29ᵛ.

[97] Ibid., fol. 30ᵛ.

[98] Ibid., fol. 40. Cf. E. F. Jacob, *Essays in the Conciliar Epoch*, 79.

When overtaken by a malady the bishop had to make his excuses for not attending Parliament or Convocation. He detailed all his symptoms and referred to his unsightly appearance. He was troubled by slanderous gossip that his illness was feigned. The abbot of Evesham sent him a monk who was skilled in medicine by whose help he recovered. By the hands of the same monk he sent a letter of thanks and commendation back to the abbot.[99] He asked a bishop in Wales for twelve of his hunting dogs, 'quibus non vidimus meliores.' His estates were being plagued by wolves that raided the livestock of his tenants taking lambs and poultry. He himself had lost six cygnets. He was eagerly looking forward to receiving these dogs to check these depredations.[100]

An agreeable side to Richard Clifford's character appears in his manumissions of villeins and his promotion of servants, examples of which appear in the Liber Albus. Here his letters of manumission are recorded as examined and agreed to by the prior and convent of the cathedral church.[101] In the last two years of his tenure of the diocese these occur and some are dated shortly before his translation to London. The servants who were rewarded included Thomas Alder, custodian of his palace and gaol who was given this office for life.[102] In the course of his last visit to his diocese the bishop showed favour to the prioress and nuns of Whistones in the suburbs of Worcester city. Their slender resources had been much diminished and the frequent demands on their charity were, they said, beyond their power to meet. They petitioned for relief in the form of an appropriation to them of the parish church of Weston-on-Avon which was of the bishop's patronage. He agreed and the King permitted it by special licence, the Statute of Mortmain notwithstanding. A suitable portion for the vicar was stipulated.[103]

---

[99] Ibid., fol. 37ᵛ. '... in cuius adventu solo nostra debilitas spe recuperande salutis cooperante non mediocriter conforta est.' Cf. Wylie, *History of England under Henry IV*, 3:132.

[100] Ibid., fol. 32.

[101] Liber Albus, fol. ccccxxiiii. 'Litteras venerabilis patris Ricardi Episcopi vidimus et inspeximus in hec verba; quorum interest noverint universi quod nos Ricardus Episcopus Wigorniensis isto quattuordecimo die mensis Octobrensis anno domini millesimo quattrocentesimo quinto Ricardum Avevant servum nostrum nativium cum tota sequela sua de consensu unanimi prioris et capitoli ecclesie nostre Cathedralis Wigorniensis manumittimus et ab omni iugo servitudinis seu nativitatis in perpetuum liberamus et omnino liberum facimus per presentes.' Cf. *X* 3. 24. 2 (C.I.C. 2:533a): 'non valet donatio quam facit praelatus inconsulto capitulo in damnum ecclesiae.'

[102] Liber Albus, fol. ccccxxxii.

[103] Ibid., fol. ccccxxxiiᵛ.

To the extent that a man's last will and testament may be a guide to his interests we have a little of this in the will made by Clifford in August 1416. It was witnessed at Dover on the 20th of that month, possibly as he was departing for the Council of Constance. He left £100 for his funeral expenses and the placing of a marble stone over his grave, which was to be in the cathedral church at London if it could be done appropriately. Another £100 were to be distributed among the poor in his lands and manors. The poor cripples who were bedridden or confined should have another hundred. He left 1,000 marks to his poor scholars, present or future, in his house at Oxford, Burnell's Inn, including fellows who were going on in their studies. This sum his executors were to pay out at the rate of £40 a year until the thousand marks were expended. A very few chattels he left to individuals. There is no mention of books.[104]

From these various indications we get a picture — if somewhat sketchy — of a churchman who, although kept away from his diocese by other concerns, was not wholly unmindful of his responsibilities there. He was not an outstanding leader in the Church in England during his episcopate. He was like other churchmen in writing letters to cardinals flattering in tone.[105] Like others he had representatives at the papal court at least part of the time.[106] He deprecated the Schism and expressed the correct sentiments of abhorrence of schismatics and rebels against ecclesiastical authority. In his relationships with clergy and people he shows no harshness and there are glimpses of humane concern. The incompleteness of the *memoranda* leaves one to conjecture as to the degree of oversight he gave his diocese. No probate of wills appears. Did the prior of the cathedral chapter make any report concerning his visitation? What did the archdeacons report about theirs? What injunctions did the bishop make following these — presumed — visitations? Clifford's long record as an administrator in secular affairs under two kings disposes one to think him efficient. It may not be unreasonable to suppose that he kept an eye on his subordinates as they administered diocesan affairs in his absence, but this is conjecture.

After due credit has been given to Bishop Clifford for his humane attitudes and a degree of judicious supervision of his diocese, the conclusion

---

[104] E. F. Jacob, *Reg. Chichele*, 2:224-25.

[105] MS Bodley 859, fols. 39, 40.

[106] Ibid., fol. 36ᵛ, 39. Clifford was evidently angling for the see of London while Roger Walden, cleric of varying fortune, was bishop there. He wrote to Innocent VII asking for an exchange for Walden after he himself is provided to London (Ibid., fol. 41). Both Walden and Innocent died in 1406.

must still be that his main interests centred in London, whether those interests were ecclesiastical or secular. His long absences, the first for sixteen
months, the last for two years or more, were not consistent with a bishop's
responsibility toward his spiritual charge. However genuine his concern for
this, his continued involvement in secular affairs through these years made
him more a servant of the Crown than of the Church.

III

THE REGISTER

Bishop Clifford's register is a well preserved volume of 99 folios located
in the Registrar's Office, Worcester. Folios 1-24 are $8\frac{1}{4}'' \times 13''$; folios 25-
51 are $7\frac{1}{2}'' \times 11\frac{1}{2}''$; folios 52-99 are $8\frac{1}{4}'' \times 13''$. To try to distinguish
the different hands is hazardous. Obviously when the scribe had to get as
much on his folio as he could the letters would tend to be more constricted
than when he had more space. This may account for differences between the
rolls of knights' fees and tenements and the memoranda that precede and
follow them. At fol. 11^v a new hand appears that continues to fol. 24^v.
With the ordination lists beginning on fol. 25 there appears to have been
another change and from this point to the end the penmanship is uni-
form.[107]

The register as bound contains groups of entries according to type but
they are interspersed. Ordinations are kept together, fols. 25 to 51.
Memoranda are entered on fols. 1 to 8^v (two quaternions), are resumed,
fols. 51^v to 59^v, and continue from fol. 68 to fol. 76^v. Institutions and exchanges fill fols. 9 to 24^v, fols. 60 to 67^v, and fols. 77 to the end. Memoranda for the last three years are missing. At the foot of fol. 24^v is a
notation in a late seventeenth-century hand, *folia transponuntur vide f. 50.*
Similarly on fol. 59^v is written, *a mense Dec. 1402 usque ad mensem Junii
1403 desiderantur.* Some memoranda were found, however, including those
with particulars about appropriations of parish churches.

These groupings of contents in the bound volume just described derive
from records made originally in three categories: memoranda or letters, institutions and ordinations. The ordinations were kept on separate folios,

---

[107] Except on fol. 51^v where an aborted entry concerning a matrimonial suit was made in
a quite different hand. See # 133a.

each set having been given its appropriate heading. Memoranda and institutions and exchanges were entered on folios of larger dimensions, i.e. $8\frac{1}{4}''$ × $13''$, grouped as sets of quires.

Chronological order was not consistently kept with the memoranda. Folios 1-8, with dates from 10 October 1401, to 29 March 1402, are quite irregular in this. Folios 9-24, from 11 November 1401, to 1 June 1403, have a chronological order of entries. Folio 52 begins a series of irregular dating, some entries having no date at all. At folio 60 careful chronology is resumed, whether entries were made at London or in the diocese, from 8 June 1403, to 21 June 1404. Irregular dating appears again with folio 68, at 17 December 1402. Appropriations were grouped in a series starting at folio 71, all in April 1403. Institutions and exchanges occupy folios 77, July 1404, to the end as noted, and are in chronological order.

Ordinations show evidence of more methodical record keeping. These are on the smaller folios mentioned above, i.e. $7\frac{1}{2}''$ × $11\frac{1}{2}''$. At first the lists of ordinands contain names of regular and secular clergy in haphazard order, but with section # 114 the arrangement becomes more systematic with regular clergy listed first within each grade. The chronological order of the ordinations is observed.

Appended to the fifteenth-century register's folios is an Index in a late seventeenth-century hand. This is not classified but gives the contents of the bound folios in their numerical order. From time to time marginal notations have been made in similar handwriting which have not been given in the pages of this calendar. The mediaeval clerk discontinued his headings for institutions and exchanges on folio 92. A later clerk proceeded to supply these.

In the spelling of place-names use has been made of Volume 4 of the English Place-Name Society, W. St. C. Baddelay, *Place-Names of Gloucestershire* (Gloucester, 1913) and Vols. 38-41, A. H. Smith, *The Place-Names of Gloucestershire* (Cambridge, 1964) also the *Guide to Worcestershire Records* (4th edition, Worcester, 1964), Eilert Ekwall, *Concise Oxford Dictionary of English Place-Names* (4th edition, Oxford, 1960) and *Crockford's Clerical Directory*. Where no modernized spelling of a local name has been found, the original spelling has been kept. Fifteenth-century versions of modern place names are given in the Index of Persons and Places. Personal names are spelled as found, even where the spellings vary. With a personal name denoting local origin the spelling of the register is kept and usually the preposition *de* as well.

Certain transactions that recurred continually, such as institutions and exchanges, have not been calendared *in extenso*. The bishop who received a new clerk into his diocese normally instituted his departing clerk into his new benefice by authority of a commission by the receiving bishop. The calendaring of institutions and exchanges has included the attendant circumstances where these were other than common form. Where a vacancy was caused by death, it is so calendared. Resignations were sometimes listed as free but without further qualifying comment. Such have been calendared as they were recorded. Reciprocal resignations that preceded exchanges have been assumed to be common form and, where they do appear in the original, they have not been included in the calendar. Similarly with resignations into the bishop's hands. The register contains an occasional specimen of the letters of institution or mandates to induct that were sent to archdeacons or alternative agents in the stages of appointment to parishes. The recipients of these documents are shown in the calendar. If vicars or vicarages are listed as perpetual the calendar includes this detail.

In transcribing or in calendaring I have usually left a blank space where there was a gap but if I have filled in the gap square brackets enclose what was supplied. A series of three dots double spaced represents a break in a quotation. In the original register dates were given in the old style, i.e. the year beginning on 25 March, but in reproducing them the modern style has been taken as the norm.

Two sources that have contributed to this study are MS Oxford, Bodleian Libr., Bodley 859 and the Liber Albus in the library of Worcester cathedral. The former is a letter book written on paper in a late fourteenth century hand. The Liber Albus is a large volume in vellum that records events and transactions in which the cathedral chapter had an interest. Contemporary unpublished records in the Public Record Office, London, have contributed to the context.

Mention should be made of manuscript material consulted in the British Library. BL MS Royal 10B IX is a miscellaneous assortment on vellum of various tracts, writs, letters and formularies, some of which may be state papers. Some are in French, others in Latin, written in some half dozen different hands. A number are concerned with the Schism and the attempts to deal with it through councils. Richard II, John of Gaunt, Henry IV and archbishops of Canterbury are prominent either as source or destination of these varied documents. Numerous English notables appear among them. Some letters are addressed to popes or originate with them; a letter from Martin V to Richard Clifford as bishop of London assures him of his friendly interest and inquires after his health (fol. 57[v]).

BL Harleian MS 431 consists of copies of letters administrative and diplomatic that passed between kings, lay notables, popes and bishops and embassies, that were collected by John Prophet, a successor to Clifford as Keeper of the Privy Seal. In this collection are also copies of papal bulls, model letters and tracts: a useful collection, valued by the secretarial mind. BL MS Cotton Cleopatra F III is a similar collection in which the assiduous John Prophet had a hand. It was used by N. Nicolas for *Proceedings and Ordinances of the Privy Council of England*.

BL Additional MS 33926 is a group of drawings of Kentish seals done by Rev'd Thomas Streatfield, on paper, made for wood blocks that were intended for engravings. In some instances actual seals are attached.

I want to thank the Worcester diocesan authorities for the facilities they generously provided. I am grateful to Miss Margaret Henderson, Associate Archivist of the diocese and to Mrs. B. E. Johnston, Honorary Librarian of Worcester Cathedral, from whom I have received many kindnesses. This work has necessitated transatlantic travel together with considerable time in England and some time in Rome, for which the Canada Council made two generous grants. I should like to thank the Arts Research Committee of Queen's University for a timely travel grant and financial help in other ways. To readers of the Pontifical Institute of Mediaeval Studies, Toronto, I am much indebted for important improvements in what I had prepared. And finally, I thank my wife under whose observant eye many deficiencies in the Indexes were corrected.

W. E. L. Smith.

THE REGISTER OF RICHARD CLIFFORD

MEMORANDA OR LETTERS
(Sections 1-107)

REGISTER OF RICHARD CLIFFORD
BISHOP OF WORCESTER

A CALENDAR

fol. 1r   THE REGISTER OF LETTERS PROCEEDING FROM THE CHANCERY OF THE VENERABLE FATHER IN CHRIST, THE LORD RICHARD CLIFFORD, BY THE GRACE OF GOD TRANSLATED FROM THE CHURCHES OF BATH AND WELLS TO THE CHURCH OF WORCESTER, WHO ON THE 20 SEPT. 1401 RECEIVED THE BULLS PRESENTED TO HIM IN LONDON.[1]

1   Boniface IX to Rich., elect of Worc., citing in the usual form the cost of a long vacancy, the need to settle the situation and the advantage of the simple method of provision and translation. Bp. Tideman having died *extra Romanam curiam*, the pope reserves the appointment for this turn. Rich. Clifford's election to the see of Bath and Wells is superseded, he is absolved from any canonical obligation there and is provided by translation to Worc.

fol. 1v   The usual admonitions to the new bp. follow. Dated at St. Peter's, Rome, 19 Aug. 1401, and the twelfth year of the pontificate.[2]

fol. 2r   **2** *24 Nov. 1401, London, at his Temple Bar House.*[3] Letter from Bp. Clifford to the offl. of the ct. of Cant. whose earlier letter to him of 14 Kalends Dec. [18 Nov.] is included in this reply. Certain individuals Adam Huggus, John Kyng, John Helwys, John Offmore and Thos. Clerk and other

---

[1] On the cover appear the words 'in isto Registro continentur quattuordecim quaterniones Ricardi Clifford,' with another two lines illegible.

[2] There is a marginal note that his collation from Bath was not subsequent to enthronement there but was before taking possession; that before consecration he was translated to Worc. under date Rome, 14 Kalends Sept. [19 Aug.] in the twelfth year of Boniface IX, 1401, and afterward, 9 Oct. of the same year, was consecrated in St. Paul's, London, by Thos. Arundel, abp. of Cant. (see below, p. 54 n.10).

[3] All subsequent London entries refer to this hospice of the bishop.

inhabitants of the villagers or hamlets of *Welynchewyck* and Chadwick, dioc. of Worc., were petitioning against Dns. Wm. Delve, Chpln., Master or Preceptor of the hosp. of St. Wolfstan beyond-the-Wall, Worc., over his providing of a chpln. for the chpl. of Chadwick. They had repeatedly sought redress from the bp. but he had paid no attention; hence they had turned to the ct. of the Arches. The offl. then wrote to Bp. Clifford concerning his failure to hear the case and give justice. If the bp. refused to try this suit and did not do justice within fifteen days of receipt of the letter, on the twentieth day after the lapse of this period or on the first juridical day thereafter, Delve was to be cited before him or the ct. of the Arches and he requested Clifford to let him know what he meant to do. The bp. replied that he was so occupied with arduous duties that he could not deal with the matter within the time limit set and authorized the ct. of Cant. to hear it.

fol. 2v   **3** *23 Nov. 1401, London.* Lic. during the bp.'s pleasure for John Child or his wife or family to have mass celebrated in an oratory in their house at Northwick provided it is not to the prejudice of the p. c.

4 *1 Dec. 1401, London.* Letters dimissory to Rich Compton, r. p. c. of Sutton to be ordained to all minor and major orders by any Catholic bp. and faculty is given to the bp. who ordains him.

5 *1 Dec. 1401, London.* Dispensation according to the constitution *Cum ex eo* to the above to be absent for three years for study *ubicunque in Anglia viget studium generale* and to put his church to farm to suitable persons and enjoy the fruits. The usual stipulations for attending to obsequies, the cure of souls and having a suitable proctor, the time limit to be three years, after which he is to return to his par. and reside there.[4]

fol. 3r   **6** *... Dec. 1401, London.* Lic. to the rec. and parishioners of Hanbury-by-Wick to have their ch. reconciled after its pollution by bloodshed, by any Catholic bp. provided there is no canonical obstacle, with faculty to such bp., saving his [Clifford's] due and customary procurations.[5]

---

[4] Archbishop Arundel's first Convocation, 6 October 1399, had passed twenty-nine constitutions among which the tenth was for the recall of clerks to their cures unless studying. 'Curati quicunque in studio generali proficere non valentes et alii non residentes ad ipsorum curas per dominos episcopos revocentur' (London, Lambeth Library, Reg. Arundel 1. fol. 53). See L. E. Boyle, 'The Constitution *Cum ex eo* of Boniface VIII,' in *Mediaeval Studies*, 24 (1962), 263-302. See also R. M. Haines, 'Education of English Clergy in the later Middle Ages,' *Canadian Journal of History*, 4 (1969), 1-22.

[5] See Appendix 1.

7 *Account of Reginald le Porter, sheriff of Worc. and his co-collectors of the aid from kts.' fees for the marriage of the eldest daughter [Joan of Acre] of King Edward, son of Henry.*[6]

Hundred of Oswaldslow. From the bp. of Worc. for two fees in Northwick, Wick by Worc., Fladbury, Ripple, Bredon, Kempsey, Blockley, Tredington, Hanbury by Wickham, Hartlebury and Alvechurch. £47.

Tenants of the bp. in the above vills and elsewhere in the county and above hundreds for thirty kts.' fees and a half. £61.

a *The thirty-first year of King Edward, son of Henry [1303]. Account of Thos. de Gardinis, sheriff of Glouc. and John Langeleye collectors of the aid from kts.' fees in the county of Glouc. granted to the king for the marriage of his eldest daughter.*

b *Hundred of Bradley.* From the bp.'s manor at Withington in the king's hands *sede vacante* as appears by inquisition, nothing.

c *Hundred of Brightwellsbarrow.* The bp. of Worc. for $1\frac{1}{2}$ kt.'s fee in Bibury, nothing, *sede vacante.* 60s.

d *Hundred of Deerhurst and Tadbaldeston.* The bp. of Worc. for $1\frac{1}{2}$ kt.'s fee in Cleeve Southam, Gotherington and Brockhampton. 60s.

e *Hundred of Henbury.* The bp. of Worc. for etc. [...] in the manor of Henbury, nothing, since it is free alms.

Feudatories of the Bishop of Worcester.

fol. 3v   **f** *Whistones.* The earl of Warwick for fifteen kts.' fees which he holds of the ch. of Worc.

John Wasborne for $\frac{1}{2}$ hide in Smyte.

Beatrix Blanket for $\frac{1}{2}$ hide in Northwick, viz., $\frac{1}{13}$ kt.'s fee.

---

[6] This seventh section illustrates how the assessment in terms of knights' fees had become a financial rather than a military assessment, the money raised by hidage, each hide contributing. Cf. H. M. Chew, *The English Ecclesiastical Tenants-in-Chief* (London, 1932), 32, 124.

The prioress of Whistones for a hide in Aston and part of ½ hide formerly of Walter Burford called *Whytefe*, and ¼ virgate in Northwick formerly of Peter Flagg.

John Garfy of Wick for part of a fee called *Whytefe*.

Wm. Kerdyf for part of the said fee.

John Pensax for part of the same.

The pr. of Worc. for part of the same.

Tenants of ½ virgate formerly Perdeswoll.

Thos. Hodyngton for a hide in Hodington.

Hugh le Oter for ½ virgate in Northwick.

Rich. Porter for a virgate in Tapenhale.

Wm. Noryse for the second part of a virgate in Northwick.

g   *Wick*. Elena de Arderne for 5 virgates in Goldwick.

Mayen Gurneye for a hide in Howelmestone.

Wm. Gunthropp for a virgate at Rugg's Place (at *le Rugge*).

The pr. of Worc. for ¼ kt.'s fee in Laughern.

h   *Bredon*. Walter Pole, kt., for a hide in Kinsham.

John Power for the rest of the lands in Westmancote and Norton.

i   *Blockley*. Wm. Ranes for ¼ kt.'s fee in Ditchford.

Walter Weley for lands in Aston.

John Chyld
Thos. Walleye   }   for 1½ hides formerly
John Gyleworth   of Robt. de Clyppeston.

The same John Chyld for a hide in Northwyck, once Clypston, and ½ hide in Draycote formerly of John de Draycote.

Robt. Prodehomme for a hide formerly of Gilbert de Draycote.

John Lygger for 2 virgates in Paxford.

Hy. Chestre for 2 hides in Aston.

Hy. Jinayne for ½ virgate in Blockley.

The earl of Hereford for ½ kt.'s fee in Condicote.

j *Cleeve.* Joan Bohun, countess of Hereford for a kt.'s fee in Southam.

Rich. Brommyng for ½ kt.'s fee in Stoke formerly of Roger de Hamme.

Lord le Spencer for 1⅓ virgates in Gotherington formerly of John le Barbor.

H. Chapman for 1⅓ virgates formerly of John Gerald.

fol. 4r Tenants of 3 virgates once of Adam Haym and since of Odo de Dumbleton.

Thos. Smyth de Gotherington for 1⅓ virgates formerly of J. Page.

The abt. of Tewkesbury for a hide in Gotherington.

Tenants of 6 acres once of Thos. Ede and since of Robt. Durel.

Rich. Chawmon for 1½ virgates in Gotherington formerly of W. Chawmon.

k *Withington.* James Boteler, earl of Ormonde, for a kt.'s fee in Aston formerly of Ralph Pypard.

Thos. Crossen for 3 hides in Foxcote.

John Upcote for ½ hide in Upcote.

John Meone for a hide in Colesborne.

Tenants of ½ hide in Withington once of John Mongebred, Wm. Boneton and Walter Godman.

John Cassy for a hide in Little Compton.

The pr. of Studley for a hide in Oldeswell.

l *Bybury.* John Pocher for a hide in Eycote.

The abt. of Glouc. for lands in Aldsworth.

The abt. of Cirencester for lands in Walle.

m *Tenants of 5 hides in Barnsley.*

Fladbury. Tenants of 2 hides in Bishampton once of Rich. Sturry and formerly of Wm. Kerdyf.

Joan Waryn for 2 hides in hill and moor (*hulle and more*).

Wm. Beachamp for 5 hides in Inkberrow once of Wm. de Valens and for 3 hides in Thorndon.

The heir of Thos. de Bishopston for 2 hides in the hill.

Thos. Throkmerton for a hide formerly of John de Pickersham and 3 virgates formerly of Robt. son of Simon de Throkmorton and 2½ hides formerly of the said Robt.

Rich. Dyngeleye for ½ kt.'s fee in Thorlton formerly Hondesacre.

n *Tredington*. The abt. of Evesham for 3 hides in Tidmington, 2 hides in Admescote and a hide in Tatelynton and another parcel.

Robt. Waldone for 4 hides in Longdon formerly of Geoffrey Spenser.

Tenants of ½ hide formerly of Thos. Freoman and Nicholas Warr.

o *Hampton*. Custodian of the chty. of the ch. of Stratford for the manor of Inge.

p *Stratford*. The earl of Hereford for ½ kt.'s fee in Clifford.

fol. 4v

John James ⎫
Rich. Finnke ⎪ for 1/10 of a
Wm. Leyacre ⎬ kt.'s fee.
Thos. Grene ⎭

Tenants of ½ virgate formerly of John Begelyn and ½ virgate formerly of Nicholas Begelyn.

q *Alvechurch*. Tenants of Robt. de la Chambre for one hide and 1½ virgates in Hopwood.

John Leycestre for one hide in Cowden part in ⅕ of a kt.'s fee formerly Cover Stanton.

Hy. Sutton for a hide formerly of Nicholas of Norfolk and ½ hide that was of Hugh le Boteler and formerly of Hugh of Norfolk.

r *Kempsey*. Tenants of a hide in Norton which Lady Dudley occupies.

Thos., chty. chpln. there, for 2 virgates in Norton formerly of John Marsh.

Tenants of 3 virgates in Kereswell once of John son of Ralph de Asshe for which the rent is 4½ bushels of rye per annum.

The heir of John Clopton for 3 virgates formerly of the hill of Kereswell.

s *Ripple*. Lord le Spenser for 3 hides in Upton formerly of Peter Saltmarsh.

Tenants of 3 hides in Hill Croome formerly of John Hulle.

Wm. Golafre for ½ hide in Bywell.

Tenants of one hide formerly of Simon de Crombe in Croome and ½ hide in Newington.

Tenants of ½ hide formerly of Robt. de Sexteyneslode which is held of the lord by service of 3s. 4d.

Tenants of ½ virgate formerly of Benedict de Okyngiale which is held by service of 6s.

The parson of Ripple for a virgate in Okyngeale.

t *Henbury in Saltmarsh*. Tenants of ½ kt.'s fee in Ichington occupied by Ralph Whythe.

Maurice Russel for ½ kt.'s fee in Aust.

Maurice de Berkoley for a kt.'s fee in Stoke Giffard.

Tenants of a kt.'s fee in Yate formerly Willington, *in manu regis*.

Thos Broke, kt., for ½ kt.'s fee in Aust formerly Cantock.

John Paunton for ½ kt.'s fee in Lawrence Weston and 2 hides of land there.

Tenants of 2 hides in Henbury and 2 virgates in Shyntescomb formerly Stonore, *in manu regis*.

John Eyton for a hide in Westbury.

John Kent de Wyke for a hide in Wick.

John Hayle for ⅕ kt.'s fee in Thryddelond.

Maurice de Berkeley for 1½ hides formerly Gorneye in Shirehampton.

John de Berkeley, kt., for ½ kt.'s fee in Compton.

fol. 5r   Margaret Sebrok for a virgate in Aylmington formerly of Peter Crok.

Wm. Herbard
John Poleyn
John Weston   } for the land called Veymes
Robert Burdon

John Werkerborwe for ½ hide in Wasborough.

u *Hartlebury*. Tenants of a virgate formerly Assherugge that is held of its lord by service of 1/20 knight's fee.

Tenants of a hide formerly of Walter de Whytelynge held of its lord by service of 6s. 8d. per annum.

Tenants of a hide formerly of Elias Absolon held of its lord by service of 3s.

v *Aston*. Tenants of a virgate in Aston formerly of Richard, clk.

Tenants of ½ virgate formerly of Wm. Servant.

8 *24 Oct. 3 Henry IV [1401], Westminster.* Writ of *certiorari* to Bp. Clifford to have the registers of his predecessors searched concerning the ch. of Eston, otherwise known as Aston Cantlow, in the deanery of Warwick. Beginning with the reign of Henry son of King John, he was to ascertain what persons had been presented, instituted and inducted, by whom, at what times, by what tit. and how. This information was to be sent to the Chancery at Westminster under the bp.'s seal, together with this letter.

9 *2 Dec. 3 Henry IV Westminster.* Writ summoning Bp. Clifford to
fol. 5v Parliament to be held at Westminster, 30 Jan. He was to attend in person and order his pr. and archdcns. to be there in person. One proctor from the cath. chap. and two from the diocesan clergy were to come, all with full authority to agree to what might be ordered.

10 *10 Dec. 1401, Hadham.* Lic. from Robt. [Braybrooke], bp. of London [1382-1404] to Rich., bp. of Worc., to hold ordinations, the first tonsure, minor orders and major orders, on Ember Sat., 17 Dec. at St. Paul's or elsewhere in the city or dioc. of London.

11 *4 Feb. 1402, London.* Mand. from Bp. Clifford to Mr. Wm. Forster his commissary general and John Chewe his sequestrator. He quoted a letter he had received from the bp. of London who gave at length a letter of instructions that had come to him from Thos. [Arundel] abp. of Cant. [1396-1398, 1399-1414], primate and legate, on 14 Jan.

fol. 6r The primate, referring to man's waywardness, called the people to return to the divine commandments and to humiliation and prayer that they should escape a visitation of divine wrath for their careless lives. Present afflictions were meant to lead them to acknowledge the divine rod and to amendment of life. Bps. were to direct all clergy in their diocs., both secular and regular, to have litanies, masses and processions with ringing of bells for this purpose and for the peace and prosperity of the king and realm. The people were to expiate their offences by suitable devotion, by prayers and alms and other charitable works. Bps. were authorized to declare indulgences of forty days trusting in the merits of the Blessed Virgin, of Peter and Paul and the national martyrs Alphage and Thomas, and they were directed to report by letters patent what they had done. The abp.'s letter was dated at his manor at Charing, 10 Jan. 1402.

fol. 6v The bp. of London's letter was dated at his manor of Hadham, 15 January. He directed the bp. of Worc. to follow the abp.'s orders with all due speed and to certify to the abp. the date of his receipt of these orders and what he had done.

Bp. Clifford ordered his commissary general and sequestrator to execute these instructions in the dioc. of Worc. with all possible speed. Clergy and people were to invoke the grace of God and the merits of the B. V. M., of the confessors Oswald and Wolfstan their patrons, and of all the saints. All who took part in processions and were truly penitent and prayed devoutly were to receive indulgence of forty days. A report was to be made by Easter [26 March] of the day this letter was received and how they had carried out its instructions.

fol. 7r **12** *4 Feb. 1402, London.* Commission to Dns. John Burgeys, r. of St. Swithun's Worc., Thos., r.p.c. of St. Nicholas, Worc., and Thos. Wheler, dn. of Worc., jointly and individually, to secure from the king's justices all clks. apprehended for felonies or other crimes at Worc. or elsewhere in the dioc. and to take charge of them with power of canonical coercion.

13 *Same date.* Commission in the same terms to Dns. Thos. Yong, dn. of the coll. ch. of Blessed Mary, Warwick, and John Brid, dn. of the christianity of Warwick, for that county.

14 *Same date.* The same to Dns. Thos. Flodbury, r.p.c. of St. Michael's, Glouc., to Robt. Batman, rec. of St. John's in that place and to Walter, dn. of Glouc., for that county.[7]

15 *Same date.* The same to Br. John, abt. of St. Augustine's, Bristol, and to Mr. Wm. Bryghlamton dn. of Bristol and Thos. Lye, r. of St. Ewen's, for Bristol.

16 *10 Oct. 1401, London.* Mand. to Mr. Wm. Forster, b. ll., to examine the election of Br. John Lymnour, can. of the convl. ch. of Llanthony by Glouc. to be pr. He is to confirm or annul and is given the necessary authority to complete the business. The bp. affixed the seal that he used as dn. of York.

---

[7] Gloucestershire cases in 1402 in Gaol Delivery Rolls show Robert Batman as Bishop's Ordinary. Two men were accused in the lay court one of whom successfully claimed benefit of clergy. The jury found both guilty. The layman was sentenced to be hanged and the clerk was turned over to Batman to be put into Bishop Clifford's prison (P.R.O., J.I. 3/189, membr. 29v).

Batman appeared again in the case of Thomas Waryn, a servant of the convent of Keynsham, accused of larceny, who pleaded clergy. 'Libro tradito legit ut clericus'. The jury found him guilty just the same and since he could not make restitution he went into the king's goal (ibid., membr. 26). In Bracton's day the clerk was to be delivered over to the ordinary without any inquisition (Henry de Bracton, *De Legibus et Consuetudinibus Angliae* (ed. G. E. Woodbine and S. E. Thorne, Cambridge, Mass., 1968), 2:348).

fol. 7v   **17**   *1 Feb. 1402, Southwark.* Faculty from John [Bottlesham.] bp. of Roch. [1400-1404], to the bp. of Worc. to confer the orders of acol. and subdcn. on the same day on Wm. Aleyn, m.a. and scholar in theology of the dioc. of Roch.

18   *5 Dec. 1401, London.* Signification for the capture of Wm. Halford. From the register of his predecessor Bp. Tideman [1396-1401], it appears that Wm. Halford, *alias* Carpynter, of Halford, of the county of Warwick in the dioc. of Worc. incurred major excommunication on authority of the ordinary and has continued contumacious forty days and more. The help of the secular arm is asked.[8]

19   *1 Oct. 1401, London.* Grant of a yearly pension of 100s. to John Stone, king's clk., the see having been vacant and in the hands of the king who had nominated John for a pension. It is to be paid in equal amounts at Easter and the feast of St. Michael while Clifford holds the temporalities of the see or until Stone is provided by him with a suitable benefice.[9]

20   *3 Feb. 1402, London.* Faculty to Robt. Sklatter, acol. of his dioc., to
fol. 8r   be ordained subdcn. and dcn. by any Catholic bp.

21   *15 Mar. 1402, London.* Letters dimissory as above to John Palmer, acol., for ordination to subdcn. and dcn.

22   *29 Mar. 1402, London.* Lic. during the bp.'s pleasure to John

---

[8] P.R.O. C 85/165/1 Significations. Chancery records contain five other significations from the diocese of Worcester while Clifford was bishop there. The names were John Wythur Junior of Upton-by-Gloucester and John Janynes of Hampton Monialium, 29 Nov. 1402 (C 85/165/1, Calendar # 155), John Jury of Northleach, 30 May 1403 (C 85/165/2), John Shukkebrugh, perpetual vic. of Kington, 18 April 1404 (ibid., # 3), Henry Hothum rec. of Dalesford, 26 Sept. 1407, 'by scrutiny of episcopal register' (ibid., # 4). The bishop authorized this last one at his manor of Blockley; the first three were from his London house and the fourth from Hillingdon. Clifford's two predecessors, Wakefield and Tideman sent in a higher proportion in relation to their tenures of the see. Wakefield, 1375-95, sent forty-one (C 85/164/1-41) and Tideman, in five years, sent fifteen (ibid., 42-56).

[9] It was long established practice that a bishop or head of a religious house, on being appointed, found a place for a clerk or other servant nominated by the King. Failure to do so made him liable to be charged in the court of King's Bench. For an example of this see P.R.O. KB 27/519, Rex 20. The theory of *Eigenkirche* was never far from the thinking of the mediaeval prince. Henry IV was always ready to use the church as a property. The forfeiture of the countess of Salisbury enabled him to give to the Queen revenues of the hostel of St. Benedict in Thames Street, London (Privy Seal Warrants, P.R.O. File 2, # 4). For the development of regalian right in England, see Margaret Howell, *Regalian Right in Mediaeval England* (London, 1962). For the first three decades in the fourteenth century, see W. E. L. Smith, *Episcopal Appointments and Patronage in the Reign of Edward II* (Chicago, 1938).

Harewell, donzel, to have mass celebrated for himself, his wife and family in the oratory of his manor or houses at Shotreth by a suitable chpln., provided it is not to the prejudice of the p.c.

23 *31 Mar. 1402, London.* Lic. in the same form to John Fulwode, donzel, to have mass celebrated in an oratory in the manor of his house of Tanworth.

24 *Undated, London.* Mand. to the pr. of Worc. to exclude from the ch. all in the dioc. who are doing public penance in Ember Days; to do this with all solemnity, and on Thursday at the celebration of the Lord's Supper to receive them into the nave of mother ch. solemnly as is customary.

25 *24 Mar. 1402, London.* Letters dimissory to Robt. Sklatter, dcn., to be ordained p.

26 *7 Apr. 1402, London.* Letters dimissory to Wm. Atte Grene to be ordained to minor and major orders of subdcn. and dcn.

27 *3 May 1402, London.* Lic. to Rich. Wolusford and his wife Margaret to have mass celebrated in the oratory of their house in the village of Walford during the bp.'s pleasure.

28 *3 May 1402, London.* Lic. to John Grene, vic. of p.c. of Fairford to make a pilgrimage to Rome.

fol. 8v **29** *5 June 1402, Ipswich.* Commission of Bp. Clifford to Dns. John [Malvern], pr. of the cath. ch. of Worc., to Mr. Gilbert de Stone his vic. general in spirituals, Wm. Forster his commissary general and Rich. Wych and Thos. Wybbe, cans. of Salisbury and Wells. It had been his intention to summon all clergy of the city and archdeaconry of Worc., regular and secular, who were subject to him to the cath. ch., Mon. after the feast of St. John the Baptist [26 June] for several days to explain and treat more fully of certain urgent matters concerning himself and the ch. He is unable because of pressing royal business to attend in person on that day. He instructs them to summon the clergy and present the urgent need of a charitable subsidy for himself and authorizes them to levy and collect it.

30 *Same date and place.* Commission in the same form to Dns. Walter and Wm., mks. and abts. of Glouc. and Winchcombe and to Gilbert de Stone and Rich. Wych and Thos. Wybbe for the archdeaconry of Glouc. and for the mks. and clergy of the same, to be in the ch. of Blessed Mary before-the-Abbey Gate at Glouc., Fri. 30 June, for the above mentioned business.

fol. 9r   REGISTER OF THE REVEREND FATHER AND RULER IN CHRIST DNS. RICH
CLIFFORD, BY THE GRACE OF GOD BP. OF WORC. CONCERNING COLLATIONS,
INSTS. AND EXCHS. EFFECTED BY HIM, WHO, HAVING BEEN TRANSLATED
FROM THE SEE OF BATH AND WELLS TO THAT OF WORC. RECEIVED THE
BULLS OF HIS TRANSLATION AT LONDON, 20 SEPT. 1401.[10]

31   *11 Nov. 1401, London.* Admission of Roger Berford, p., as perp. chpln. to the chpl. or chty. of Elmley Castle. (pat.: Lady Margaret Beauchamp, countess of Warwick), vacant by the resignation of Roger Tangeley.
Letters of induction to the archdcn. of Worc.

32   *12 Nov. 1401, London.* Exch. on the authority of Edmund [Stafford],
bp. of Exeter [1395-1419], between Thos Herford, can. of the coll. ch. of
fol. 9v   Ottery St. Mary, Exeter dioc., and Wm. Rayner, r.p.c. of Rodmarton (pat.:
fol. 10r   Henry Burdon, donzel). The bp.'s letters of inst. to Rayner and Herford and
his letter of induction to the archdcn. of Glouc. follow. Also the certification to the bp. of Exeter which included in full the commission he had
originally sent to Bp. Clifford from his London house dated 5 Nov.

33   *26 Nov. 1401, London.* Exch. on the authority of Wm. [Wykeham.],
bp. of Winch. [1367-1404], between John Palmer, perp. vic. of Donameney
fol. 10v   (pat.: Walter Grendon, pr. of the hosp. of St. John of Jerusalem in
England) and Wm. Colyt, perp. vic. of Imbeshere, Winch. dioc. (pat.: p.
& c. of the convl. ch. of Blessed Mary of Southwick, Winch. Dioc.). Both
took oath to reside in person.[11] John's letter of inst. from Bp. Clifford is
given. Wm. had letters of inst. and mand. to induct to the archdcn. of
Glouc.

34   *1 Dec. 1401, London.* Resignation of the hosp. or chty. of Holy
Trinity, Longbridge by Berkeley, into the bp.'s hands by the last incumbent

---

[10] *Marginal note as above,* p. 43, n.2: This collation of the reverend father from Bath and
Wells was not subsequent to enthronement there but before taking possession; before consecration he was translated to Worc. under date Rome 14 Kalends Sept. [19 August] in the
twelfth year of the pontificate of Boniface IX, 1401, and later, on 9 Oct. of that year, was
consecrated in St. Paul's, London, by Dns. Thos. Arundel, abp. of Cant.
[11] 'iuxta formam constitucionum dominorum Othonis et Othoboni ... in hac parte
editarum...'. Cf. Constitutiones Othonis et Othoboni, Tit. 9, *De Residentia Vicariorum.*
Lyndwood, pp. 95 ff. See also Powicke and Cheney, *Councils and Synods,* 2:757.

Thos. Bristowe and collation and inst. of Thos. Thame, p., as master or perp. chpln. who has sworn to observe all the terms of the foundation, and had letters of collation and induction to the archdcn. of Glouc.

fol. 11r **35** *5 Dec. 1401, London.* Admission and inst. of Dns Rich. Wylkyns, p., to the perp. vicge. of p.c. of Butler's Marston (pat.: a. & c. of Alcester), vacant by resignation of Dns. John Kynges. Robt. Moreshom, clk., acting as proctor. Letters of inst. and mand. to induct to the archdcn. [*blank*].

36 *22 Dec. 1401, Hillingdon.* Admission and inst. of John Petche, clk., to p.c. of Comberton on presentation by the king, vacant and in his hands through custody of the land and heir of Thos., late earl of Warwick, a tenant *in capite*. Letters of inst. and induction to the archdcn. of Worc.

fol. 11v **37** *1 Feb. 1402, London.* Exch. between Robt. Cavell, r.p.c. of Alcester (pat.: Katherine, prioress and c. of Cook Hill), and John Piry, r.p.c. of Kinwarton of the bp.'s collation. Letters of inst. collation and induction [*unspeficied*].

38 *10 Feb. 1402, London.* Exch. between Rich. Hewet, warden of the chty. of St. Michael of Winterbournebradston (pat.: Thos. Bradston, squire) and John Martyn, r.p.c. of St. Nicholas of Hertford, Lincoln dioc. Rich. had letters of inst. *sub forma debita*; John had letters of induction to the archdcn. [*blank*].

39 *13 Feb. 1402, London.* Exch. between Dns. John Stokton, *alias* Mathew, r.p.c. of Peopleton (pat.: Lord John Russell, kt.), and John Dalby, r.p.c. of Iken, Norwich dioc., Dalby acting as proctor for John Stokton. Letters of inst. Dalby had letters of induction to the archdcn. [*blank*].

fol. 12r **40** *15 Feb. 1402, London.* Admission and inst. of Dns. Ralph Pyng, p., to the perp. vicge. of Grimley, vacant by resignation of Mr. John Derlton (pat.: pr. and chap. of the cath. ch. of Worc.), Thos. Lancastell, squire, acting as proctor. Letters of inst. and induction to the custodian of the peculiar of Grimley.

41 *23 Feb. 1402, London.* Admission and inst. of Dns. John Molsham, p., to p.c. of St. Werburgh's, Bristol, (pat.: a. & c. of Blessed Mary of Keynsham) vacant by the death of Dns. John Warewyke, John Sperey, notary public acting as proctor. Letters of inst. and induction to the archdcn. of Glouc.

fol. 12v **42** *23 Mar. 1402, London.* Admission and inst. of Br. Thos. Paas, can. of p.c. of Halesowen to the perp. vicge. of p.c. of Clent (pat.: a. & c. of Halesowen) vacant by the death of Br. Robt. de Atherstone, can. of the same, Thomas Birchecar, clk., acting as proctor for Br. Thos. Letters of inst. and induction to the archdcn. [*blank*].

43   *30 Mar. 1402, London*. Collation and inst. of Dns. Thos. Knyght, p., to the recy. of p.c. of Upton-on-Severn. Letters of collation and induction to the archdcn. of Worc.

44   *11 Apr. 1402, London*. Admission and inst. of Dns. Rich. Ferne, p. to the perp. vicge. of Hampton Lucy (pat.: Mr. John Burbach, rec. of Hampton). Letters of inst. and induction to Mr. Wm. Forster, commissary general, or in his absence to the said Mr. John [Burbach], rec.

fol. 13r   **45**   *12 Apr. 1402, London*. Exch. between Dns. Walter Trelewith, r.p.c. of Littleton (pat.: a. & c. of Malmesbury, Salisbury dioc.) and John Collyng, perp. vic. of p.c. of Tuddenham, Hereford dioc. Letters of inst. John had mand. to induct to the archdcn. of Glouc.

46   *25 Apr. 1402, London*. Exch. between Dns. Walter Stonyng, r.p.c. of St. Andrew's, Eastleach (pat.: a. & c. of Tewkesbury), and Dns. Robt. Bowyer, r.p.c. of Taplow, Lincoln dioc. Letters of inst. Robt. had letters of induction to the archdcn. of Glouc.[12]

47   *25 Apr. 1402, London*. Exch. between Dns. John Wade, r.p.c. of Idlicote (pat.: p. & c. of Kenilworth, Coventry and Lichfield dioc.) and Dns. John Kynarton, r.p.c. of Knossington, Lincoln dioc. Wm. Penford acting as proctor. Letters of inst. John Kynarton had letters of induction to the archdcn. of Worc.

fol. 13v   **48**   *28 Apr. 1402, London*. Admission and inst. of Dns. Rich. Newbold, p., to p.c. of Alcester (pat.: prioress and conv. of Cook Hill), vacant by resignation of Dns. John Piry, Thos. Lancastre *literatus* acting as proctor. Letters of inst. and mand. to induct to the archdcn. of Worc.

49   *28 Apr. 1402, London*. Admission and inst. of Dns. John Piry, p., to the perp. vicge. of p.c. of Old Sodbury (pat.: Br. Thos. Hertlebury, sacristan of the cath. ch. of Worc.), vacant by resignation of Dns. Thos. Baker, Robt. de Moreshom acting as proctor. Letters of inst. and induction to the archdcn. of Glouc.

[12] See Appendix 2.

50 *4 May 1402, London.* Collation and inst. of Dns. Rich. Clifford, p., to the ch. of Hampton Lucy, vacant by the death of Mr. John Burbach. Letters of collation and induction...

fol. 14r **51** Transactions of Mr. Gilbert de Stone, can. of the ch. of Hereford and vicar-general in spirituals of Bp. Clifford who is to be engaged abroad[13] from 6 May 1402, on which day he left London for the territories of the Emperor for the marriage between his son and Lady Blanche, daughter of King Henry IV, until 29 July, 1402, on which day Bp. Clifford returned to London from overseas.

The bp. gave the following instructions.

52 *4 May 1402, London.* The bp. refers to his departure abroad on important business of the king and realm compelling him to be away from his dioc. He is concerned for his flock and appoints Stone his vicar-general in spirituals, giving him full powers in the city and diocese to admit and institute clergy into vacant ch. benefices and to induct them or cause them to be inducted. He has authority to examine elections in religious houses and confirm or annul and to induct and instal those whose election is confirmed. He can hear and decide all cases within the diocesan spiritual jurisdiction and execute the decision. He can initiate and conduct probate of estates whether there is a testament or not. He is to inquire into crimes among his fol. 14v subjects to correct or punish canonically. Whatever pertains to the office by right or custom he is to execute or cause to be executed with power of spiritual coercion. It is not intended that the power already given to Mr. Wm. Forster as commissary general be revoked in any way.

53 *9 May 1402, London.* Admission and inst. by the above vic. in spirituals of Mr. Robt. Esbach, clk., to the recy. of St. Andrew's, Worc. (pat.: pr. and chap. of the cath. ch. of Worc.). Letters of inst. and mand. to induct to archdcn. of Worc.

54 *18 May 1402, London.* Admission and inst. by the vic. in spirituals of Mr. John Pavy, clk., to the recy. of St. Martin's, Worc. (pat.: pr. and chap. of the cath. ch. of Worc.), Thos. Birchecarr, clk., acting as proctor. Letters of inst. and mand. to induct to the archdcn. of Worc.

55 *21 May 1402, London.* Admission and inst. by the vic. in spirituals of Dns. John Benson, p., to the perp. vicge. of p.c. of Berkeley (pat.: a. & c. of

---

[13] *in remotis.*

St. Augustine's by Bristol), vacant by the death of Mr. John Trevisa. Letters of inst. and mand. to induct to archdcn. of Glouc.

fol. 15r **56** *28 May 1402, London.* Exch. between Mr. Edward Dauntesey, r.p.c. of Yate, and Mr. Roger Smyth, preby. or holder of part of a preb. which Rich. Bray recently obtained in the ch. of St. Probus, Exeter dioc. (pat.: King Henry by reason of the custody of the lands and heir of the late John de Welyngton, tenant *in capite* of Richard II, lately King, having been in that King's hands.) Letters of collation and inst. Roger had mand. to induct to archdcn. of Glouc.

57 *31 May 1402, London.* Exch. between Dns. Thos. Chapman, r.p.c. of Hampton Meysey (pat.: Dns. Rich. de St. Maur, kt.), and Dns. Nicholas fol. 15v Stoke, can. and preby. in the coll. ch. of St. Thomas the Martyr, Glaseney and r.p.c. of Withleigh (pat.: p. & c. Bodmin, Exeter dioc.). The text of the letter of collation and inst. from the vic. in spirituals to Thos. follows. It stated that the collation to the canonry and preb. belonged to the bp. of Exeter, it detailed the particulars of the exch. which were normal, and sealed it with the seal of the Worc. officiality.[14] Letters of collation and inst. Nicholas had mand. to induct to the archdcn. of Glouc.

58 *22 June 1402, Worc.* Admission and inst. of John Pokulchurch, clk., to Beverston ch. (pat.: a. & c. of St. Peter, Gloucester), vacant by the resignation of the last rec., Robt. Deyson, *alias* Sumnor, acting as proctor. Letters of inst. and mand. to induct to the archdcn. of Glouc.

fol. 16r **59** *25 June 1402, Worc.* Writ *quod admittatis* dated 14 June, from Sir Wm. Thirnyng, Chief Justice of the King's Bench, stating that the king had recovered in ct. presentation to Aston, *alias* Aston Cantlowe, against the pr. of Studley. The vic. in spirituals was ordered to admit the royal presentee, Thos. Burdet, clk., which he did, with John Charleton, clk., acting as proctor.[15] Letters of inst. and mand. to induct to the archdcn. of Worc.

60 *27 June 1402, Worc.* Admission and inst. of Wm. Merston, p., to Loxley vicge. (pat.: p. & c. of Blessed Mary of Kenilworth) as perp. vic. Letters of inst. and mand. to induct to the archdcn. of Worc.

---

[14] 'In quorum testimonium sigillum officialitatis Wygorniensis quo utimur in officio presentibus est appensum.'

[15] The royal writ refers to the last Hilary Roll, lxxviii. Henry IV promised his first Parliament that if there was a dispute about his right to present to a church benefice, the Ordinary could refuse to admit his presentee until the royal claim had been upheld by due process of law (*Rot. Parl.*, 3:438). See Calendar # 142n.

61 *30 June 1402, Glouc.* Exch. between John Webbe, r.p.c. of Icomb (pat.: pr. and chap. of the cath. ch. of Worc.), and Wm. Ibote, r.p.c. of Halling (pat.: a. & c. of Winchcombe). Wm. had letters of inst. and induction to the dn. of Stowe of the archdeaconry of Glouc. because the archdcn. of Glouc. has no jurisdiction in the ch. of Icomb. John had letters to the above archdcn.

fol. 16v   **62** *1 July 1402, Glouc.* Admission and inst. of Wm. Ayse, chpln., to p.c. of Haseleton (pat.: a. & c. of Winchcombe) vacant by the resignation of Mr. John Bradeley, *alias* Wynchecombe. Letters of inst. and mand. to induct to the archdcn. of Glouc.

63 *1 July 1402, Glouc.* Admission and inst. of John Monk, p., to p.c. of Oldbury (pat.: Lady Joan Burdon of Oldbury), vacant by the resignation of Dns. John Bathe. Letters of inst. and mand. to induct to the archdcn. of Glouc.

64 *18 July 1402, London.* Exch. between Robt. Child, r.p.c. of Lighthorn and Wm. Kydermystre, r.p.c. of St. Nicholas Acon, London (pat.: a. & c. of Malmesbury). Wm. was presented by King Henry who had the wardship of Rich., son and heir of Thos., late earl of Warwick. Letters of inst. Wm. had mand. to induct to the archdcn. of Worc.

fol. 17r   **65** *14 July 1402, London.* Collation of Nicholas Herbury, clk., kinsman of Bp. Clifford, to the preb. in the coll. ch. of Westbury commonly called Brianes Provendre, the preb. being vacant by the death of Dns. Thos. Butiller. The commission, dated at London, 6 May, authorizing the vic. in spiritualis to collate to a benefice *sine cura* is recited. The letter of collation and the order to the dn. of Westbury to induct follow.[16]

fol. 17v   *Completion of the transactions of the vic. [in spirituals] and resumption of activity by the bp.*

66 *8 Aug. 1402, London.* Admission and inst. of Thos. Stanford, p., to the chty. of Beauvale in Coberley (pat.: John Asscheton, r.p.c. of Coberley) vacant by the resignation of Dns. John Godehyne, p. Letters of inst. and mand. to induct to archdcn. of Glouc.

67 *21 Aug. 1402, Hillingdon.* Exch. between Thos. Hoppeley, perp. vic. of p.c. of Tanworth (pat.: p. & c. of Blessed Mary the Virgin and St.

---

[16] See Appendix 3.

fol. 18r Michael the Archangel of Maxstoke, Coventry and Lichfield dioc.) and William Bakon, perp. vic. of p.c. of Crich, same dioc., (pat.: a. & c. of Blessed Mary of Darley, same dioc.), Robert Moreshom, clk., acting as proctor for Thos. Letters of inst. Wm. had mand. to induct to archdcn. of Worc.

68 *23 Aug. 1402, Hillingdon.* Exch. between Dns. John Couper, r.p.c. of Belbroughton (pat.: Dns. John Cheyne, kt., John Kyrkeby, Thos. Cole, Wm. Ofchurch and John Knyghtley), and Dns. Nicholas Hambury, r.p.c. of Horton (pat.: Mr. Nicholas Danyell, can. of Salisbury and preby. of Horton). Letters of inst. and mand. to induct, Nicholas to the archdcn. of Worc. and John to the archdcn. of Glouc.

fol. 18v **69** *26 Aug. 1402, Hillingdon.* Admission and inst. of Wm. Gereward, p., to the ch. or chpl. of Oddingley (pat.: Dns. Edward Charleton, kt.), vacant by the resignation of Dns. Thos. Gereward. Letters of inst. and induction to Dns. John Bele, r.p.c. of St. Helen's, Worc.

70 *1 Sept. 1402, Hillingdon.* Admission and inst. of John Gerlethorp, clk., of York dioc., to the perp. vicge. of p.c. of Inkberrow (pat.: Dns. Wm. de Beauchamp, lord of Bergevenny, John Prat, clk., Thos. Reed, Thos Walwayn, Wm. Wenlok, John Olney, squires). Letters of inst. and induction, directed to the archdcn. of Worc. refer to a papal dispensation for Gerlethorp to continue in minor orders for ten years.[17]

fol. 19r **71** *28 Sept. 1402, Hillingdon.* Admission and inst. of Dns. Adam Drake, p., to the perp. vicge. of p.c. of Giffardstoke (pat.: p. & c. of Little Malvern). Letters of inst. and mand. to induct to the archdcn. of Glouc.

72 *12 Oct. 1402, London.* Exch. between Dns. John Stevenes, vic. of Coln St. Aldwyn and Dns. Wm. Asshford, vic. of Churcham, Hereford dioc. both on presentation by a. & c. of St. Peter's, Glouc. both vicges. perp. Letters of inst. Wm. had letters of induction to the archdcn. of Glouc.

fol. 19v **73** *13 Oct. 1402, London.* Exch. between Dns. John Chaumbreleyn, r.p.c. of St. Michael's, Bristol (pat.: a. & c. Tewkesbury) and John Hokere, r.p.c. of Cotleigh, Exeter dioc. Letters of inst. John Hokere had mand. to induct to the archdcn. of Glouc.

[17] The thirteenth constitution of the Council of Lyons, 1274, had required that any clerk instituted in a church must go on to priest's orders within a year and be resident. Exemptions were numerous. Cf. F. M. Powicke and C. R. Cheney, *Councils and Synods*, 2:857.

74 *14 Oct. 1402, London.* Admission and inst. of John Newent, clk., of Hereford dioc. to p.c. of Tonworth (pat.: John Veel, squire), vacant by the resignation of the incumbent, Mr. Edmund Kempley. Dns. John Monk, p., acting as proctor. Letters of inst. and induction to the archdcn...

75 *19 Oct. 1402, London.* Exch. between Dns. Nicholas Stoke, r.p.c. of Hampton Meysey (pat.: Dns. Rich., lord of St. Maur, kt.) and Dns. Rich. Norreys, r.p.c. of Combe Martin, Exeter dioc. Letters of inst. and mand. to induct to the archdcn. of Glouc.

fol. 20r **76** *3 Nov. 1402, London.* Admission and inst. of Thos. Malle, p., to the perp. vicge. of p.c. of Kidderminster (pat.: p. & c. of Blessed Mary of Maiden Bradley, Salisbury dioc.), John Haukyn, p., acting as proctor. The bp. reserved for himself and his successors the right to order a suitable part of the fruits of the ch. to be kept for the support of the vic.[18] Letters of inst. and induction to the archdcn. of Worc.

77 *8 Nov. 1402, London.* Admission and inst. of Thos. de Kyrkeby, p., to the perp. vicge. of p.c. of Sherbourne by Warwick, presented by the *locum tenens*[19] of the prior of the hospital of St. John of Jerusalem in England, the pr. himself being away. Letters of inst. and induction to the archdcn. of Worc.

fol. 20v **78** *19 Nov. 1402, London.* Exch. between Dns. Rich. Ulkerthorp, r.p.c. of Llanharan, Llandaff dioc. and Dns. Lewis Stalwarth, r.p.c. of Rockhampton (pat.: Dns. Francis Court, kt.), Thomas Mathewe acting as proctor for Lewis Stalwarth. Letters of inst. Rich. had letters of induction to the archdcn. of Glouc.

79 *1 Dec. 1402, London.* Admission and inst. of Mr. Geoffrey Wyke, p., to the preb. which Rich. Bromlee, clk., obtained in the coll. ch. of Warwick, now vacant by Rich.'s death (pat.: King Henry). Letters of inst. and mand. to induct to the dn. of the coll. ch.

80 *28 Dec. 1402, Windsor Castle.* Admission and inst. of John de Gerlethorp, dcn., to the perp. vicge. of p.c. of Inkberrow (pat.: Wm. de Beauchamp, lord of Bergevenny, John Prat, clk., Thos. Reed, Thos. Walwayn, Wm. Wenlok and John Olney, squires). Letters of inst. and induction to the archdcn. of Worc.

---

[18] See # 231.
[19] ad presentacionem locumtenentis.

fol. 21r   **81** *20 Jan. 1403, Hillingdon.* Admission and inst. of Mr. John Kerby, m.a., to p.c. of Oddington (pat.: Wm. Kerby, precentor in the cath. ch. of Blessed Peter, York), vacant by the resignation of Dns. Wm. Assherug. Letters of inst. and induction to the archdcn. of Glouc.

82 *14 Feb. 1403, Hartlebury Castle.* Exch. between Dns. Rich. Shirbourne, r.p.c. of Coln-Rogers (pat.: a. & c. of St. Peter's, Glouc), and Dns. John Couper, perp. vic. of p.c. of Dudley (pat.: p. and c. of St. James of Dudley, Coventry and Lichfield dioc.) Letters of inst. and mand. to induct to the archdcn. of Glouc. for John, of Worc., for Rich.

83 *19 Feb. 1403, Pershore.* Admission and inst. of Dns. Thos. Alford, p., to p.c. of Strensham (pat.: John Russell, kt.). Letters of inst. and induction to the archdcn.

84 *28 Feb. 1403, Hartlebury Castle.* Admission and inst. of Mr. Wm. Wotton, *alias* Ludelowe, clk., to p.c. of Broadwell (pat.: a. and c. of Evesham OSB) vacant by the resignation of Dns. Wm. Malle. Letters of inst. and induction to the archdcn.

fol. 21v   **85** *12 Mar. 1403, Glouc.* Admission and inst. of John Godhyne, p., to p.c. of Edgeworth (pat.: Thos. Ralegh de Charles, lord of Farnborough), vacant by the resignation of Robt. Swynford. Letters of inst. and induction to the archdcn.

86 Chty. of Beauvale in the ch. of Coberley. [*No entry*].

87 *15 Mar. 1403, Hartlebury Castle.* Exch. between Dns. John Wayte de Wodehous, perp. vic. of p.c. of Ebrington (pat.: a. & c. of Biddlesden, Lincoln dioc.), and Dns. John Drew, r.p.c. of Steane, Lincoln dioc. Letters of inst. and mand. to induct to the archdcn. of Glouc.

fol. 22r   **88** *15 Mar. 1403, Hartlebury Castle.* Admission and inst. of Dns. John Bucke, p., to the perp. vicge. of p.c. of Paineswick (pat.: p. & c. of Llanthony by Glouc. OSA). Letters of inst. and induction to the archdcn. of Glouc.

89 *18 Mar. 1403, Hartlebury Castle.* Admission and inst. of Dns. Thos. French, p., to the perp. vicge. of p.c. of St. Owen's, Glouc. (pat.: p. & c. of Llanthony by Glouc.). Letters of inst. and induction to the archdcn. of Glouc.

90 *15 Mar. 1403, Hartlebury Castle.* Admission and inst. of Dns. Stephen Doun, p., to the perp. vicge. of p.c. of Prestbury (pat.: p. & c. of Llanthony by Glouc.). Letters of inst. and induction to the archdcn. of Glouc.

fol. 22v   **91**   *25 Mar. 1403, Hartlebury Castle.* Admission and inst. of Dns. John Whylde, p., to the perp. vicge. of p.c. of Overbury (pat.: pr. and chap. of the cath. ch. of Worc.). Letters of inst. and induction to the archdcn. of Worc.

92   *28 Mar. 1403, Hartlebury Castle.* Admission and inst. of Dns. John Cook, p., to p.c. of Spetchley (pat.: Wm. Spechesley, donzel). Letters of inst. and induction to the archdcn. of Worc.

93   *9 Apr. 1403, Hartlebury Castle.* Exch. between Dns. Thos. Thame, pr. or master of the Hosp. of the Holy Trinity, Longbridge by Berkley (pat.: Dns. Thos. Berkeley, lord of Berkley) and Mr. Reginald Pony, r.p.c. of Oddington, Lincoln dioc., John Colevyle, *literatus*, acting as proctor. Letters of inst. Reginald had mand. to induct to the archdcn. of Glouc.

fol. 23r   **94**   *9 Apr. 1403, Hartlebury Castle.* Admission and inst. of Mr. Thos. de Lye, p., to p.c. of St. Peter's, Bristol (pat.: a. & c. of Tewkesbury, OSB). Letters of inst. and induction to the archdcn. of Glouc.

95   *12 Apr. 1403, Worc.* Admission and inst. of Dns. Wm. Halle, p., to the perp. vicge. of p.c. of Lower Swell, vacant by the resignation of Dns. Rich. Wodeford, (pat.: a. & c. Notley, Lincoln dioc.). Letters of inst. and induction to the archdcn. of Glouc.

96   *13 Apr. 1403, Worc.* Admission and inst. of Dns. Thos. Eklessale, p., to the perp. vicge. of p.c. of Blessed Mary before the Gate of Glouc. Abbey (pat.: a. & c. of St. Peter's, Glouc., OSB), John Calverhull, clerk acting as proctor.[20] Letters of inst. and induction to the archdcn. of Glouc.

97   *13 Apr. 1403, Worc.* Admission and inst. of Dns. Robt. Grene, p., to the perp. vicge. of p.c. of Toddington (pat.: a. & c. of Hailes, O. Cist.). Letters of inst. and induction to the archdcn. of Glouc.

fol. 23v   **98**   *13 Apr. 1403, Worc.* Admission and inst. of Dns. Wm. Wrenneford, p., to the perp. vicge. of p.c. of Holy Trinity, Glouc. with the annexed chpl. of Graslone (pat.: a. & c. of St. Peter's, Glouc., OSB).[21] Letters of inst. and induction to the archdcn. of Glouc.

99   *14 Apr. 1403, Worc.* Admission and inst. of Nicholas Hulle, p., to the perp. vicge. of p.c. of Himbleton (pat.: pr. and chap. of the cath. ch. of Worc.).[22] Letters of inst. and induction to the archdcn. of Worc.

[20] Cf. # 227.
[21] Cf. # 228.
[22] Cf. # 225, 226, 229.

100   *18 Apr. 1403, Worc.* Admission and inst. of Dns. Salamon Haywode, p. to p.c. of Boxwell (pat.: a. & c. of St. Peter's, Glouc., OSB). Letters of inst. and induction to the archdcn. of Worc.

101   *28 Apr. 1403, Hampton Lucy.* Admission and inst. of Dns. John Wethy, p., to the perp. vicge. of p.c. of Pillerton-Hersey, vacant by the resignation of Dns. John Colet (pat.: d. & c. of the coll. ch. of Blessed Mary of Warwick). Letters of inst. and induction to the archdcn.

fol. 24r   **102**   *15 May 1403, Hillingdon.* Admission and inst. of Dns. Thos. Whitenhurst, p., to p.c. of St. Andrew's, Wick (pat.: p. & c. of Deerhurst). Letters of inst. and induction to the archdcn. of Worc.

103   *19 May 1403, Hillingdon.* Exch. between Dns. John Martyn, custodian of the chty. of Winterbournebradston (pat.: Thos. Bradston, lord of Winterbournebradston, donzel), and Dns. Robt. Warreys, r.p.c. of Ditteridge, Salisbury dioc. Letters of inst. Robt. had mand. to induct to the archdcn. of Glouc.

104   *19 May 1403, Hillingdon.* Exch. between Dns. Thos. Kyngham, r.p.c. of Blessed Mary of Oversley (pat.: Wm. Sloughtre, lord of Clent in the county of Glouc.) and Dns. John Tymmes *alias* Tyso, rec. of Shaw, Salisbury dioc. Letters of inst. John had mand. to induct to the archdcn. of Glouc.

fol. 24v   **105**   *21 May 1403, Hillingdon.* Exchange between Mr. Thos. Felde, doctor of laws, of Hartlebury, and Dns. John Cresset, r.p.c. of Ross, Hereford dioc. Collation of respective diocesans. Letters of inst. John had mand. to induct to the archdcn. of Worc.

106   *22 May 1403, Hillingdon.* Admission and inst. of Thos. Shelford, clk., to p.c. of Aston Cantlow (pat.: p. & c. of Studley), vacant by the death of Thos. Burdet. Letters of inst. and induction to the archdcn. of Worc.

107   *1 June 1403, London.* Exch. between Dns. John Robilet, perp. vic. of p.c. of Wolford (pat.: warden and scholars of the scholars' house of Merton in Oxford), and Dns. John Ragbrok, r.p.c. of Baynton, Salisbury dioc. Robt. Staunton acting as proctor for Robilet. Letters of inst. John Ragbrok had mand. to induct to the archdcn.

THE REGISTER OF RICHARD CLIFFORD

ORDINATION LISTS
(Sections 108-133)

THE REGISTER OF THE VENERABLE FATHER IN CHRIST, THE LORD RICHARD CLIFFORD OF ORDINATIONS CONFERRED, THE WHICH REVEREND FATHER WAS TRANSLATED FROM THE SEE OF BATH AND WELLS TO THE SEE OF WORCESTER IN THE YEAR 1401.

fol. 25r **108** *Ember Sat., 17 Dec. 1401, London. Orders celebrated by the bp. in the chpl. of his London House by special lic. of Robt. [Braybrook], bp. of London [1382-1404], whose lic. dated 10 Dec. precedes the ordination lists.*[1]

Acolytes

Mr. Roger Bottall, b. ll., York dioc., d.o.

Roger Bolter, r.p.c. of Blackawton, Exeter dioc., d.o.

John Cook, Lincoln dioc., d.o.

Br. Wm. Harngey, OSA, London.

Br. Wm. Petwode
Br. Roger Albon
Br. Stephen Chart
Br. Robt. Laxton
Br. Rich. Caleys
Br. Hermann Coleyn
} O. Carm., London

fol. 25v Wm. Wynwyk, r.p.c. of Beeby, Lincoln dioc., d.o.

Walter Counterfet, London dioc., d.h.t.

Philip Polton, Salisbury dioc., d.o.

Nicholas Harbury of London, d.h.t.

John Mareys, Exeter dioc., d.o.

John Dygon.

Br. Hy. Wareyne, OP, London.

Br. Nicholas Wockyng
Br. John Blokley
Br. Lawrence Man
Br. Roger Wylton
} OSB, Chertsey, Winch. dioc.

Thos. Ryngold
Adam Gyvecok
} vicars choral of St. Paul's, London, d.h.s.

Owem Coneway, r.p.c. of Llanmuair.

[1] See Appendix 4.

Subdeacons

Mr. Roger Bottall, b.ll., York dioc., d.o. and tit. of pry. of Thurgarton, same dioc.

Roger Bolter, r.p.c. of Blackawton, Exeter dioc., d.o., t.b.s.

John Elys, Exeter dioc., d.o. and tit. of pry. of St. Mary Overy in Southwark, Winch. dioc.

John Bernard, Norwich dioc., d.o. and tit. of St. Leonard's hosp., Newport, London dioc.

John Waryn, Lincoln dioc., d.o. and tit. of the pry. of Haliwell, London dioc.

Br. John Berly
Br. Geoffrey London } cans. of the church of Blessed Mary Overy in Southwark
Br. Hy. Werkworth Winch. dioc.

Rich. Gatyn, Winch., d.o. and t.p.s.

Br. Cornelius Hugan, OSA, London conv.

Br. Thos. Cheyne
Br. John Bernyngham } O. Carm., London
Br. Robt. Laxton

fol. 26r   Rich. Skydemore, r.p.c. of Shillingford, Exeter dioc., d.o. and t.b.s.

Stephen Doun, York dioc., d.o. and tit. of the pry. or hosp. of Blessed Mary-without-Bishopsgate, London dioc.[2]

Br. John Embrigge, can. of the hosp. of St. Mary-without-Bishopsgate, London dioc.

John Scot de Terlynge, London dioc., d.h.t. and tit. of the monas. of Beeleigh, same dioc.

Wm. Wynwyk, r.p.c. of Beeby, Lincoln dioc., d.o., t.b.s.

Br. Nicholas Wockyng
Br. John Blokley
Br. Lawrence Man } OSB, Chertsey, Winch. dioc., d. (etc.)
Br. Roger Wylton

John Mareys, Exeter dioc., d.o. and tit. of the monas. of Bodmin, same dioc.

[2] Hospital of St. Mary of Bethlehem.

Deacons

Mr. Walter Honyngton, London dioc., s.d. and tit. of a. & c. of Keynsham, Bath and Wells dioc.

John Swyft, tit. of Ditcheat, Bath and Wells dioc., d.o., t.b.s.

John Cristemesse, Ely dioc., tit. of the mons. of Blessed Mary and St. John the Evangelist of Leighs, London dioc., d.o.

Ancelm Kylmyngton, York dioc., tit. of the house of Kirkstead, d.o.

John Hornsee, York dioc., d.o. and tit. of p. & c. of Merton, Winch. dioc.

David Michell, Bath and Wells dioc., d.h.p. and of p. & c. of Poughley, Salisbury dioc.

Br. Peter de Argentina, OP, London.

John Wellys, London dioc., tit. of a. & c. of St. John, Colchester, London dioc., d.h.t.

Thos. Call, perpetual choral vic. of the cath. ch. of Wells, t.s.s., d.o.

fol. 26v Mr. Wm. Lambert, York dioc., tit. of a. & c. of Osney, Lincoln dioc., d.o.

Br. John Odyham, OSB, Chertsey, Winch. dioc., d.o.

John Barnes, York dioc., tit. of priory of St. Mary Magdalen of Monk Bretton, same dioc., d.o.

Br. Andrew Canntirbury
Br. Wm. Beklee   } O. Carm., Maldon, London dioc.
Br. John Handesacre

Priests

Walter Muskham, London dioc., tit. of the hosp. of St. Mary of Elsing Spital, London.

Thos. atte Hythe, Salisbury dioc., d. etc., tit. of p. & c. of Bisham, same dioc.

John Kaulyn, London dioc., tit. of the monas. of Beeleigh, same dioc.

John Markham, York dioc., tit. of the hosp. of Blessed Mary of Bootham-by-York, s.d.

John Walden *alias* Spark, London dioc., s.d. tit. of the monas. of Osney, Lincoln dioc.

Wm. Clethe, Lincoln dioc., tit. of the monas. of Missenden, s.d.

Mr. Thos. Malton, b. ll., r.p.c. of Lydiard Millicent, Salisbury dioc., t.b.s.

John Mabbe, Exeter dioc., s.d. tit. of St. Bartholomew's hosp. in Smithfield by London.

Br. John Stanfeld, mk. of the Carthusian house, London, s.d.

Br. James Pagham of St. Thos. hosp. in Southwark s.d.

Br. John Lord, can. of the pry. of Berden, London dioc.

John Carsewell, r.p.c. of St. Leonard's in St. Vedast Lane, London, tit. of St. Martin's le Grand, London, s.d.

Wm. Lyne, Lincoln dioc., tit. of p. & c. of Chicksands, s.d.

fol. 27v John Eyre, Worcester dioc., tit. of St. John's hosp., Lechlade.

Thos. Macy, Salisbury dioc., tit. of the pry. of Tortington.

Wm. Beynyn, Exeter dioc., tit. of the pry. of St. Andrew of Cowick, same dioc.

Alexander atte Beare, Exeter dioc., tit. of the monas. of Canonsleigh, same dioc., s.d.

John Tryvet, Exeter dioc., tit. of the monas. of Dunkeswell, same dioc. s.d.

Br. Nigel Wasshyngton
Br. Nicholas Tewkesbury } OP, London
Br. Thos. Mannyng

John Baldewyne, London dioc., tit. of the house of nuns of Henham at-the-Castle, same dioc.

Robt. Fountayne, Lincoln dioc., tit. of the house of Woburn s.d.

Nicholas Hulle, Bath and Wells dioc., d. etc., tit. of the monas. of Keynsham, same dioc.

John Prechet, London dioc., s.d. tit. of the monas. of Waltham, same dioc.

John Knyfe, Bath and Wells dioc., s.d. tit. of Forde.

Br. John Dorem
Br. Rich. Spaydyng } O. Carm., London

fol. 27v **109** *Ember Sat., 18 Feb. 1402. London, Orders celebrated by the bp. of Worcester in the chpl. of his London house by special lic. of the bp. of London, The lic. follows.*

Acolytes

John Smyth de Gamlingay, Ely dioc., d.o.

John Gurdon, London dioc., d.o.

Wm. Hodyrsall, York dioc., d.o.

Br. Nicholas Rowe, O. Carm., London.

Thos. atte Mylle, Lincoln dioc., d.o.

Mr. Wm. Aleyn, Roch. dioc., d.h.s.

Subdeacons

Mr. John Coll, can. of St. Paul's, London, d.o., t.b.s.

Mr. John Woghope, Cant. dioc., fellow of Merton Hall, Oxford, tit. of the said hall, d.o.

John Bele de Wisbech, Ely dioc., tit. of the pry. of St. Radegund, of Cambridge, same dioc., d.o.

Wm. Treberneth, Exeter dioc., tit. of the monas. of Osney, Lincoln, d.o.

Wm. Rauf, Exeter dioc., tit. of the pry. of Bodmin, same dioc., d.o.

Br. Hermann of Cologne
Br. Rich. Caleys
Br. Wm. Petwode   } O. Carm., London.
Br. John Londe

Wm. Wade, London, tit. of the monas. of Langdon, Cant. dioc., d.o.

Philip Polton, Salisbury dioc., tit. of the new hosp. of Blessed Mary of Strood, Roch. dioc., d.o.

Mr. Thos. Morton, r.p.c. of Brinkley, Ely dioc., t.b.s., d.h.t.

John Walys, Exeter dioc., tit. of the house or pry. of St. Germans, Exeter dioc., d.o.

fol. 28r   John Gobyen, Exeter dioc., tit. of the pry. of Bodmin, same dioc., d.o.

Mr. Wm. Aleyn, fellow of Clare Hall, Cambridge, tit. of the said hall, d.o.

Adam Jevecok, vic. choral of the cath. ch. of St. Paul, London, t.s.s.

Deacons

Stephen Doun, York dioc. tit. of the bp. of Worc., d.o.

Rich. Skydmore, r.p.c. of Shillingford, Exeter dioc., t.b.s., d.o.

Rich. Triby, Exeter dioc., tit. of the house of Tavistock, same dioc., d.o.

Wm. Aleyn, Exeter dioc., tit. pry. of Bodmin, same dioc., d.o.

Mr. Roger Bottall, b. ll., York dioc., tit. of the pry. of Thurgarton, same dioc., d.o.

Wm. Dypford, Exeter dioc., tit. of the hosp. of St. Lawrence-by-Bristol, Worc. dioc., d.o.

John Elys, Exeter dioc., tit. of the pry. of St. Mary Overy in Southwark, Winch. dioc., d.o.

Richard atte Kyrke, r.p.c. of Widmerpool, York dioc., t.b.s., d.o.

John Bernard, Norwich dioc., tit. of St. Leonard's hosp. Newport, London dioc., d.o.

Robt. Bengrove, Worc. dioc., tit. of St. Wolfstan's hosp., Worc.

William Bryt, Salisbury dioc., tit. pry. of Christ Ch. of Twineham, Winch. dioc., d.o.

Br. Thos. Barlee ⎫ cans. of the convl. ch.
Br. Geoffrey London ⎬ of Blessed Mary Overy in
Br. Hy. Werkeworth ⎭ Southwark, Winch. dioc.

John Waryn, Lincoln dioc., tit. of the pry. of Haliwell, London dioc., d.o.

Br. John Blokley ⎫
Br. Lawrence Mann ⎬ OSB, Chertsey, Winch. dioc.
Br. Rich. Wylton ⎭

fol. 28v   Br. Robt. Laxton, O. Carm., London.

John Mareys, Exeter dioc., tit. of the pry. of Bodmin, same dioc., d.o.

Stephen Monynden, Cant. dioc., tit. of the monas. of St. Gregory, Cant., d.h.t.

Rich. Gatyn, Winch. dioc., t.p.s., d.o.

Br. Thos. Wendylbury, O. Cist. Rewly, Lincoln dioc., d.o.

Wm. Pylton, r.p.c. of Shifnal, Coventry and Lichfield dioc., t.b.s., d.o.

John Barfote de Higham-Gobion, Lincoln dioc., tit. of the pry. of Chicksands, d.h.t.

John Skot, London dioc., tit. of the monas. of Beeleigh, same dioc., d.h.p.

Robt. Fyssher, York dioc., tit. of the coll. ch. of Southwell, same dioc., d.h.p.

Matthew Newton, St. Asaph dioc., tit. of the patrimony of Meredud ap David ap Ll[ewelyn] of the same dioc., d.o.

Br. John Hembrigge, can. of the pry. or hosp. of Blessed Mary-without-Bishopsgate, London, d.h.t.

Priests

Thos. Call, vic. choral of the cath. ch. of Wells, tit. of his vicge., d.o.

John Barnes, York dioc., tit. of the monas. of St. Mary Magdalen of Monk Bretton, same dioc., d.o.

Peter Allerton, York dioc., tit. of the pry. of Michelham, Chich. dioc., d.o.

Wm. Hurte, Exeter dioc., tit. of the monas. of St. Frideswide, Oxford, Lincoln dioc., d.o.

Matthew Symon, Exeter dioc., tit. of the above monas., d.o.

Mr. Walter Hanyton, London dioc., tit.

John Elvestowe, r.p.c. of Tarporley, Coventry and Lichfield dioc., t.b.s., d.o.

John Welles, London dioc., tit. of the house of St. John, Colchester, same dioc., d.h.d.

Rich. Smyth de Wymondley, Lincoln dioc., tit. of the pry. of Wymondley, same dioc., d.o.

John Hornsee, York dioc., tit. of the pry. of Merton, d.o.

fol. 29r   Br. Nicholas Davy of the house of St. Thos. of Acon, London, d.h.t.

Br. John Hatfeld
Br. John Leghton   } OSB, of St. Albans.
Br. Rich. Luton
Br. Robt. Bever

Br. Wm. Manfeld, OSB, cath. ch. of Roch., d.o.

Ancelm Kylnyngton, York dioc., tit. of the house of Kirkstead, same dioc., d.o.

Mr. Thos. Sloughtre, r.p.c. of Baunton, Worc. dioc., t.b.s.

John Swyft, r.p.c. of Ditcheat, Bath and Wells dioc., t.b.s.

Br. Thos. Dalby
Br. Wm. Sozreys   } OSB, Westminster.

Br. Thos. Axebrygge can. of the house of the Holy Trinity, London.

110   *Sat. when Sitientes is sung [Sat. preceding Passionweek], 11 Mar. 1402, London, Orders celebrated by the bp. in the chpl. of his London house by special lic. of the bp. of London.*

Subdeacons

Thos. Hereford, r.p.c. of Rodmarton, Worc. dioc., t.b.s.

fol. 29v   Br. Nicholas Rowe, O. Carm., London.

John Smyth de Gamelyngey, Ely dioc., tit. of the pry. of Ickleton, d.o.

Deacons

Mr. John Woghope, Cant. dioc., fellow of Merton Hall, Oxford, tit. of the same hall, d.o.

Wm. Treberneth, Exeter dioc., tit. of the monas. of Osney, d.o.

Robt. Sklatter, Worc. dioc., tit. of the monas. of Bruern, same dioc., (*sic*).

Philip Polton, Salisbury dioc., tit. of the hosp. of Blessed Mary of Strode, Roch. dioc., d.o.

Wm. Lymyngton, Bath [and Wells] dioc., tit. of the hosp. of St. John the Baptist, Wells, d.o.

Wm. Rauf, Exeter dioc., tit. of the pry. of Bodmin, same dioc., d.o.

John Polglas, Exeter dioc., tit. of the abbess of Wherwell Winch. dioc., d.o.

Thos. de Bergevenny, Llandaff dioc., tit. of the house of St. Mark, Bristol, Worc. dioc., d.o.

Robt. Couche, Salisbury dioc., tit. of the nuns of Blessed Mary, Winch., d.o.

John Bullouk, Winch. dioc., tit. of the pry. of Tortington, Chich. dioc., d.o.

Wm. Wade, London dioc., tit. of the monas. of Langdon, Cant. dioc., d.o.

Thos. Coffyn, Exeter dioc., tit. of the house of Newenham, same dioc., d.o.

John Walys, Exeter dioc., tit. of the pry. of St. Germans, same dioc., d.o.

Priests

Rich. Halbarne, York dioc., tit. of Balliol Hall, Oxford, d.o.

fol. 30r Mr. John White, St. David's dioc., tit. of the house of Osney, d.o.

Wm. Aleyne, Exeter dioc. tit. of the pry. of Bodmin, same dioc., d.o.

John Elys, Exeter dioc., tit. of the pry. of St. Mary Overy, Winch. dioc., d.o.

John Mareys, Exeter dioc., tit. of the pry. of Bodmin, same dioc., d.o.

Nicholas North, Salisbury dioc., tit. of the monas. of Lacock, same dioc., s.d.

Edmund Taunton, Bath [and Wells] dioc., tit. of the pry. of Selborne, Winch. dioc., d.o.

Br. Hy. Werkworth, can. of the ch. of Blessed Mary Overy, Winch. dioc., d.o.

Rich. Skydmore, r.p.c. of Shillingford, Exeter dioc., t.b.s., d.o.

Rich. Gatyn, Winch. dioc., t.p.s., d.o.

Robt. Bengrove, Worc. dioc., tit. of St. Wolfstan's hosp., Worc.

Roger Leget, Roch. dioc., tit. of the nuns of Dartford, same dioc., s.d.

Robt. Fyssher, York dioc., tit. of the coll. ch. of Southwell, same dioc., d.o.

Wm. Pylton, rec. of Shifnal, Coventry and Lichfield dioc., t.b.s., d.o.

111 *1 Apr. 1402, Eltham.* Memorandum that on Sat. in the Vigil of Easter, vid. 2 Apr. 1402, in the ch. of Eltham manor, King Henry IV being present, the bp. ordained Mr. Wm. Aleyn, fellow of Clare Hall, Cambridge, to the priesthood, by special lic. of John Bottlesham, bp. of Roch. [1400-1404], tit. of said hall, s.d.h.p.[3]

fol. 30v   **112** *Ember Sat., 23 Sept. 1402, Hillingdon. Orders celebrated by the bp. in the chpl. of his house at Hillingdon, by special lic. of the bp. of London.*

Acolytes

Thos. Burdet, Lincoln dioc., d.o.

John Dyer ⎫
John Smyth ⎬   Worc. dioc.
Wm. Grene ⎭

Deacons

Wm. Stacy, Worc. dioc., tit. of the monas. of Hailes, same dioc.

John Graunger, Salisbury dioc., tit. of the pry. of Poughley, d.o.

Priests

Stephen Doun, York dioc., tit. of the pry. or hosp. of Blessed Mary-without-Bishopsgate, London dioc., d.o.

fol. 31r   **113** *Ember Sat., 23 Dec. 1402. Orders celebrated by the bp. in the chpl. of his house at Hillingdon by special lic. of the bp. of London.*

Acolytes

John Sandale, Dublin dioc., d.o.

Thos. Pyle, Worc. dioc.

John Milward, Salisbury dioc., d.o.

John Petsche, r.p.c. of Comberton Magna, Worc. dioc.

Subdeacons

John Dyer, Worc. dioc., tit. of the monas. of St. Augustine, Bristol, d.o.

John Smyth, same dioc., tit. of the pry. of Cold Norton, d.o.

John South, Salisbury dioc., tit. of the pry. of nuns of Littlemore, d.o.

Br. Wm. Harngey, OSA, London.

[3] Easter Day was 26 March. If the Vigil referred to Easter Week the date ought to have been 1 April.

Thos. Halywell of the par. of All Saints in Broad Street, London, of the immediate jurisdiction of the abp. of Cant., tit. of King Henry IV, d.o.

John Petche, r.p.c. of Comberton Magna, Worc. dioc., t.b.s.

Walter Countrefynt, Lincoln dioc., tit. of the pry. or hosp. commonly called Elsing Spital, London, d.o.

Deacons

Alexander Clympyng, Salisbury dioc., tit. of the monas. of Tarrant, d.o.

Br. Nicholas Wokkyng, OSB, Chertsey, Winch. dioc., d.o.

John Gerlethorp, York dioc., tit. of Rich., bp. of Worc., d.o.

Priests

John Graunger, Salisbury dioc., tit. of the pry. of Poughley, d.o.

Wm. Stacy, Worc. dioc., tit. of the monas. of Hailes.

Br. John Odyham	OSB, Chertsey,
Br. John Blokkeley	Winch. dioc.
Br. Rich. Wylton	

Br. Hy. Dancastre, OP, London.

fol. 31v   Wm. Hodersall, York dioc., tit. of the monas. of Blessed Mary of Whalley, Coventry and Lichfield dioc.

Wm. Lyngeyn, Worc. dioc., tit. of St. Wolfstan's hosp., Worc.

Walter Fyssh, Salisbury dioc., tit. of the nuns of Tarrant, d.o.

114   *Sat. of first week of Lent, 10 Mar. 1403. Orders celebrated by the bp. in the conv. ch. of Llanthony by Glouc.*

Acolytes

Br. John Norton	
Br. John Twynyng	OSB, Tewkesbury
Br. Robt. Berwe	
Br. John Wyrcetre	

Br. Rich. Budyer, OFM, Gloucester.

Walter Wynley
Hy. Grafton
Hy. Spelly
John Adam
Walter Robert

Thos. Swalowe
Thos. Yate
Hy. Wawe
Wm. Camme } of the dioc. of Worc.
Thos. Lake
Wm. Whitchened
Robt. Piers
Nicholas Kynges

Hy. Asshe, Coventry and Lichfield dioc., d.o.

fol. 32r *Subdeacons*

Br. Wm. Preston
Br. Wm. Malvern } OSB, St. Peter's, Glouc.
Br. Walter Stanley
Br. Rich. Horton

Br. John Norton
Br. John Twynyng
Br. John Berwe } OSB, Tewkesbury
Br. John Wyrcetre
Br. Roger Bristowe

Br. Nicholaus Lekhampton
Br. Thos. Chiltenham } cans. of Cirencester
Br. Thos. Sturmy
Br. Wm. Lechelade

Br. John Bussh, OFM, Gloucester.

John Collyt, Exeter dioc., tit. of the pry. of St. Nicholas, Exeter, d.o.

Wm. Joye, Worc. dioc., tit. of the monas. of Studley, d.o.

John Willyys, same dioc., tit. of the hosp. of Lechlade, d.o.

Robt. Stanley, same dioc., tit. of the hosp. of St. Oswald by Whistones, d.o.

John Bristowe, same dioc., tit. of the monas. of Alcester, d.o.

Wm. Wode, same dioc., tit. of the nuns of Cook Hill, d.o.

Hy. Wawe, same dioc., tit. of the monas. of Winchcombe, d.o.

John Kerby, rec. of Oddington, same dioc., t.b.s.

Wm. Brereley, fellow of Merton Hall, Oxford, Lincoln dioc., tit. of the same hall, d.o.

Deacons

Br. John Gloucestre
Br. Wm. Newenton } OSB, Pershore

Br. Wm. Spert
Br. Rich. Calne } cans. of Llanthony

Br. Thos. Frompton, OSB, Hailes.

Br. Wm. Bristowe, O. Cist., Kingswood.

Br. John Claveryng, OFM, Gloucester.

Robt. Ferys, Exeter dioc. tit. of a. & c. of Beaulieu, Winch. dioc., d.o.

John James, Worc. dioc., tit. of the monas. of Evesham, d.o.

John Smyth, Worc. dioc., tit. of the pry. of Cold Norton, d.o.

John Paradys, same dioc., tit. of the pry. of Poulton, d.o.

Robt. Fossard, Ossory dioc., of the monas. of Blessed Mary of Rewley, Oxford, d.o.

Wm. Nicholles, Worc. dioc., tit. of the nuns of Cook Hill, d.o.

Thos. Geffrays, Hereford dioc., t.p.s., d.o.

John Petche, rec. of Comberton [Magna], Worc. dioc., t.b.s.

John Kemmeys, Hereford dioc., tit. of the chty. of Winforton, d.h.t.

Priests

Br. Wm. Froncetre, OSB, St. Peter's, Glouc.

Br. Thos. Circetre
Br. Thos. Brightwelton } OSB, Winchcombe

Br. Thos. Pershore, OSB, Pershore.

Br. Wm. Wotton
Br. Roger Gloucestre } OSB, Hailes

Br. John Wodelond, OSB, Kingswood.

Br. John Walsch, OFM, Glouc.

John Pole, rec. of Cardynham, Exeter dioc., t.b.s., d.o.

Roger Bolter, r.p.c. of Blackawton, Exeter dioc., t.b.s., s.d.

John Nicholas of the city of Hereford, tit. of the pry. of Hereford, s.d.

Roger Werkman, Chich. dioc., tit. of the pry. of Clifford, s.d.

John Turnor, Hereford dioc., tit. of Abbey Dore, s.d.

fol. 32v

115 *Sat. when Sitientes is sung, 31 Mar. 1403. Orders celebrated by the bp. in the chpl. of his castle at Hartlebury.*

fol. 33r   *Acolytes*

Br. Thos. Wircestre OSA, Wick, Worc. dioc.

Thos. Crosse ⎱
John Colynes ⎟
Thos. Levyet ⎟
Rich. Ambresley ⎬   of Worc. diocese
John Northwode ⎟
John Cropthorn ⎟
Thos. Hullor ⎰

John Aston of Worc. city.

Subdeacons

Mr. Roger Smyth, rec. of Yate, Worc. dioc., t.b.s.

Thos. Beteryng of the city of London, tit. of the bp. [of Worc.], d.o.

Thos. Crosse, Worc. dioc., tit. of St. Wolfstan's hosp., Worc.

Thos. Lake of the city of Worc., tit. of the said hosp.

Thos. Yate, Worc. dioc., tit. of the monas. of Malmesbury.

Rich. Porter, same dioc., tit. of the prioress and c. of Henwood.

Hy. Grafton, same dioc., tit. of St. Bartholomew's hospital, Glouc.

Peter Buryman, same dioc., tit. of St. Oswald's hosp., Worc.

Hy. Spelly, same dioc., tit. of same hosp. of St. Oswald.

Rich. Geek, Exeter dioc., tit. of the monas. of St. Stephen, Launceston, d.h.t.

John Sendale, Dublin dioc., tit. of the hosp. of Blessed Mary-without-Bishopsgate, London, d.o.

John Kyng, Exeter dioc., tit. of the pry. of St. Frideswide, Oxford, d.o.

Deacons

John Bristow, Worc. dioc., tit. of the monas. of Alcester.

Wm. Joy, same dioc., tit. of the pry. of Studley.

John Wyllyys, same dioc., tit. of St. John's hosp., Lechlade.

Wm. Wode, same dioc., tit. of the nuns of Cook Hill.

Robt. Stanley, same dioc., tit. of St. Oswald's hosp., Worc.

John Kerby, rec. of Oddington, same dioc., t.b.s.

Roger Bovet, Exeter dioc., tit. of the pry. of Bodmin, s.d.

John Mayow, Exeter dioc., tit. of said pry., s.d.

John Alvethcote, Exeter dioc., tit. of the pry. of Frithelstock, d.o.

John Colle, Exeter dioc., tit. of the pry. of St. Nicholas, Exeter, d.o.

Thos. Broke, Exeter dioc., tit. of the pry. of St. Germans, d.o.

fol. 33v Thos. Shere, Exeter dioc., tit. of the pry. of St. Germans, d.o.

Wm. Champion, same dioc., tit. of prioress and c. of Littlemore, Lincoln dioc., d.o.

John Collyt, Exeter dioc., tit. of the pry. of St. Nicholas, Exeter, d.o.

Rich. Philip, same dioc., tit. of the pry. of St. Frideswide, Oxford, d.o.

Wm. Brereley, fellow of Merton Hall, Oxford, tit. of said hall, d.o.

Thos. Odbryght, Lincoln dioc., tit. of the pry. of Bicester, same dioc., d.o.

Thos. Gamman, St. David's dioc., t.p.s., d.o.

Priests

John Gerlethorp, vic. of Inkberrow, Worcester dioc., t.b.s., s.d.

John Dyer, Worcester dioc., tit. of the monas. of St. Augustine, Bristol.

John Smyth, Worcester dioc., tit. of the pry. of Cold Norton, same dioc.

Br. Thos. Radclyffe, OSA, Wick, same dioc.

John Paradys, Worc. dioc., tit. of the pry. of Poulton.

John [Petche] rec. of Comberton Magna, Worc. dioc., t.b.s.

John James, same dioc., tit. of the monas. of Alcester.

Wm. Nicholles, same dioc., tit. of the nuns of Cook Hill.

Robt. Farley, ... dioc., tit. of the pry. of Little Malvern, d.o.

Alexander Clympyng, Salisbury dioc., tit. of the nuns of Tarrant, d.o.

John Cork, Exeter dioc., tit. of the monas. of Tavistock, d.o.

Robt. Fossard, Ossory dioc., tit. of the monas. of Blessed [Mary] of Rewley, Oxford, d.o.

John Doyngel, Exeter dioc., tit. of the pry. of St. Germans, same dioc., d.o.

Rich. Whitlampe, Coventry and Lichfield dioc., tit., of the monas. of Darley, d.o.

Robt. Ferys, Exeter dioc., tit. of the monas. of Beaulieu, Winch. dioc., d.o.

John Shryvenham, Lincoln dioc., tit. of the nuns of Lacock, d.o.

Mr. Roger Bottall, York dioc., tit. of the pry. of Thurgarton, d.o.

fol. 34r **116** *Holy Sat., 14 Apr. 1403. Orders celebrated by the bp. in his cath. ch. of Worc.*

Subdeacons

Walter Roberdes, Worc. dioc., tit. of St. Bartholomew's hosp., Glouc., d.o.

Wm. Mortymer, of the city of Worc., t.p.s.

John Couper, Coventry and Lichfield dioc., tit. of St. Oswald's hospital by Worc., d.o.

Deacons

Thos. Beteryng, of the city of London, tit. of the bp. of Worc., d.o.

Thos. Lake, of the city of Worc., tit., of St. Wolfstan's hospital by Worc.

Mr. Roger Smyth, rec. of Yate, Worc. dioc., t.b.s.

Thos. Crosse, same dioc., tit. of St. Wolfstan's hosp.

John Kyng, Exeter dioc., tit. of the pry. of St. Frideswide, Oxford, d.o.

Priests

John Kerby, rec. of Oddington, Worc. dioc., t.b.s.

Mr. Wm. Brereley, fellow of Merton Hall, Oxford, Lincoln dioc., tit. of said hall, d.o.

John Bristowe, Worcester dioc., tit. of the monas. of Alcester, same dioc.

Robt. Stanley, same dioc., tit. of St. Oswald's hosp. by Worc.

fol. 34v Wm. Joye, Worc. dioc., tit. of the pry. of Studley, same dioc.

John Collyt, Exeter dioc., tit. of the pry. of St. Nicholas, Exeter, d.o.

Roger Benet, same dioc., tit. of the pry. of Bodmin, d.o.

John Colle, Exeter dioc., tit. of the said pry. of St. Nicholas, d.o.

Thos. Gamman, St. David's dioc., t.p.s., d.o.

John Braklee, Lincoln dioc., tit. of the nuns of St. Michael-by-Stamford, same dioc., d.o.

Thos. Odbryght, Lincoln dioc., tit. of the pry. of Bicester, same dioc., d.o.

117 *9 June 1403. Orders celebrated by the bp. in St. Stephen's Chpl. in the palace of Westminster by special lic. of the bp. of London.*

Subdeacon

John Heanok, Exeter dioc., tit. of the house of the Holy Trinity, London, d.o.

Deacons

Peter Buryman, Worcester dioc., tit. of St. Oswald's hosp., Worc.

Wm. Whitchirch, York dioc., tit. of the pry. of Blessed [Mary] of Folkstone, Cant. dioc., d.o.

Rich. Geek, Exeter dioc., tit. of the pry. of St. Germans, same dioc., d.o.

Priests

Br. John Wormenhale, can. of the pry. of St. Frideswide, Oxford, Lincoln dioc., d.o.

fol. 35r Mr. Roger Smyth, rec. of Yate, Worc. dioc., t.b.s.

Thos. Beterynge of the city of London, tit. of the bp. of Worc., d.o.

Thos. Crosse, Worc. dioc., tit. of St. Wolfstan's hosp., by Worc.

Rich. Philipp, Exeter dioc., tit. of the pry. of the said St. Frideswide, d.o.

118 *Ember Sat., 22 Dec. 1403. Orders celebrated by the bp. in the chpl. of his house at Hillingdon by special lic. of the bp. of London.*

fol. 35v Thos. Wylcotes, r.p.c. of Burton, Worc. dioc., t.e.s., to be deacon.

fol. 36r **119** *First Sat., in Lent, 15 Feb. 1404. Orders celebrated by the bp. in the chpl. of his London house by special lic. of the bp. of London.*

Acolytes

John Flynt, Roch. dioc., tit. of the hosp. of Blessed Mary-without-Bishopsgate, London dioc., d.o.

Thos. Agas, Lincoln dioc., tit. or said hospital, d.o.

Walter Fraunceys, Exeter dioc., d.o.

John Burgonn, r.p.c. of St. Olave's, Exeter, d.o.

Wm. Spridlyngton, r.p.c. of Springthorpe, Lincoln dioc., d.o.

Subdeacons

Stephen Petit, Exeter dioc., tit. of the monas. of Thame, Lincoln dioc., d.o.

Edward Legh, Exeter dioc., tit. of the monas. of Buckfast, same dioc., d.o.

John Beaufitz, Exeter dioc., tit. of the pry. of St. Nicholas, Exeter, d.o.

Wm. Grendon, Exeter dioc., tit. of the said pry. of St. Nicholas, d.o.

Wm. Whateley, Bath [and Wells] dioc., tit. of the monastery of Kingswood, d.o.

fol. 36v John Knouston, Exeter dioc., tit. of the monas. of Torre, same dioc., d.o.

John Borngan, Exeter dioc., tit. of the pry. of Bodmin, same dioc., d.o.

Michael Carnebon, Exeter dioc., tit. of said pry., d.o.

John Treher, Exeter dioc., [tit.] of same pry., d.o.

John Burgonn, Exeter dioc., r.p.c. of St. Olave's Exeter, t.b.s., d.o.

Wm. Boneton, Worc. dioc., tit. of the pry. of Studley, same dioc.

Robt. Wale, Lincoln dioc., tit. of the pry. of Cold Norton, d.o.

Edward Myldenhale, Norwich dioc., tit. of the pry. or hosp. commonly called Elsing Spital, London, d.o.

Wm. Sprydlyngton, r.p.c. of Springthorpe, Lincoln dioc., t.b.s., d.o.

Deacons

John Wyche, Bath and Wells dioc., tit. of the pry. of Bruton, d.o.

John Bragge, Exeter dioc., tit. of the monas. of Osney, d.o.

John Gayle, Lincoln dioc., tit. of the monas. of Bruern, same dioc., d.o.

Hy. Wawe, Worc. dioc., tit. of the monas. of Winchcombe, same dioc.

Priests

John Chawelowe, Salisbury dioc., tit. of the pry. of Poughley, same dioc., d.o.

John Southe, Salisbury dioc., tit. of the nuns of Littlemore, d.o.

John Remys, Chichester dioc., tit. of the pry. of Cotham by Arundel, same dioc., d.o.

John Coryngham, r.p.c. of Deene, Lincoln dioc., t.b.s., d.o.

fol. 37r **120** *Holy Sat., 19⁴ Mar. 1404. Orders celebrated by the bp. in the chpl. of his house at Hillingdon by special lic. of the bp. of London.*

Priests

Philip ap 3enn ap Rees, r.p.c. of Mounton, St. David's dioc., s.d., t.b.s.

John Beaufitz, Exeter dioc., tit. of the pry. of St. Nicholas, Exeter, d.o.

⁴ *Sic.* It should read, 29 March.

Walter Roberdes, Worc. dioc., tit. of St. Bartholomew's hospital, Glouc., same dioc.

Wm. Boneton, Worc. dioc., tit. of the pry. of Studley, same dioc.

121 *24 May 1404. Orders celebrated by the bp. in the chpl. of his house at Hillingdon, Whit. Sat. by special lic. of the bp. of London.*

Acolytes

Br. Thos. Gloucestre, OSB, Alcester, Worc. dioc.

Br. Wm. Muchelley, can. (*sic*) of Kingswood, same dioc.

Br. Thos. London
Br. Rich. Merfeld } OSB Chertsey, Winch. dioc., d.o.
Br. Peter Stoke

fol. 37v. Rich. Brugge, Hereford dioc., s.d.h.p.

Subdeacons

Br. Wm. Intebergh
Br. Thos. Gloucestre } OSB, Alcester, Worc. dioc.

Br. Wm. Muchelley, can. of Kingswood, same dioc.

Br. Thos. London
Br. Rich. Merfeld } OSB, Chertsey, Winch. dioc., d.o.
Br. Peter Stoke

Deacons

Br. Hy. Weston
Br. John Otenell } OSB, Chertsey, Winch. dioc., d.o.

Mr. Rich. Kyngeston, same dioc., tit. of the monas. of Chertsey.

Thos. Corman, Worc. dioc., tit. of the pry. of Poulton, Salisbury dioc., (*sic*).

Rich. Porter, Worc. dioc., tit. of the nuns of Henwood.

Priests

Br. Wm. Romsey, mk. of the monas. of Dorchester, Lincoln dioc., s.d.

Br. Wm. Brystow, can. of Kingswood, Worc. dioc.

John Knouston, Exeter dioc., tit. of the monas. of Torre, d.o.

122 *Ember Sat. 20 Sept. 1404. Orders celebrated by the bp. in the convl. ch. of Llanthony by Glouc.*

fol. 38r   *Acolytes*

Br. John Brystowe
Br. Wm. Abendon   } OSA,
Br. Robt. de Norwych   Bristol

Br. Wm. Poywyke
Br. John Frompton   OSB, St. Peter's, Glouc.,
Br. Adam Grene   Worc. dioc.
Br. Rich. Stafford

Br. John Sudbury, OSB, cath. ch. of Worc.

Br. Robt. Acton, can. of Kingswood.

Br. John Prous   } O. Carm.,
Br. Wm. Hayton   Glouc.

Br. Rich. Beer OFM, Glouc.

Nicholas Barstaple
Walter Aysshelworth
John Palmer
John Wethurherd
Thos. Messager
John Hulle
John Brugge   secular acols. of
Robt. Wodeman   Worc. dioc.
John Tryst
John Warylowe
Wm. Lane
John Parlebien
Thos. Strongfere
Thos. Chiryton

Wm. Spelly of Worc. city.

Wm. Eggedon, Hereford dioc., *dimissus ad ordines accolitatus et subdiaconatus.*

John Carpenter, same dioc., *dimissus ad ordines acol. et subd.*

Subdeacons

Br. Wm. Poywyk
Br. John Frompton   OSB, St. Peter's,
Br. Adam Grene   Glouc.
Br. Rich. Stafford

fol. 38v   Br. Rich. Cowern, OSB, cath. ch. of Worc.

Br. John Keynesham, can. of St. Augustine's, Bristol, Worc. dioc.

Br. Walter Wynley, can. of the pry. of Llanthony by Glouc., same dioc.

Br. Nicholas Curteys, OP, Glouc.

Br. Rich. Bodyer, OFM, Glouc.

John Wheton, Worc. dioc., tit. of St. John's hosp., Lechlade, d.o.

Thos. Honyborne, Worc. dioc., tit. of the monas. of Cold Norton, d.o.

Rich. Malvern, Worc. dioc., tit. of the monas. of Stonely, d.o.

John Grene, Worc. dioc., tit. of a. & c. of Pershore.

Thos. Maltman, Worc. dioc., tit. of the house or hosp. of St. Bartholomew, Glouc.

John Snard, Worc. dioc., tit. of a. & c. of Bordesley.

John Carpentere, Worc. dioc., tit. of the monas. of Hailes.

Thos. Symond, Worc. dioc., tit. of the monas. of Great Malvern.

Wm. Eggedon, Hereford dioc., [tit.] of p. & c. of Llanthony by Glouc. and their house at Duddeston, d.o.

Rich. Brugge, Hereford dioc., tit. of the above, d.o.

Deacons

Br. Rich. Brugge, OSB, cath. church of Worc.

Br. Nicholas Lechampton
Br. Thos. Cheltenham   } cans. of Cirencester,
Br. Thos. Sturmy   Worc. dioc.
Br. Wm. Lechelade

Br. John Norton
Br. John Twynyng   } OSB, Tewkesbury,
Br. Roger More   Worc. Dioc.
Br. John Wyrcetre

Br. Wm. Grene   } cans. of the pry. of Llanthony
Br. John Heghamstede by Glouc., Worc. dioc.

Br. Wm. Intebergh   } OSB, Alcester, Worc.
Br. Thos. Gloucestre   dioc.

Br. Wm. Muchelley, can. of Kingswood, said dioc.

Br. Wm. Thurkyl, OP, Gloucester.

Br. David Sylby   }   OFM,
Br. John Rok   Glouc.

fol. 39r   Br. John Blebury
Br. Thos Aumbresley   OSB, Malmesbury,
Br. Thos. Evesham   Salisbury dioc.
Br. Geoffrey Bristowe

Rich. Wawe, Worc. dioc., tit. of a. & c. of Bordesley.

Rich. Porter, Hereford dioc., tit. of a. & c. of Wigmore, d.h.t.

Philip Croyne, St. David's dioc., tit. of d. & c. of Hereford, s.d.

Priests

Br. Wm. Preston
Br. Wm. Malvern   OSB, St. Peter's,
Br. Rich. Horton   Glouc., Worc. dioc.

Br. John Hambury   }   OSB, cath.
Br. John Alcetre   ch. of Worc.

Br. Wm. Newenton, OSB, Pershore, Worc. dioc.

Br. Wm. Spert   }   cans. of the pry. of Llanthony
Br. Rich. Calne   by Glouc., Worc. dioc.

Br. Thos. Brystowe, O. Carm., Bristol, same dioc.

Br. Thos. Longe   }   OP, Glouc.
Br. Thos. Howell

Br. Rich. Gy   }   OFM, Bristol
Br. Roger Newman

Br. David Raydor, O. Carm.

Wm. Wode, Worc. dioc., tit. of the pry. or monas. of Cook Hill, same dioc.

Henry Wawe of Worc., tit. of the monas. of Winchcombe, d.o.

Walter Blankete, Worc. dioc., tit. of the college of Oxford, d.o.

Thos. Corman, Worc. dioc., tit. of p. and c. of Poulton, Salisbury dioc.

Hy. Spelly, Worc. dioc., tit. of St. Oswald's hosp. by Whiston, d.o.

Robt. Wynchestre, Bath [and Wells] dioc., tit. of the monas. of Keynsham, d.o.

Rich. Geek, Exeter dioc., tit. of the pry. of St. Germans, same dioc., d.o.

John Janynes, Hereford dioc., tit. of the pry. of Llanthony by Glouc., d.h.t.

John Wyford, Hereford dioc., tit. of p. & c. of the said pry. of Llanthony and their house of Duddeston, d.o.

Rich. Wodeward, Hereford dioc., l.d.o.s., tit. of the said house.

fol. 39v **123** *First Sat. of Lent, 14 Mar. 1405 London. Orders celebrated by the bp. in the convl. ch. of the Order of Preachers by special licence of Thomas, abp. of Canterbury, London sede vacante, and commission of Mr. Wm. Stortford, can. of St. Paul's and custodian of spiritualities.*

Acolytes

Br. John Brokman
Br. Robt. Lynne } OSA, cans. of Leighs,
Br. John Welles London dioc.

Br. Wm. Ybyngho } OP, London.
Br. Wm. Woderoue

fol. 40r Mr. John Bremore, can. of the cath. ch. of St. Paul, London.

Stephen Menyot, Norwich dioc., d.o.

Robt. Panter, Roch. dioc., d.o.

Reginald Panter, same dioc., d.o.

Hy. Guernon, warden of the sinecure chpl. of Stanford-le-Hope, London dioc.

John Corkeby, Carlisle dioc., d.o.

John Bagot, York dioc., d.h.t.

Subdeacons

Br. John Brokeman
Br. Robt. Lynne } OSA, cans. of Leighs,
Br. John Welles London dioc.

Br. Robt. Grafton, mk. of the Cistercian order and house of Stratford, London dioc.

Br. Milo Stabler } OP, Dunstable.
Br. Wm. Ybyngho

Mr. John Bremore, can. of St. Paul's, London, t.b.s.

Thos. Gylis, Chich. dioc., tit. of Br. Robt. Normanton, *locum tenens* of the pry. of the hosp. of St. John of Jerusalem in England, s.d.

John Alvyngton, London dioc., tit. of the bp. of Worc., d.o.

Wm. Tynker, Worc. dioc., tit. of the house or hosp. of St. John the Baptist, Warwick, d.o.

Deacons

Br. John Bywell, mk. of the house or monas. of St. Albans, Lincoln dioc., d.h.t.

Br. Thos. Stratford } O. Cist. of Stratford, London
Br. Wm. Berkyng dioc.

Br. John Haywode, OP, London.

Br. John Gwynnowe, same order.

Simon Abbot, Lincoln dioc., tit. of the pry. of St. John the Baptist of Haliwell-without-Bishopsgate, London dioc., d.o.

John Wyllys, Bath [and Wells] dioc., tit. of the house of St. Mark of Bidswick by Bristol, Worc. dioc., d.o.

Thos. Aude, r.p.c. of St. Michael's, Southampton, Winch. dioc., t.b.s., d.o.

John Grene, Worc. dioc., tit. of the monas. of Pershore, d.o.

John Wheton, Worc. dioc., tit. of St. John's hosp. Lechlade, d.o.

John Snard, Worc. dioc., tit. of the monas. of Bordesley, d.o.

John Cergeaux, r.p.c. of St. Martin-by-Looe, Exeter dioc., d.o.

Philip Lovecok, London dioc., tit. of the pry. of Blessed Mary of Southwark, Winch. dioc., d.o.

Reginald Holbeche, London dioc., tit. of the master and confraternity of St. Bartholomew's hosp. of West Smithfield, London dioc., d.o.

Thos. Agas, Lincoln dioc., tit. of the hosp. of Blessed Mary-without-Bishopsgate, London dioc., d.o.

fol. 40v Peter Glook, Salisbury dioc., tit. of the pry. of Poughley, same dioc., d.o.

Wm. Edmund, Exeter dioc., tit. of a. & c. of Osney, Lincoln dioc., d.o.

John Stoke, r.p.c. of High Ongar, London dioc., t.b.s., s.d.

Nicholas Chilton, Cant. dioc., tit. of the pry. of St. Gregory, Cant., d.o.

Priests

Br. John Badley, OSB, Eynsham, Lincoln dioc., p.d.

Br. Wm. Intebergh } OSB, Alcester
Br. Thos. Gloucetre same dioc.

Wm. Chirchehey, Worcester dioc., tit. of the pry. of Ivychurch, OSA, Salisbury dioc. d.o.

Robt. Malvern, Worc. dioc., tit. of abt. of Stonely, d.o.

Thos. Warden, Roch. dioc., tit. of a. & c. of Malling, same dioc., d.o.

Rich. Trippe, London dioc., tit. of the nuns of Cheshunt, p.d. of the custodian of the spiritualities of London, *sede ibidem vacante.*

Wm. Wylflete, rec. of East Ham, London dioc., t.b.s., *in hac parte dimissus.*

John Cole, Chich. dioc., tit. of the prioress of Easebourne, same dioc., d.o.

Wm. del Holme, Carlisle dioc., tit. of the monas. of St. Frideswide, Oxford, d.o.

John Lansell, Canterbury dioc., tit. of the monas. of Beeleigh of the Premonstratensian order, d.o.

fol. 41r **124** *Holy Sat., 18 Apr. 1405. Orders celebrated by the bp. in the Hillingdon p.c. by special lic. of the abp. of Cant., London, sede vacante.*

Acolyte

John Dyra, Exeter dioc., d.o.

Subdeacons

John Hylle, Exeter dioc., tit. of the monas. of Newenham, d.h.t.

John Corkeby, Carlisle dioc., tit. of the hosp. of St. John the Baptist-with-out-East Gate, Oxford, Lincoln dioc., d.o.

Deacons

Mr. John Bremore, can. of the cath. ch. of St. Paul, London, t.b.s., d.o.

John Melbury, Exeter dioc., d.o., tit. of a. & c. of Torre, same dioc.

John Bagot, York dioc., tit. of the pry. of Luffield, d.o.

Priest

John Luytylton, Worc. dioc., tit. of p. & c. of Studley, same dioc., d.o.

fol. 41v **125** *Whit Sat., 13 June 1405. Orders celebrated by the bp. in the chpl. of his London house by special lic. and commission of Mr. Wm. Stortford, official, London sede vacante.*

Acolytes

Br. Wm. Herry OSA, London, p.d.

Br. Thos. Brys. O. Carm., Newington, Canterbury dioc., p.d.

John Salewey, Worc. dioc.

John Labowe, Worc. dioc.

Hugo Mauncell, St. David's dioc.

Subdeacons

Br. Wm. Stokesby of the house of Ashridge, Lincoln dioc., p.d.

Thos. Messenger, Worc. dioc., tit. of a. & c. of Hailes, same dioc.

John Truste, Worc. dioc., tit. of p. & c. of St. Bartholomew's hosp., Glouc., same dioc., d.o.

John Labowe, Worc. dioc., tit. of Prioress and c. of Cook Hill, same dioc., d.o.

John Salewey, Worc. dioc., tit. of the pry. of Studley, same dioc., d.o.

John Blesard, Worc. dioc., tit. of a. & c. of Bordesley, same dioc., d.o.

Wm. Bery, Worc. dioc., tit. of St. Bartholomew's hospital, Glouc., d.o.

Thos. Chaumbreleyn, [Coventry and] Lichfield dioc., d.o., tit. of the pry. of Christchurch, London.

John Enot, Lincoln dioc., tit. of the monas. of Notley, same dioc., d.o.

Edmund Lake, Exeter dioc., d.o., tit. of Simon, pr. of St. Mary Magdalen of Barnstaple, same dioc.

fol. 42r *Deacons*

Br. Robt. Lynne
Br. John Welles   } cans. of the pry. of Leighs,
Br. John Brokeman   London, dioc.

Thos. Honyborn, Worc. dioc., tit. of the monas. of Cold Norton, Lincoln dioc., d.o.

Rich. Yaneworth, Worc. dioc., tit. of the pry. of Longleat, d.o.

Br. John Becclis   } OSA, London.
Br. Matthew Clerc

John de Walesby, rec. of Walesby, Lincoln dioc., d.o., t.b.s.

John Hylle, Exeter dioc., tit. of a. & c. of Newenham, same dioc., d.o.

Robt. Panter, Roch. dioc. tit. of pr. and chap. of the cath. ch. of Roch., d.o.

Reginald Panter, same dioc., tit. of prioress and c. of Minster-in-Sheppey, d.o.

Henry Guernon, custodian of the sinecure chpl. of Stanford-le-Hope, London dioc., t.b.s., d.o.

John Thoralby, tit. of Eccleston, [Coventry and] Lichfield dioc., d.o., t.b.s.

Priests

Br. John Bywell, mk. of St. Albans, London dioc., (*sic*) p.d.

Br. John Stephenes
Br. John Talbot   } OP, London
Br. John Haywode

Mr. John Bremore, can. of the cath. ch. of St. Paul, London, t.b.s., d.o.

John Penne, r.p.c. of Fleet, Lincoln dioc., t.b.s., d.o.

Rich. Porter, Worc. dioc., tit. of prioress and c. of Henwood.

John Wheton, same dioc., tit. of pr. and confraternity of St. John's hosp., Lechlade, d.o.

Thos. Malteman de Cheltenham, Worc. dioc., tit. of Br. John pr. of St. Bartholomew's hosp., Glouc., d.o.

John Strugg, Worc. dioc., tit. of p. & c. of Studley, same dioc., d.o.

fol. 42v   **126** *Ember Sat., 19 Sept. 1405. Orders celebrated by Nicholas [Duffield], bp. of Dunkeld in the convl. ch. of Cirencester by commission of the bp. of Worc.*

The bp. gives his involvement in affairs of the realm as his reason for not officiating himself.[5]

Acolytes

Br. John Malteby
Br. Wm. Bengeworth   } OSB, Malmesbury,
Br. Thos. Brystowe   Salisbury dioc., p.d.

Br. Thos. Fleter OP, Glouc.

Wm. Hasulton, warden of the perp. house of scholars of Wotton-under-Edge, Worc. dioc., tit. of same house.

John Jones
Wm. Curteys
Rich. Parker   } Worc. dioc.

[5] See Appendix 5.

John Hogell
John William
John Kenet

fol. 43r   *Subdeacons*

Br. Robt. Acton, O. Cist., Kingswood, Worc. dioc.

Br. John Malteby
Br. Wm. Bengeworth   OSB, Malmesbury,
Br. Thos. Brystowe   Salisbury dioc., p.d.

Br. John Sulthorn   cans. of Osney, Lincoln
Br. John Westbury   dioc. p.d.

Br. John Pecok   OP, Glouc.
Br. Thos. Fleter

Br. Thos. Ingleby, OSA, Bristol.

Nicholas Herbury, archdcn. of Glouc., tit. of his archdeaconry.

Wm. Spelly, Worc. dioc., tit. of St. Oswald's hosp. by Worc.

Wm. Hasulton, warden of the perp. house of scholars of Wotton-under-Edge, Worc. dioc., tit. of same house.

John Otewey, Worc. dioc., tit. of monas. of Hailes, same dioc.

Thos. Wotton, Salisbury dioc., tit. of St. John's Hosp., Lechlade, d.o.

Wm. Wyse, Exeter dioc., tit. of the monas. of Dunkeswell, same dioc., d.o.

Walter Morangill, Durham dioc., tit. of the monas. of Rewley by Oxford, d.o.

Deacons

Br. John Sudbury   OSB, Worc. pry.
Br. Rich. Cowern

Br. Walter Wynley, can. of the pry. of Llanthony by Glouc.

Br. Rich. Norton OSA, Droitwich, Worc. dioc.

Nicholas Lucy, r.p.c. of Stratton-by-Cirencester, Worcester dioc., t.b.s.

Thos. Messanger, Worc. dioc., tit. of the monas. of Blessed Mary of Hailes.

John Carpentere, Worc. dioc., tit. of same.

Robt. Halyday, *alias* Unet, Hereford dioc., tit. of the pry. of Little Malvern, d.h.t.

fol. 43v John Ledwell, Worc. dioc., tit. of the nuns of Westwood, d.o.

Wm. Tynker, Worc. dioc., tit. of the hosp. of St. John the Baptist, Warwick.

Nicholas Mykelton, Worc. dioc., tit. of St. Wolfstan's hosp., Worc., d.o.

John Labowe, Worc. dioc., tit. of the nuns of Cook Hill, d.o.

Wm. Bery, Worc. dioc., tit. of St. Bartholomew's hosp., Glouc., d.o.

John Truste, Worc. dioc., tit. of same, d.o.

Robt. Spynys, York dioc., tit. of St. John's hosp., Leicester, d.o.

Priests

Br. Rich. Brugge, OSB, Worc. pry.

Br. John Bristowe
Br. John Keynesham   } cans. of the monas. of
Br. Wm. Abendon   St. Augustine, Bristol,
Br. Robt. Northwych   Worc. dioc.

Br. Nicholas Lechamton
Br. Thos. Chyltenham   } cans. of Cirencester,
Br. Thos. Sturmy   Worc. dioc.
Br. Wm. Lecchelade

Br. Wm. Michelney O. Cist., Kingswood, Worc. dioc.

Br. Thos. Slade   cans. of Osney, Lincoln
Br. Thos. Weston   } dioc., p.d.

Br. John Brystowe OSA, Bristol.

Br. Wm. Redymere, OP, Glouc.

John Brugge, Worc. dioc., tit. of the house of St. Mark of Billeswick by Bristol, Worc. dioc., d.o.

John Snard, Worc. dioc., tit. of the monas. of Bordesley, d.o.

Thos. Honyborn, Worc. dioc., tit. of the monas. of Cold Norton, Lincoln dioc., d.o.

Rich. Yaneworth, Worc. dioc., tit. of the pry. of Longleat, d.o.

Wm. Skynner, Hereford dioc., tit. of the monas. of Flaxley, s.d.

Rich. Cokk, Hereford dioc., tit. of the monas. of Hailes, d.o.

fol. 44r Thos. Whyte, Hereford dioc., tit. of d. & c. of the cath. ch. of Hereford, s.d.h.p.

Hugh Lucas, same dioc., tit. of a. & c. of Flaxley, s.d.h.p.

John Corby, Carlisle dioc., tit. of the hosp. of St. John the Baptist-without-East Gate, Oxford, d.o.

Rich. Jordan, St. David's dioc., t.p.s., s.d.

127 *Holy Sat., 10 April 1406. Orders celebrated by the bp. in the chpl. of his London house, by special lic. of Mr. Wm. Stortford, official and custodian of the spiritualities, London, sede vacante.*

Priests

Mr. Wm. Congesbury, r.p.c. of St. Werburgh's, Worc. dioc., t.b.s.

John Colyns, Worc. dioc., tit. of p. & c. of Studley, same dioc., d.o.

John Hylle, same dioc., tit. of same p. & c., d.o.

John Clayton, r.p.c. of Croxby, Lincoln dioc., t.b.s., d.o.

128 *Ember Sat., 18 Sept. 1406. Orders celebrated by the bp. in the chpl. of his house at Hillingdon by special lic. of Mr. Wm. Stortford, official etc.*

fol. 44v   *Acolytes*

Br. Wm. Myssenden } cans. of the monas. of
Br. Rich. Wendovre } Missenden, Lincoln dioc., s.d.

Rich. Lydgate OESA, London.

John More, Worc. dioc.

Wm. Kyrkham, r.p.c. of St. Matthews, Ipswich, Norwich dioc., s.d.h.p.; t.e.s.

Adam Dalton, York dioc., p.d. of his diocesan.

Subdeacons

Simon Thomson de Holbeche, Lincoln dioc., s.d.h.p., tit. of a. & c. of Blessed Mary of Swineshead-in-Holland, same dioc.

John Benet, Lincoln dioc., s.d.h.p., tit. of rec. and conv. of the house of Ashridge, same dioc., d.o.

John Cokerell, York dioc., s.d.h.p., tit. of the pry. of Merton, Winch. dioc., d.o.

Hermann Perys, London dioc., s.d., tit. of the master and chplns. of the college of All Saints, Maidstone, Cant. dioc., d.o.

Wm. Boneton, Worc. dioc., tit. of a. and c. of Alcester, same dioc., d.o.

Br. Wm. Missenden
Br. Rich. Wendovre } cans. of Missenden, Lincoln dioc., s.d.

Br. Thos. Thorp OESA, London.

John Jones, Worc. dioc., tit. of p. and c. of St. Bartholomew's hosp., Glouc., d.o.

Wm. Kyrkham, r.p.c. of St. Matthew's, Ipswich, Norwich dioc., s.d.h.p., t.e.s.

Deacons

Mr. Nicholas Herbury, archdcn. of Glouc., in the church of Worc., t.b.s.

Mr. Adam Redyforth, York dioc., tit. of the house of Notley, d.o.

John Holteby, York dioc., tit. of the master or warden of the hosp. of Blessed Mary by Bootham, same dioc., d.o.

Br. Peter Stoke, mk. of the monas. of Chertsey, Winch. dioc., s.d.h.p.

Br. Thos. Capgrave OESA, London.

Br. John Mendham O. Carm., Aylesford.

Rich. Compton, rec. of Sutton, Worc. dioc., t.b.s.

fol. 45r John Fax, Exeter dioc., tit. of the pry. of Poughley, Salisbury dioc., s.d.h.p.

John Gyles, Exeter dioc., s.d.h.p., tit. of p. & c. of St. Mary of Hurley, d.o.

Priests

Br. John Hermondesworth
Br. Nicholas Wokkyng } OSB, Chertsey, Winch. dioc., s.d.h.p.
Br. Lawrence Mann

Br. Thos. Hanyngton, can. of the monas. of Notley, Lincoln dioc., s.d.h.p.

Br. Wm. Churchehull, OSB, Eynsham, Lincoln dioc., d.o.

Br. John Rokell
Br. Nicholas Corby } OP, London.
Br. Robt. Chalk

Br. Stephen Chart
Br. John Prince } O. Carm., Aylesford.

Br. Thos. Broke OSA, London.

Br. Robt. Heywode, OP, Dunstable.

John Carpenter, Worc. dioc., tit. of the monas. of Hailes, d.o.

Wm. Farceux de Preston, Lincoln dioc., p.d., tit. of the monas. of Croyland, d.o.

John Tuttebury, Worc. dioc., tit. of the pry. of Dudley, same dioc., d.o.

Thos. Hykkes, Llandaff dioc., tit. of the master or warden of St. Lawrence hosp. by Bristol, d.o.

Rich. ap Guillam, r.p.c. of Bridell, St. David's dioc., d.o., t.b.s.

fol. 45v **129** *Ember Sat., 18 Dec. 1406. Orders celebrated by the bp. in the chpl. of his London house by special lic. of Nicholas [Bubwith] bp. of London, [1406-1407].*

Acolytes

Ninian Coden
Ralph Hyllary
Walter Smale   } Exeter dioc., d.o.
Thos. Bounde

John Frenssh, Coventry and Lichfield dioc., s.d.h.p.

Rich. Gabriell, r.p.c. of Pyworthy, Exeter dioc., s.d.

Subdeacons

Mr. Thos. Noreys, Salisbury dioc., tit. of Queen's Hall College, Oxford, d.o.

Henry Eton, r.p.c. of Doddinghurst, London dioc., t.b.s.

Rich. Gabriell, r.p.c. of Pyworthy, Exeter dioc., s.d.h.p., t.e.s.

John Frenssh, Coventry and Lichfield dioc., s.d.h.p., tit. of the pry. of Stone, same dioc.

Deacons

John Robyn, Exeter dioc., s.d.h.p., tit. of the pry. of St. Germans, same dioc.

Wm. Kyrkham, r.p.c. of St. Matthews, Ipswich, Norwich dioc., t.e.s., d.o.

Thos. Burton, r.p.c. of Withy Brook, Coventry and Lichfield dioc., s.d.h.p., t.e.s.

Priests

Nicholas Herbury, archdcn. of Glouc. in the ch. of Worc., t.b.s.

Mr. Rich. Flemyng, can. of York and preby. of Southnewbold in same, d.o., tit. of his preb.

Mr. John Castell, York dioc., s.d.h.p., tit. of the hosp. of St. John the Baptist-without-East Gate, Oxford.

Mr. John Cowlyng, Exeter dioc., d. tit. of the pry. of Bodmin, same dioc., d.o.

fol. 46r **130** *Ember Sat., 18 Dec. 1406. Orders celebrated by Nicholas bp. of Dunkeld in Compton p.c. by commission of the bp. of Worc.*

Religious Acolytes

Br. John Haselore can. [*sic*] of the monas. of Alcester.

Br. Francis Circetre can. of Llanthony pry.

Br. John Alcetir
Br. John Henley   } OSB, Hailes
Br. John Hembury
Br. Hy. Alcetir

Br. Thos. Wynchecombe } OSB, Winchcombe.
Br. Thos. Penwortham

Secular Acolytes

Wm. Grene, Worc. dioc.

Mr. Robt. Burton, Durham dioc., p.d.

Walter Fouler, r.p.c. of Longwatton, Lincoln dioc., s.d.

John Besseford
John Palmer
Wm. Wattes
Thos. Gybbes
John Gybbes
John Baron
Rich. Thorn   } Worc. dioc.
Nicolas Baldewyn
Rich. Swyft
John Wheler
Rich. Othale
John Warre
David Wroxham
John Benet

Robt. de Barre [Coventry and] Lichfield dioc., p.d.

Thos. Bayton
John Gase
Thos. Holtham
John Banard

 Worc. dioc.

fol. 46v   *Religious Subdeacons*

Br. John Haselore, OSB, Alcester.
Br. Thos. Wynchecombe
Br. Thos. Penwortham

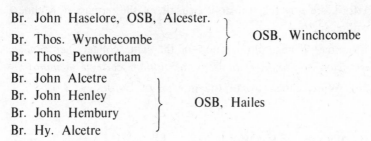 OSB, Winchcombe

Br. John Alcetre
Br. John Henley
Br. John Hembury
Br. Hy. Alcetre

OSB, Hailes

Secular Subdeacons

Mr. Robt. Burton, Durham dioc., p.d., tit. of the hosp. of St. John the Baptist-without-East Gate, Oxford, Lincoln dioc., d.o.

Walter Fouler, r.p.c. of Longwatton, Lincoln dioc., p.d., t.b.s.

Robt. Wodeman, Worc. dioc., tit. of the hosp. of Lechlade, same dioc., d.o.

Thos. Strongefere, Worc. dioc., tit. of St. Bartholomew's hosp., Glouc., d.o.

Hy. Kempe, Worc. dioc., tit. of said hosp. d.o.

John More, Worc. dioc., tit. of the pry. of Cook Hill, d.o.

John Warlowe, r.p.c. of Dodington, Worc. dioc., t.b.s.

John Edward, Worc. dioc., tit. of the monas. of Hailes, d.o.

Robt. Barre, [Coventry and] Lichfield dioc., p.d.

John Kemotes, Worc. dioc., tit. of St. Bartholomew's hosp. Glouc., d.o.

Thos. Barbour, Worc. dioc., tit. of the hosp. of St. John the Baptist, Warwick.

Wm. Wattes, Worc. dioc., tit. of the hosp. of St. John the Baptist-without-East Gate, Oxford, d.o.

John Banard, Worc.dioc., tit. of the nuns of Westwood, same dioc., d.o.

Wm. Camme, Worc. dioc., tit. of St. Bartholomew's hosp., Glouc., d.o.

John Gase, Worc. dioc., tit. of the nuns of Cook Hill, same dioc., d.o.

Secular Deacons

Wm. Spelly, Worc. dioc., tit. of St. Oswald's hosp. by Worc. city, d.o.

Wm. Boneton, Worc. dioc., tit. of the monas. of Alcester, d.o.

Wm. Hasulton, master of the perp. house of scholars of Wotton-under-Edge, Worc. dioc., tit. of the same.

John Carpenter, Worc. dioc., tit. of St. Bartholomew's hosp. Glouc., d.o.

Mr. John Pole, Salisbury dioc., fellow of the college of Blessed Mary of Winch.,[6] Oxford, s.d., by the Apostolic See, tit. of the monas. of Malmesbury, same dioc., d.o.

Mr. Wm. Mounter, Winch. dioc., fellow of the same college, *per eandem sedem apostolicam consimiliter dimissus ad titulum collegii memorati.*

John Blesard, Worc. dioc., tit. of the monas. of Bordesley, d.o.

Religious Priests

Br. Thos. Colchestre OSA, Oxford, p.d.

Br. John Turney OFM, Oxford, p.d.

Br. Henry Wolfton
Br. John Fauconer } OFM, Worc.

Br. Wm. Poywyk
Br. John Frompton
Br. Adam Grene } OSB, Glouc.
Br. Rich. Stafford

Br. Thos. Frompton, OSB, Hailes.

Br. John Norton
Br. Roger More } OSB, Tewkesbury

Br. Walter Wynley, can. of Llanthony by Glouc.

Secular Priests

Nicholas Lucy, rec. of Stratton-by-Cirencester, Worc. dioc., t.b.s.

Rich. Compton, rec. of Sutton, Worc. dioc., t.b.s.

Wm. Blakemore, Coventry and Lichfield dioc., tit. of d. and c. of the coll. ch. of Blessed Mary, Warwick, d.o.

Thos. Symondes, Worc. dioc., tit. of the pry. of Great Malvern.

Rich. Meyre, Worc. dioc., tit. of the pry. of Studley, d.o.

John Otewy, Worc. dioc., tit. of the monas. of Hailes, same dioc., d.o.

---

[6] New College.

fol. 47v   **131**   *Holy Sat., 16 Mar. 1407. Orders celebrated by the bp. in Withington, p.c.*

Acolytes

Hugh Penne, Worc. dioc.

John 3ate, same dioc.

Robt. Pynchebek, Lincoln dioc., s.d.

Hy. Wyse
Rich. Sherberd
Wm. Saundres
Wm. Colles
} Worc. dioc.

Subdeacons

Walter Tonker, Bath and Wells dioc., p.d., tit. of St. Mark's house, Bristol, d.o.

John Smyth de Lechelade, Worc. dioc., tit. of St. John's hosp. Lechlade, d.o.

John Shaw, r.p.c. of St. John the Baptist, Bristol, Worc. dioc., t.e.s.

Walter Taillour, Worc. dioc., tit. of the pry. of Little Malvern, d.o.s.

John 3ate, Worc. dioc., tit. of the monas. of Halesowen, d.o.

Robt. Perys, Worc. dioc., tit. of St. Bartholomew's hospital, Glouc., d.o.

Robt. Pynchebek, Lincoln dioc., p.d., tit. of the hosp. of St. John the Baptist-without-East Gate, Oxford, d.o.

Adam Dalton, York dioc., p.d., tit. of the pry. of Holy Trinity in the city of London, d.o.

Religious Deacons

Br. John Haselore
Br. John Alcetre
Br. Hy. Alcetre
Br. John Hembury
Br. John Henlee
} OSB, Alcester,
Worc. dioc.

fol. 48r   *Secular Deacons*

John Palmer, Worc. dioc., tit. of the hosp. of St. John the Baptist, Warwick, d.o.

Robt. Wodeman, Worc. dioc., tit. of St. John's hosp., Lechlade, d.o.s.

John,[7] Worc. dioc., tit. of the nuns of Cook Hill, d.o.s.

John Jones, Worc. dioc., tit. of the pry. of St. Bartholomew, Glouc., d.o.s.

Thos. Vyncent, Worc. dioc., tit. of St. Bartholomew's hosp. Gloucester, d.o.s.

Thos. Newport, r.p.c. of Pontvane St. David's dioc., p.d., t.b.s.

Wm. Brystowe, r.p.c. of St. Peter-the-Little, York, p.d., t.b.s.

Augustine Strode, Exeter dioc., p.d., tit. of the monas. of Tavistock, same dioc., d.o.

John Banard, Worc. dioc., tit. of the nuns of Westwood, d.o.

John Wheler, Worc. dioc., tit. of St. Oswald's hosp. by Worc., d.o.

John Nycoll, Exeter dioc., p.d., tit. of the pry. of St. Nicolas, Exeter, d.o.

Thos. Bayton, Worc. dioc., tit. of the hosp. of St. John the Baptist, Warwick, d.o.

John Kemotes, Worc. dioc., tit. of St. Bartholomew's hosp. Glouc., d.o.

Priests

Robt. Ewardby, Lincoln dioc., p.d., tit. of the monas. of St. Germanus de Selby, York dioc., d.o.

Thos. Barbour, Worc. dioc., tit. of the hosp. of St. John the Baptist, Warwick, d.o.

John Sowey, Bath and Wells dioc., p.d., tit. of the monas. of Athelney, same dioc., d.o.

John Sexteyne, Bath and Wells dioc., p.d. tit. of the monas. of Keynsham, same dioc., d.o.

Wm. Spelly, Worc. dioc., tit. of St. Oswald's hosp. by Worc., d.o.

John Adames, Worc. dioc., tit. of the nuns of Cook Hill, d.o.

Walter Smale, Exeter dioc., p.d., tit. of the monas. or pry. of Barlinch, Bath and Wells dioc., d.o.

John More, Worc. dioc., tit. of the nuns of Cook Hill, same dioc., d.o.

Hy. Kemp, Worc. dioc., tit. of St. Bartholomew's hosp., Glouc., d.o.

Wm. Boneton, Worc. dioc., tit. of the monas. of Alcester, d.o.

Thos. Strongefere, Worc. dioc., tit. of St. Bartholomew's hosp., Glouc. d.o.

---

[7] No surname given. Probably John More, *see* # 130.

fol. 48v *Deacons*[8]

John Edward, Worc. dioc., tit. of the monas. of Blessed Mary of Hailes, d.o.

John Carpentere, Worc. dioc., tit. of St. Bartholomew's hosp., Glouc., d.o.

Thos. Burton, b. ll., Winch. dioc., fellow of the college of Blessed Mary of Winch., Oxford, by authority of special apostolic privilege granted to that college and its fellows, s.d.h.p., tit. of the same college.

Walter Colswayn, b.a., Winch. dioc., fellow of the said college, by the aforesaid privilege s.d., tit. of that college.

Robt. Barre, Coventry and Lichfield dioc., p.d., tit. of the hosp. of St. John the Baptist-without-East Gate, Oxford, d.o.

John Blesard, Worc. dioc., tit. of the monas. of Bordesley, d.o.

John Truste, Worc. dioc., tit. of St. Bartholomew's hosp., Glouc., d.o.

132 *Whit. Sat., 21 May 1407. Orders celebrated by the bp. in Blockley p.c.*

Religious Acolytes

Br. Wm. Bermengeham, can. of the monas. of Halesowen, Worc. dioc.

Br. Wm. Pershore } O. Cist., Bruern,
Br. John Sonyngwell   Lincoln dioc., p.d.

Br. John Blokkeley } OSB, Pershore,
Br. John Bosbury   Worc. dioc.

Br. Wm. Henley, OSB, Hailes, same dioc.

Secular Acolytes

Wm. Sterlyng
Thos. Grene
Rich. Warde
Wm. Lorkyn
John Smyth de Clyve
Rich. Phelpes   } Worc. dioc.
Robt. Sprenge
John Wryght
John Elmeley

[8] Three of these men were already deacons: Blesard (#130), Carpenter (#130), Truste (#126).

Wm. Mountfort
Edmund Eustas
Thos. James
Wm. Smyth

Religious Subdeacons

Br. Wm. Henley, OSB, Hailes, Worc. dioc.

Br. John Blokley } OSB, Pershore,
Br. John Bosbury   same dioc.

Br. Wm. Pershore } O. Cist., Bruern,
Br. John Sonnyngwell   Lincoln dioc., p.d.

Secular Subdeacons

Rich. More de Forthampton, Worc. dioc., tit. of St. Bartholomew's hosp., Glouc., d.o.

John Howes, Worc. dioc., tit. of the house of the Holy Sepulchre, Warwick, d.o.

Rich. Garsdale, York dioc., fellow of the house of Blessed Mary, Oxford, p.d., tit. of said house, d.o.

Walter Clerc, Worc. dioc., tit. of the monas. of Bruern, d.o.

Rich. Clyve, Worc. dioc., tit. of the monas. of Hailes, d.o.

Religious Deacons

Br. Thos. Dodeley
Br. Thos. Belgrave } OSB, Hailes, Worc.
Br. Hy. Wyghtwyke   dioc.

Br. John Abendon
Br. Robt. Kelmescote } O. Cist., Bruern, Lincoln
Br. Thos. Hertfeld   dioc., p.d.

Br. Thos. Wynchecombe } OSB, Winchcombe
Br. Thos. Penwortham

Br. Rich. Wyrcetre } OSB, cath.
Br. Thos. Colwell   ch. Worc.

Secular Deacons

Robt. Pynchebek, Lincoln dioc., p.d., tit. of the hosp. of St. John the Baptist-without-East Gate, Oxford, d.o.

John Holdernesse, York dioc., p.d., tit. of said hosp., d.o.

Adam Dalton, York dioc., p.d., tit. of the pry. of Holy Trinity, London, d.o.

Robt. Perys, Worc. dioc., tit. of St. Bartholomew's hosp. Glouc., d.o.

John Smyth, Worc. dioc., tit. of St. John's hosp., Lechlade, d.o.

John Shawe, r.p.c. of St. John the Baptist, Bristol, Worc. dioc., t.e.s.

John 3ate, Worc. dioc., tit. of the monas. of Halesowen, same dioc., d.o.

fol. 49v Mr. Thos. Noreys, Salisbury dioc., p.d., tit. of Queen's Hall College, Oxford, d.o.

Religious Priests

Br. Thos. Warde OFM, Gloucester.

Br. John Clyfton, can. of the monas. of Dorchester, Lincoln dioc., p.d.

Br. John Wyrcetre, OSB, Tewkesbury, Worc. dioc.

Br. Howel 3eyl
Br. Wm. Cheytwode   }   OP, Warwick
Br. Stonefeyld

Br. John Alcetre
Br. John Henley   }   OSB, Hailes, Worc. dioc.
Br. Hy. Alcetre

Secular Priests

John Kemottes, Worc. dioc., tit. of St. Bartholomew's hosp., Glouc., d.o.

Walter Markere, Exeter dioc., p.d., tit. of the monas. of Tavistock, same dioc., d.o.

Mr. John Barton, b. ll., r.p.c. of Lamyat, Bath and Wells dioc., p.d., t.b.s.

John Wheler, Worc. dioc., tit. of St. Oswald's hosp. by Worc.

Thos. Warre, r.p.c. of Lammana, Exeter dioc., p.d., t.e.s.

John Gase, Worc. dioc., tit. of the nuns of Cook Hill, same dioc.

133 *Ember Sat., 24 Sept. 1407. Orders celebrated by the bp. in Blockley, p.c.*

Religious Acolytes

Br. Thos. Hertlebury OP, Worc. city, p.d.

Br. Rich. Tyberton, OSB, cath. ch. of Worc.

Br. John London, OSB, Winchcombe, Worc. dioc.

Secular Acolytes

Rich. Shelwyke
Rich. Aston } Worc. dioc.
Rich. Parys
John Gerneys

John Revell, Lincoln dioc., p.d.

Wm. Fosteby, fellow of New College, Oxford, p.d. by the apostolic see and by indult to him and to its fellows.

Religious Subdeacons

Br. Thos. Hertlebury, OP, Worcester, p.d.

Br. Rich. Tyberton, OSB, cath. ch. of Worc.

Br. John London, OSB, Winchcombe.

Secular Subdeacons

Wm. Lenchewyk, Worc. dioc., tit. of the pry. of Studley, same dioc., d.o.

Henry Wyse, same dioc., tit. of the monas. of Great Malvern, same dioc., d.o.

Wm. Boldynge, same dioc., tit. of the master or warden of the brs.' and sisters' hosp. of St. John the Baptist, Coventry, d.o.

Thos. Grene, same dioc., tit. of the monas. of Bordesley, d.o.

John Besford, Worc. dioc., tit. of the coll. ch. of Warwick, d.o.

Hugh Pen, Worc. dioc., tit. of the pry. of Little Malvern, d.o.

John Smyth de Clyve, same dioc., tit. of St. Bartholomew's hosp. Glouc., d.o.

Rich. Ward, same dioc., tit. of the monas. of Pershore, d.o.

Nicholas Bailly de Bishampton, Worc. dioc., tit. of the nuns of Cook Hill, d.o.

Rich. Parys, Worc. dioc., tit. of the hosp. of St. John the Baptist of Ludlow, d.o.

Thos. Strange, said dioc., tit. of the monas. of Alcester, d.o.

John Revell, Lincoln dioc., p.d., tit. of the monas. of Osney, Oxford, d.o.

Religious Deacons

Br. John Blokkeley } OSB, Pershore
Br. John Bosbury

Br. Wm. Pershore
Br. John Sonnyngwell   }   O. Cist., Bruern.
Br. Wm. Henle, OSB, Hailes.

Secular Deacons

Rich. More de Forthampton, Worc. dioc., tit. of the pry. of St. Bartholomew's hosp. Glouc., d.o.s.

fol. 50v   John Howes, Worc. dioc., tit. of the house of the Holy Sepulchre, Warwick, d.o.

Rich. Clyve, Worc., tit. of the monas. of Halesowen, d.o.

Walter Clerc, Worc. dioc., tit. of the monas. of Bruern, d.o.

Thos. Baillemounde, Salisbury dioc., scholar and fellow of New College, Oxford University, by authority of a privilege given by the Apostolic See to that college and its fellows, *dimissus in hac parte*, tit. of the college.

Walter Taillour, Worc. dioc., tit. of the pry. of Little Malvern, d.o.

Religious Priests

Br. John Sudbury   OSB, cath.
Br. Rich. Cowern   }   ch. of Worc.

Br. John Twenyng, OSB, Tewkesbury.

Br. Thos. Wynchecombe, OSB, Winchcombe.

Br. John Aas   OSB, Abingdon,
Br. John Westbury   }   Salisbury dioc., p.d.

Br. Hy. Weston   OSA, cans.,
Br. William Shrovesbury   }   Kenilworth, p.d.

Br. John Abendon   O. Cist.,
Br. Robt. Kelmescote   }   Bruern, p.d.

Secular Priests

John Smyth, Worc. dioc., tit. of St. John's hosp. Lechlade, d.o.

John Banard, same dioc., tit. of the nuns of Westwood, d.o.

Robt. Perys, same dioc., tit. of St. Bartholomew's house, Glouc., d.o.

Thos. Rede, same dioc., tit. of the pry. of St. Bartholomew by Smithfield, London, d.o.s.

John Warlowe, r.p.c. of Dodington, Worc. dioc., t.b.s.

John 3ate, same dioc., tit. of the monas. of Halesowen, d.o.

Robt. Wodeman, same dioc., tit. of St. John's hosp., Lechlade, d.o.

Thos. Vyncent, same dioc., tit. of St. Bartholomew's house, Glouc., d.o.

John Shaw, r.p.c. of St. John, Bristol, Worc. dioc., t.b.s.

John Palmer, same dioc., tit. hosp. of St. John the Baptist, Warwick, d.o.s.

Thos. Bayton, Worc. dioc., tit. of the same hosp., d.o.s.

Adam Dalton, York dioc., p.d., tit. of the pry. of Holy Trinity, London, d.o.s.

Robt. Pynchebek, Lincoln dioc., p.d., tit. of the house of St. John the Baptist-without-East Gate, Oxford, d.o.s.

fol. 51r Geoffrey ap 3ennor, St. David's dioc., p.d., tit. of the president and chap. of the [*cath.*] ch. of Hereford, d.o.s.

THE REGISTER OF RICHARD CLIFFORD

MEMORANDA
(Sections 133a-368)

fol. 51v **133a** *No date*. Rich. Mannyng, doctor of decretals, of the officiality of the Worc. consistory to Dns. Nicholas Morys of Severn Stoke, Worc. dioc., greetings etc. Thos. Power of Kempsey in a matrimonial case in the said consistory between himself and one Alice Smyth of the same. [*The rest of the folio is blank*].

fol. 52r **134** *28 June 1402, Worc.* Lic. from Gilbert Stone, can. of Hereford and vic. in spirituals, the bp. being abroad, to Br. John [Malvern] pr. of the cath. ch. of Worc. to have Br. Thos. Ledebury, mk. in dcn.'s orders, advanced to the priesthood by any Catholic bp.

135 *7 Apr. 1402, London.* Letter testifying that the bp., by lic. of the bp. of London, ordained Rich. Gatyn, acol. of Winch. dioc., to the following orders and on these dates, he having shown letters dimissory from his diocesan d.o.s. Orders were celebrated in the chpl. of his London house. To subdcn., Ember Sat., viz., 17 Dec. 1401: to dcn., Sat. of the first week of Lent, viz. 18 Feb. following: to p., Sat. when Sitientes is sung, viz. 11 Mar. following. Rich. was ordained to tit. of his patrimony with which he declared himself content.

136 *2 July 1402, Glouc.* Lic. from Gilbert Stone, vic. in spirituals, to the pr. of Llanthony by Glouc., OSA [John Lymnor], to have Brs. Wm. Spert, Wm. Grene, Rich. Calne and John Heyhamstede, cans. and acols., promoted to subdiaconate by any Catholic bp. notwithstanding they are professed religious.

fol. 52v **137** *24 June 1402, Worc.* Dispensation to collect a tenth and half tenth. Gilbert Stone, vic. in spirituals as above, to the p. and c. of Great Malvern concerning the collection of a tenth and half tenth for the King. He recites the royal letter of 14 June to Bp. Clifford or his vicar-general which he received 23 June. This refers to Bp. Tideman, late bp. of Worc., and the other prelates and clergy of Cant. province having met in convocation at St. Paul's, London, 26 Jan. of the second year of his reign [1401] when they granted a tenth and half tenth from taxable benefices. These were to be paid, one half at Trinity [29 May] next following, one half at the next feast of St. Andrew [30 Nov.] and the third half at the following nativity of John the Baptist [24 June], hosps. and poor nunneries to be exempt. The collectors were not to use royal authority except by writ *de significavit* as hitherto. Bp. Tideman had appointed the p. & c. of Great Malvern collectors of the third half tenth in the archdeaconry of Worc. as appeared by inspection of the Exchequer rolls. They have complained that no letters from Bp. Tideman came to them about this nor could they be held responsible in any way, for he was now dead. They claimed that to make them levy and collect this half tenth would be to the injury of the king and the manifest impoverishment of the p. & c. unless a suitable compensation was provided. The king, desiring to allow their supplication, as is just, orders the bp. to depute either the p. & c. or other trustworthy clergy, as he wishes, to collect the third half tenth in the archdeaconry of Worc. and answer by the quin-

fol. 53r

zaine of John the Baptist to the Treasurer and barons of the Exchequer, and by the octave of the same give them the collectors' names. Sealed at Westminster, 14 June, 3 Henry IV per memoranda roll of the third year, county records, and memoranda roll of the second year, Easter records touching the certification of [Bp.] Tideman.

The vic. in spirituals proceeded to direct the p. and c. to collect, according to the form of the grant, the third half tenth from beneficed clergy in the archdeaconry of Worc. who customarily paid tenths. The cath. chap. and the clergy of the city were to be included and all others who held portions or pensions or benefices at farm. Recalcitrants were to be subject to sequestration of their benefices and ecclesiastical censures and their names reported and if necessary the secular arm was to be invoked.

138 *25 June 1402, Worc.* Notification of the vic. in spirituals to the Treasurer and barons of Exchequer that in accordance with the tenor of the royal writ of 23 June he has appointed the p. & c. of Great Malvern to be collectors of the third half tenth in the archdeaconry of Worc.

fol. 53v

139 *24 July 1402, Worc.* Notification in the same form that the vic. in spirituals has appointed the a. & c. of Hailes by letters patent collectors of the third half tenth in the archdeaconry of Glouc. and later notified the Treasurer and barons of the Exchequer of the names of these collectors by letters under date of 15 July.

140 *14 Aug. 1402, Westminster.* Writ of summons to the bp. to Parliament at Westminster which has been postponed from the morrow of the Exaltation of the Holy Cross [15 September] to the morrow of St. Michael [30 September]. He is to attend personally and likewise the pr. and archdcns. One member of the cath. chap. is to come and two proctors of the clergy.

141 *10 July 1402, Westminster.* Royal writ of *Certiorari* to the bp. or his vicar-general in spirituals. The king wants to know what and how many persons have been presented to the vicge. of Aston, otherwise called Aston Cantlow from the first regnal year of Henry son of King John, at whose presentation, by whom the vicge. was founded and endowed, when and in what manner. Let the episcopal registers be searched and notify chancery of what is found, returning this writ.

fol. 54r

142 *30 Jan. 1402, Hartlebury.* Reply to king attesting that earlier registers were searched and it was found that Dns. Adam Horleton [Bp. Orleton, 1327-1333] instituted John Beurepor in the vicge. on presentation by Mr. John Maudyt rec. of Aston *alias* Aston Cantlow by an exch. with Robt Alve then vic. there, for the ch. of Wolverdington, 1 July 1329, but by whom or at whose presentation Robt. was earlier presented and instituted could not be found in the registers.

Item 17 July, 1344, Bp. Wolfstan [1339-1349] instituted Thos. de Normanton by an exch. of his vicge. of Boddington with Anthony Fossor then vic. of Aston but at whose presentation there is no mention and nothing could be found in the register as to how he was instituted.

Item 17 July 1349, Bp. Wolfstan instituted Nicholas Sheldon in the vicge. vacant by the death of Thos. de Normanton (pat.: p. & c. Maxstoke).

Item 14 September 1361, Bp. Reginald Bryan [Reynold Brian, 1356-1361] instituted Rich. de Walford in the vacancy made by the death of Nicholas Sheldon (pat.: p. & c. Maxstoke).

Item 5 February 1365, Bp. Wm. Witlesey [Whittlesey, 1364-1368] instituted Robt. Bircheley by exch. of his vicge. of Arley with Rich. de Walford (pat.: p. & c. Maxstoke).

Item 22 Nov. 1375, Bp. Wm. Lynne [Lynn, 1369-1375] instituted Rich. Pulteney in the vacancy made by the death of Robt. Bircheley (pat.: p. & c. Maxstoke).

Item 17 Jan. 1389, Mr. Rich. Wych, vicar-general in spirituals of Dns. Bp. Tideman, instituted John de Aston in the vicge. (pat.: p. & c. Maxstoke). Concerning the inductions of these persons nothing else is found except mands. to the archdcn. of Worc. or their officials to induct them.

fol. 54v

By further search in the archives and registers of the cath. ch. of Worc. it is found that Dns. Walter Cantelupe [1237-1266] gave the ch. of Aston to the p. & c. of Studley to maintain hospitality and a hostel for the poor outside the pry. gate in June, 1253. There is no mention of the day of the month it was appropriated and before that date the vicge. was assigned in the ch. of

Aston. It does not say who founded or endowed it because the registers of earlier bps. perished in the fire a long time ago.[1]

143 *No date.* Invitation of Bp. Clifford to his clergy to come to his enthronement, 4 Feb. He has been absent unwillingly and now the heavy necessity of ruling, together with gratitude for the liberality of all the clergy that he has experienced, and the law of seemliness especially, urge him to make haste to come nearer to those parts to see his fair spouse. He asks them along with the more prominent people and prelates, for his own honour and that of the ch., to attend both in the solemnities and at table. Although he does not venture to promise luxurious entertainment, nevertheless the intercourse of so many friends as they come together will serve them with a greater enjoyment in place of luxurious fare, and afterwards, he hopes, they will have a merry countenance and a grateful heart.

144 *21 Sept. 1402, Hillingdon.* Letters dimissory to Thos. Hereford, r.p.c. of Rodmarton, to be ordained p.

fol. 55r **145** *23 Sept. 1402, Hillingdon.* Offer of an indulgence of forty days for two years, by divine grace and the merits of Mary and confessors Oswald and Wolfstan, to parishioners of the dioc. who, having confessed and being penitent, will repair the royal road between Southall and Wycombe, in the London dioc., which is deep in mud in winter and dangerous to pedestrians and riders, wheeled vehicles and animals, and causes loss and damage to goods. The indulgence is available also to those who collect for the work, make bequests or otherwise give assistance.

---

[1] Exchequer records, ecclesiastical, have a number of documents on this complicated case (E 135). Priors of Studley claimed the patronage and were opposed by successive priors of Maxstoke (E 135/19/4). The case went to the court of King's Bench in Hilary term 1402, at which point King Henry intervened, claiming that the benefice was of lay fee and his by escheat. The case was decided in June when the judges found for him (E 135/23/7) and he presented (Calendar # 59). The death of his presenteee opened the way for the prior and convent of Studley to present (Calendar # 106). The prior of Maxstoke challenged their presentation. The King intervened again, secured the presentation, then 'out of grace' gave it to the prior and convent of Maxstoke to be held in free and perpetual alms in recognition of their prayers for the Queen, his parents and himself (E 135/4/6). The prior and convent of Studley appealed, first to the Archbishop of Canterbury (E 135/23/6), then to Rome (E 135/9/5), where they lost. A bull of Innocent VII of 9 August 1405, recognized the claim of the prior and convent of Maxstoke, as having been in possession 'forty years and more' (E 135/16/5). In December the prior of Studley who continued to resist was excommunicated by the Primate (E 135/18/16). See also *Reg. Arundel*, 1, fols. 369, 370.

146 *18 Sept. 1402, Hadham.* A letter from the bp. of London directs Bp. Clifford to execute Abp.'s Arundel's mand. calling Convocation, the tenor of which follows. The abp. refers to his preference for quietly guarding the prelates and clergy from troublesome and costly hardships that they might serve the King of kings more freely. However, urgent and arduous matters touching the state of the universal ch. compel him, unwillingly and contrary to his earlier intention, to call them together. The bp. of London is directed to order the summoning of his fellow bps. and suffragans in the province of Cant. and, if absent, their vicars-general in spirituals and through them deans and prs. of cath. chs. and their individual chaps. Archdcns. abts. and prs. of convs. and other prelates exempt and non-exempt of chs. and clergy are to attend in person, each cath. chap. to be represented by one clk. and the clergy of each diocese by two qualified proctors, all to appear 21 October next in St. Paul's before the abp. or his *locum tenens* or commissaries if he himself should be prevented from being present.

fol. 55v The purpose is to deal in the following days with urgent matters affecting the interest of the universal ch. and to agree and order what should be just and necessary. The bp. of London is ordered to execute what applies to his own city and dioc. and is summoned to appear with all his other suffragans. The foregoing carries no intention to the prejudice of the privileges of the prelates of exempt houses, non-mendicant, of any order, whether of his dioc. or those of his fellow bps. Absence, unless excused for proven necessity, will be contumacy and is to be punished. All suffragans and vics. are ordered to certify clearly by letters patent the names of those summoned. The bp. of London is to report the day he received this mand. and what he has done about it, giving the names of those summoned in his own dioc. in a separate schedule. Given in the manor of Otford, 1 Sept. 1402. By authority of this mandate the bp. of London cites Bp. Clifford to appear in person before the abp. or his *locum tenens* or commissaries on the day set and to execute fully the requirements of the mand. as they apply in his own city and dioc. certifying to the abp. that he has done as required. Given in his manor of Hadham, 18 Sept. 1402.

fol. 56r **147** *28 Sept. 1402, Hillingdon.* Mand. from Bp. Clifford to Mr. Wm. Forster, his commissary general, in the foregoing terms for convocation of the clergy before the abp., 21 Oct. 1402 at St. Paul's. He specifies the archdcns. of Worc. and Glouc. Only proven necessity will excuse absence: not that it is intended, however, to punish for contumacy those who may happen to be absent at that time.[2] The clergy are to be called together to appoint proctors. The bp. requires reports with names in a separate schedule by 18 Oct.

fol. 56v **148** *18 Oct. 1402, London.* Report to the abp. of Cant. that the pr. and chap. of the cath. ch., the archdcns. of Worc. and Glouc., the abts. of convs. in the bp.'s obedience and other prelates exempt and non-exempt have been summoned as directed, with the disciplinary clause as ordered. The names of those cited follow.

NON-EXEMPT HOUSES

John, pr. and chap. of the cath. ch. of Worc.

Mr. Wm. Rocombe, archdcn. of Worc.

Mr. Rich. Wynchecombe, archdcn. of Glouc.

Dn. and college of Westbury.

Dn. and college of Warwick.

Walter, abt. of Glouc.

Thos., abt. of Tewkesbury.

John abt. of St. Augustine's, Bristol.

John abt. of Cirencester.

Wm., abt. of Winchcombe.

Thos., abt. of Pershore.

John, abt. of Alcester.

Peter, pr. of Studley.

John, pr. of Dodford.

Rich. pr. of Little Malvern.

John, pr. of Llanthony by Glouc.

Wm. Lane, master of St. Mark's Bristol.

EXEMPT HOUSES

Wm., abt. of Evesham.

Walter, abt. of Kingswood.

John abt. of Hales[owen].

---

[2] *non intendit quin pocius canonice punire contumacias eorumdem si quos contingit tunc abesse.*

Robt., abt. of Hailes.

John, pr. of Great Malvern.

John, abt. of Bordesley.

Clergy of the city and dioc. of Worc.

149 *Morrow of St. Michael, [30 Sept.] 1402, Hillingdon.* Mand. to Thos. Wybbe, rec. of Hanbury-by-Wick, to collect the charitable aid of 12d. in the mark on temporals and spirituals from benefices taxed and not taxed that was lately granted by the clergy of the archdeaconry of Worc., with authority to use canonical coercion.[3]

fol. 57r **150** *9 Oct. 1402, London.* Mand. to Mr. John Pavy, r.p.c. of St. Martin's, Worc., and Mr. John Chew, clk., on behalf of John Gerlethorp perp. vic. of p.c. of Inkberrow. His immediate predecessor John had left serious deficiencies at his death both in the chancel of the ch. and in respect of the furnishings of the manse and buildings and enclosures for which replacement is due.[4] John Gerlethorp has asked for a remedy and John Pavy and John Chew are instructed to go there and personally investigate, calling together clergy and laity to make sworn statements, and summoning the executors, if any, that the late vic. had. They are to estimate defects and cost of repairs and cause ecclesiastical property of the deceased to that amount in the dioc. to be sequestrated and to be kept safe until the deficiencies are made good or John Gerlethorp is satisfied in other ways. The bp. is to be informed of the amount of the deficiencies and their character and the estimated cost.

fol. 57v **151** *29 Aug. 1402, Hillingdon.* Mand. to Mr. Wm. Forster, commissory general and Mr. John Chew, clk. It refers to the letter from the king, etc. Since the various bps.' registers are in their hands and have not come to him, Bp. Clifford orders them to make a search concerning the said vicge.[5] from the first regnal year of King Henry son of King John to find out who were presented and instituted in it, by whose presentation, by whom it was founded and endowed, when and in what manner.

152 *No date.* Mand. to Mr. Wm. Forster, b. ll., commissary general concerning the charitable aid granted by the abts., prs., and other prelates and

---

[3] *Marginal note*: Similar commission to Mr. William Forster for the archdeaconries of Worcester and Gloucester to be noted in the next folio.

[4] 'Si rector alicujus Ecclesiae decedens domos Ecclesiae reliquerit dirutas vel ruinosas, de bonis ejus Ecclesiasticis tanta portio deducatur quae sufficiat ad reparandum haec et alios defectus Ecclesiae supplendos'. Lyndwood 3:27, *De Ecclesiis Aedificandis.* p. 250.

[5] Presumably Aston Cantlow. This entry is in the wrong place. See # 142.

clergy of the archdeaconry of Glouc. in the same form as that sent to Mr. Thos. Webbe (*sic*), for its collection in the archdeaconry of Worc. as shown in the preceding folio.

153 *No date*. Grant of charitable aid granted to the bp. by the religious and prelates of the archdeaconry of Worc. of 12d. in the mark from benefices and ecclesiastical goods both temporal and spiritual, according to true and customary taxation, the first half to be paid at the feast of St. Michael [29 Sept.] next following or within fifteen days after, and the second half at the Annunciation [25 Mar.] or fifteen days after, submitting themselves to ecclesiastical censures of suspension, excommunication and interdict if in default of the whole or part, and renouncing any appeals or fol. 58r relief at law that would impede the collection. The form of the grant by the clergy of the archdeaconry follows: 'In Dei nomine Amen, nos totus clerus Archidiaconatus Wygorniensis...' in the same terms.

154 *No date*. Grant of the same in manner and form by prelates and clergy of the archdeaconry of Glouc.

155 *No date*. Notice by the archdcn. of Glouc. that John Wythir, Jr., of Upton-by-Gloucester, John Janynes of Hampton Monialium and John Whitknyght of Framilode of his dioc. are under greater excommunication and are more than forty days contumacious to the peril of souls and a pernicious example. He asks the bp. to apply for the help of the secular arm 'secundum regni Anglie consuetudinem laudabilem.'

156 *26 Oct. 1402, Hillingdon*. Signification to the king of the foregoing, fol. 58v invoking the royal authority and asking that the sheriff of Glouc. be ordered to arrest the contumacious.

157 *31 Oct. 1402, London*. Letters dimissory to Wm. Chichelhey, clk., to all orders minor and major of subdcn. and dcn.

158 *5 Nov. 1402, London*. Mand. to Mr. Wm. Forster, commissary general. The pry. of the Holy Sepulchre, Warwick, having become vacant by the death of the pr., Peter Warrewyk, the brs. have elected Br. John Staunford in his stead. The bp. has been asked to confirm the election but since he is engaged in other duties he cannot investigate the matter. He instructs Forster to examine, calling before him the co-electors and any who are opposed, examining them in legal form, and he is to confirm or disallow within fifteen days, after which he is to send his report of the entire process, *opportuno tempore.*[6]

fol. 59r **159**   *8 Nov. 1402, London.* Letters dimissory to John Dyer of his dioc. acol., to the holy orders of subdcn. and dcn.

160   *16 Nov. 1402, London.* Permission granted to John Ely, r.p.c. of Chokenhill to be absent for a year, to put his church to farm to suitable persons and to receive its revenues. Services and cure of souls are not to be neglected and in particular the obsequies of Mr. John Prophet, the king's secretary. This special privilege is granted provided that he sends in a suitable proctor who will answer to the ordinaries in his place. By the bp.'s direction the disadvantage of his absence is to be compensated for by the liberal distribution of alms in the parish.

161   *17 Nov. 1402, London.* Mand. to the dean of Kington and to Dns. Rich., par. chpln. of Preston-on-Stour and to the recs., vics. and chplns, of the deanery. Joan, widow of John Smyth of Preston-on-Stour, is being maliciously defamed by statements of people unknown to her by name, that when robbers broke into the house and killed her husband she consented and aided them. Those who so defame and injure her incur greater ex-fol. 59vcommunication. These clergy are charged, singly and collectively, to make this excommunication known for three Sundays in the ch. of Preston-on-Stour and in all chs. of the deanery and anywhere else where Joan may say it should be done. It is to be done in the presence of the people and in the solemnities of the mass, with cross erect in their hands, bells tolling and candles lighted, and then these are to be extinguished and cast to the ground as the denunciation is uttered. The dn. and Rich. are told to hold an inquisition and if the parties to the crime are found and are recalcitrant their names are to be sent to the bp.

162   *26 Nov. 1402.* Lic. to Wm., r.p.c. of Barnsley to be non-resident for one year and to put his ch. to farm under the usual form with the clause for the obsequies of Wm. Stourton of Salisbury dioc., donzel.

163   *27 Nov. 1402, London.* Lic. to Mr. Rich. Roche of the p.c. of Blessed Mary in-the-Market, Bristol, to be non-resident for one year and put his ch. to farm.

[6] See Appendix 6.

164 *3 Dec. 1402, London.* Permission during the bp.'s pleasure to Agnes Jonet that wherever in his diocese she might happen to stay mass might be said, provided that nothing be in prejudice of the mother chs. or parsons of the place. Lic. is given to her and to ps. in her presence.

165 *10 Dec. 1402, Hillingdon.* Grant of faculty to Wm., abt. of Winchcombe, to have Thos. Circestre and Thos. Bryghtwelton, mks. of that monas. and dcns., ordained to the priesthood by any Catholic bp., notwithstanding they are professed in a regular order.

fol. 60r   **166** *8 June 1403, London.* Admission and inst. of Mr. Robt. Neuby, p., to the perp. vicge of p. c. of Tetbury (pat.: a. & c. of Blessed Mary of Eynsham, OSB, Lincoln dioc.) vacant by the death of Dns. John Philyper. Letters of inst. and induction to the archdcn. of Glouc.

167 *10 June 1403, London.* Exch. between Dns. John Assheton, r.p.c. of Coberley (pat.: Dns. Thos. Berkeley, lord of Coberley), and Dns. Nicholas Boteler, perp. vic. of p.c. of Westbury-by-Newenham, Hereford dioc. Letters of inst. Nicholas had mand. to induct to the archdcn. of Glouc.

168 *19 June 1403, Alvechurch.* Admission and inst. of Dns. John Severle, p., to the perp. vicge. of p.c. of Newbold Pacey (pat.: Thos. Carlele, provost of Queen's Hall, Oxford, and the fellows and scholars) vacant by the resignation of Dns. Wm. Burton. Letters of inst. and induction to the archdcn. of Worc.

fol. 60v   **169** *22 June 1403, Alvechurch.* Collation to the vicge of p.c. of Ebrington of Dns. Rich. Dene, p.; the collation having devolved to the bp. for that turn. Letters of inst. and induction to the archdcn. of Worc. or his offl. or in their absence to Mr. John Pavy, r.p.c. of St. Martin's, Worc.

170 *25 June 1403, Alvechurch.* Admission and inst. of Dns. Robt. Stanley, p. to the vicge. of Himbleton p.c. (pat.: pr. and chap. of the cath. ch. of Worc.). Letters of inst. and induction to the archdcn. of Worc.

171 *2 July 1403, Alvechurch.* Admission and inst. of Dns. Brian Richardes, p., to the perp. chty. of Blessed Mary in the cemetery of p.c. of Kidderminster (pat.: Dns. Wm. de Beauchamp, kt.) vacant by the resignation of Dns. Wm. Malpas. Letters of inst. and induction to the archdcn. of Worc.

fol. 61r   **172** *13 July 1403, Alvechurch.* Admission and inst. of Dns. John Graunger, p., as perp. vic. of p.c. of Bisley (pat.: rec. of the first portion of Bisley ch.) vacant by the resignation of Dns. John Wolrugge. Letters of inst. and induction to the archdcn.

173 *16 July 1403, Alvechurch.* Exch. between Dns. Nicholas Howet, r.p.c. of Blessed Mary in Aust, Glouc. (pat.: p. & c. of Llanthony by Glouc., OSA) and Dns. John Burgeys, r.p.c. of Tholweston, Salisbury dioc. Letters of inst. John had mand. to induct to the archdcn. of Glouc.

174 *18 July 1403, Worc.* Admission and inst. of Thos. Bruet, p., to p.c. of Coaley (pat.: a. & c. of Pershore, OSB) vacant by the resignation of Thos. Alforde. Letters of inst. and induction to the archdcn. of Glouc.

fol. 61v **175** *21 July 1403, Worcester.* Exch. between Dns. Robt. Belde, perp. vic. of p.c. of Acton Turville (pat.: Geoffrey Crompe, custodian of p.c. of Tormarton) and Dns. Wm. Godefray, perp. vic. of p.c. of Rowington (pat.: a. & c. of Reading). John Leycestre, *literatus*, acting as proctor for William. Letters of inst. and mand. to induct to Wm., archdcn. of Glouc. and Robt., archdcn. of Worc.

176 *3 Aug. 1403, Hanbury.* Admission and inst. of Dns. Rich. Aldryngton *alias* Colcomb, p., to the free chpl. of St. Katherine in the manor of Compton (pat.: bp. of Exeter), vacant by the death of Dns. Wm. Styward. Letters of inst. and induction to the archdcn. of Glouc.

177 *4 Aug. 1403, Alvechurch.* Collation, it having devolved on the bp. for that turn, of Dns. John Laury, p., to p.c. of St. Ewen, Bristol. Letters of inst. and induction to the archdcn. of Glouc. or his offl. or in their absence to Mr. Wm. Forster, commissary general.

fol. 62r **178** *8 Aug. 1403, Blockley.* Exch. between Dns. Wm. Ybote, r.p.c. of Icomb (pat.: pr. of the cath. ch. of Worc.) and Dns. Edmund Knyght, perp. vic. of Winterbourne-Monketon, Salisbury dioc., who was represented by Thos. Jay, *literatus*, as proctor, John Monkton, *literatus*, acting as proctor for Wm. Ybote. Letters of inst. Edmund had mand. to induct to Mr. Wm. Forster, commissary general, and the dn. of Stowe.

179 *14 Aug. 1403, Blockley.* Exch. between Dns. Wm. Assheford, perp. vic. of p.c. of Coln St. Aldwyn (pat.: a. & c. of St. Peter's, Glouc.) and Dns. John Basely, r.p.c. of Havering, Lincoln dioc. Letters of inst. John had mand. to induct to the archdcn. of Glouc.

fol. 62v **180** *29 Aug. 1403, Chipping Norton.* Admission and inst. of John Mortimer, clk., to Wick Rissington (pat.: Dns. Hugh Burnell, kt., lord of Holgot and Weoley) vacant by the resignation of Dns. John Hewys. Letters of inst. and induction to the archdcn. of Glouc.

181   *24 Sept. 1403, Hillingdon.* Exch. between Dns. Wm. Cheyny, r.p.c. of Albrighton (pat.: a. & c. of Pershore, OSB) and Dns. Thos. Haccorn, chpln. or custodian of the chpl. or chty. of Westratton, Winch. dioc. Letters of inst.   Thos. had mand. to induct to the archdcn. of Worc.

182   *25 Sept. 1403, Hillingdon.* Admission and inst. of Dns. Wm. Yonge, p., to p.c. of Basingdene, vacant by the resignation of Dns. Robt. Tolle (pat.: William Quenyngton and John Yonge, chplns. of the chty. of the Holy Trinity and St. Mary in the ch. of St. John the Baptist, Cirencester, lords of Basingdene). Letters of inst. and induction to the archdcn. of Glouc.

fol. 63r **183**   *1 Oct. 1403, Hillingdon.* Exch. between Dns. Stephen Doun. perp. vic. of p.c. of Prestbury (pat.: p. & c. of Llanthony by Glouc., OSA) and Dns. Thos. Kyngham, r.p.c. of Shaw, Salisbury dioc. Letters of inst. Thomas had mand. to induct to the archdcn. of Glouc.

184   *8 Oct. 1403, London.* Admission and inst. of Dns. Hy. Portlond, p., to the perp. chty. of the Calenders' Fraternity in All Saints Church, Bristol, vacant by the death of Dns. John Wylford (pat.: John Stephenys, the mayor of Bristol; nomination by the pr. and brs. of the fraternity by letters under their seal.), Mr. John Chew acting as proctor. Letters of inst. and induction to the archdcn. of Glouc.

185   *12 Nov. 1403, Hillingdon.* Admission and inst. of Dns. Robt., p.,[7] to the perp. vicge. of the p.c. of Blessed Mary before the great gate of the Abbey, Glouc. (pat.: a. & c. of St. Peter's). Letters of inst. and induction to the archdcn. of Glouc.

fol. 63v **186**   *18 Nov. 1403, Hillingdon.* Exch. between Dns. John Yonge, r.p.c. of Harnhill (pat.: King Henry) and Dns. John Bryd, perp. vic. of p.c. of Marden, Salisbury dioc. Letters of inst.   John Bryd had mand. to induct to the archdcn. of Glouc.

187   *18 Nov. 1403, Hillingdon.* Admission and inst. of Mr. John Fytone to p.c. of Arrow (pat.: Dns. Thos. Burdet, kt.), vacant by the death of Mr. Robt. Rouley. Letters of inst. and induction to the archdcn. of Worc.

188   *18 Nov. 1403, Hillingdon.* Exch. between Dns. Wm. Hull, r.p.c. of Bradley (pat.: King Henry) and Dns. John Neweton, perp. vic. of p.c. of

---

[7] No surname. See # 227.

Wilsford, Salisbury dioc. Letters of inst. John had mand. to induct to the can. of Bibury.

fol. 64r **189** *22 Dec. 1403, Hillingdon.* Exch. between Dns. John Ragbroke, perp. vic. of p.c. of Wolford (pat.: warden and scholars of Merton house in Oxford) and Dns. John Hereward, perp. vic. of p.c. of Notley, Winch. dioc. Letters of inst. John Hereward had mand. to induct to the archdcn. of Worc.

190 *23 Dec. 1403, Hillingdon.* Admission and inst. of John Bremore, clk., to the recy. of p.c. of Suckley (pat.: King Henry). Letters of inst. and induction to the archdcn. of Worc.

191 *14 Jan. 1404, London.* Admission and inst. of Dns. John Wade, p., fol. 64v to the preb. in the coll. ch. of Blessed Mary, Warwick vacant by the death of Mr. Robt. Rouley (pat.: Dns. Rich. de Beauchamp, earl of Warwick), Dns. John Boys, p., acting as proctor. Letters of inst. and induction to the dn. of the college of Warwick.

192 *16 Jan. 1404, London.* Exch. between Dns. Wm. Ingleby, perp. vic. of the prebendal ch. of Bitton (pat.: Mr. Robt. Hallum, can. of the cath. ch. of Blessed Mary, Salisbury and preby. of Bitton) and Dns. Walter Eymer, perp. vic. of p.c. of Burford, Lincoln dioc., who had as proctor Mr. John Penne, notary public. Letters of inst. Walter had mand. to induct to the archdcn. of Glouc.

193 *24 Jan. 1404, London.* Exch. between Dns. Rich. Carpenter, r.p.c. of Condicote (pat.: King Henry) and Dns. John Moryene, r.p.c. of Bradley Winch. dioc. The king presented by reason of his custody of the land and fol. 65r minor heir of Ralph Stonore a tenant-in-chief of R[ichard] II, late King of England. Letters of inst. John had mand. to induct to Mr. Wm. Forster, commissary general.

194 *25 Jan. 1404, London.* Admission and inst. of Dns. Thos. Curteys, p. *secundum formam fundacionis* to the perp. chty., newly founded in the chpl. of Blessed Mary in the p.c. of Winchcombe (pat.: Richard Wynchcombe, archdcn. of Glouc., on nomination by Rich. Chaumberleyn and Walter Ponchard). Letters of inst. and induction to the archdcn. of Glouc.

195 *16 Feb. 1404, London.* Certification by the d. & c. of Hereford of an exch. between Dns. John Randolf, perp. vic. of p.c. of Southrop (pat.: Br. Robt. Normanton, *locum tenens* of the pr. of the hosp. of St. John of Jerusalem in England, the pr. *in remotis*), and Dns. Nicholas Barton, perp.

vic. of p.c. of Holmer, Hereford dioc. Nicholas had mand. to induct to the archdcn. of Glouc.

fol. 65v **196** *18 Feb. 1404, London.* Exch. between Dns. John Botyler, r.p.c. of Winterbournebradston (pat.: Thos. Bradston, donzel, lord of Winterbournebradston), and John Prentys, clk., r.p.c. of Castleford, York dioc. Letters of inst. John Prentys had mand. to induct to the archdcn. of Glouc.

197 *26 Feb. 1404, London.* Exch. between John Prentys, clk., r.p.c. of Winterbournebradston (pat.: Thos. Bradston, squire) and John Dautre, master or custodian of the house or hosp. of St. Bartholomew by the bridge called Fromebridge, Bristol (pat.: the Reverend Thos. La Warre, Lord La Warre). Letters of inst. and mand. to induct to the archdcn. of Glouc.

198 *17 Mar. 1404, London.* Admission and inst. of Mr. Wm. Forster to the p.c. of Wotton-under-Edge (pat.: Thos. Berkeley, lord of Berkeley). Letters of inst. and mand. to induct.

fol. 66r **199** *9 Apr. 1404, Hillingdon.* Admission and inst. of Dns. John Clerk, p., as perp. custodian or chpln. of the chpl. or chty. of Harescombe (pat.: p. & c. of Llanthony by Gloucester) with the annexed chpl. of Pichencombe, he having sworn to observe the terms of the foundation. Letters of inst. and induction to the archdcn. of Glouc.

200 *21 Apr. 1404, Hillingdon.* Admission and inst. of Dns. Rich. Dene, p., to the recy. of p.c. of Fretherne (pat.: Anselm Gyse, John Harsefeld, Thos. Alford, lately rec. of Coaley and Matthew Clifford). Letters of inst. and induction to the archdcn. of Glouc.

201 *24 Apr. 1404, Hillingdon.* Admission and inst. of Dns. Wm. White, p., to the recy. of p.c. of Dereham (pat.: Dns. Maurice Russell, kt.). Letters of inst. and induction to the archdcn. of Glouc.

fol. 66v **202** *2 May 1404, London.* Exch. between Dns. John Coupere, r.p.c. of Coln-Rogers (pat.: a. & c. of St. Peter's, Glouc.), and Dns. Rich. Budden, perp. vic. of p.c. of Bradley, Salisbury dioc. Letters of inst. Richard had mand. to induct to the archdcn. of Glouc.

203 *2 May 1404, London.* Admission and inst. of Dns. Wm. Seman, p., to the perp. vicge. of p.c. of Newbold Pacey, vacant by the resignation of Dns. John Severley, on presentation by John Sharp, senior fellow and acting provost of the college of Queen's Hall, Oxford, the office of provost being vacant, and the fellows and scholars. Letters of inst. and induction to the archdcn. of Worc.

204   *5 May 1404, London.* Exch. between Dns. Robt. Warreys, guardian or custodian of the perp. chty. in the p.c. of Winterbournebradston (pat.: Thos. Bradston lord of Winterbournebradston) and Dns. Wm. Stoke, perp. vic. of p.c. of Lesenes, Roch. dioc. Robt. Warreys was admitted to Lesenes vicge. by commission of John Launce, clk. and b. ll., vicar-general and custodian of spirituals, Roch., *sede vacante.* Letters of inst.   Wm. had mand. to induct to the archdcn. of Glouc.

fol. 67r   **205**   *7 May 1404, London.* Exch. between Dns. John Dautre, r.p.c. of Winterbournebradston (pat.: Thos. Bradston) and Dns. Walter Fitzpers, r.p.c. of Acle, Norwich dioc., Rich. Aston, clk., acting as proctor. Letters of inst. Walter had mand. to induct to the archdcn. of Glouc.

206   *23 May 1404, Hillingdon.* Admission and inst. of Dns. John Hoo, p., to the perp. vicge. of p.c. of Ebrington (pat.: a. & c. of Biddlesden, O. Cist., Lincoln dioc.). Letters of inst. and induction to the archdcn. of Glouc.

fol. 67v   **207**   *29 May 1404, Hillingdon.* Exch. between Dns. Wm. Bataile, r.p.c. of Colesborne (pat.: p. & c. of Llanthony by Gloucester, OSA) and Dns. John Mason perp. vic. of p.c. of Budbrooke (pat.: d. & c. of the coll. ch. of Blessed Mary, Warwick). Letters of inst. and mands. to induct, Wm. to the archdcn. of Worc. and John to the archdcn. of Glouc.

208   *13 June 1404, Hillingdon.* Admission and inst. of Dns. Rich. Thomas, p., to the perp. vicge. of p.c. of Chedworth (pat.: King Henry IV). Letters of inst. and induction to the archdcn. of Glouc.

209   *21 June 1404, Hillingdon.* Certification by Henry [Bowet], bp., Bath and Wells [1401-1407], of an exch. between Andrew Swynford, perp. vic. of the prebendal ch. of Bedminster and Radcleve, Bath and Wells dioc., and Wm. Dudelbury, r.p.c. of Stowe (pat.: a. & c. of Evesham). Direction to the archdcn. of Glouc.[8]

fol. 68r   **210**   *17 Dec. 1402, Hillingdon.* Mand. and a general monition for the return of stolen articles, sent to the r.p.c. of Arrow and the perp. vic. of p.c. of Alcester. The rec., Wm. de Kyngeley, has complained to the bp. that certain persons unknown to him by name broke into his house at Kingley and

---

[8] The form changed in this instance. 'Scriptum fuit ut moris est Archdiacano Gloucestrie vel eius officiali ad inducendum juramento obediencie recepto primitus ab eodem.' This form occurs in numerous subsequent memoranda of collations.

carried off memoranda, charters and muniments concerning the rights and obligations of himself and his heirs together with other goods and have kept them hidden, to the great injury of himself and heirs and danger to their own souls. The bp. orders that in the chs. of Arrow and Alcester when there are large congregations on Sundays and festivals, public warning be given that full restitution is to be made within fifteen days under penalty of major excommunication, and if the malefactors do not appear as a result of the monitions, then when there is a full congregation at mass on Sundays the sentence of major excommunication is to be declared with cross erect, bells tolling, candles lighted, etc., and is not to cease until the malefactors come for absolution or the rec. and vic. receive some other directive from the bp.

211 *23 Dec. 1402, Hillingdon.* Dispensation in accordance with *Cum ex eo* to Thos. Willicote, r.p.c. of Burton, subdcn., to be absent for two years to study *ubicunque in Anglia viget studium generale*, to put his ch. to farm to suitable persons and receive the fruits. The usual injunctions about cure of souls, obsequies and proctor. After two years he must come back and reside.[9]

fol. 68v **212** *3 Feb. 1403, London.* Letters dimissory to Robt. Sklatter, acol. to be advanced to the orders of subdcn. and dcn.

213 *1 Dec. 1402, Westminster.* Writ *Significavit* to the sheriff of Glouc. for the arrest of the manifestly contumacious John Wythur, Jr. of Upton-by-Gloucester who has disregarded the excommunication of the ch.

214 *3 Feb. 1403, Worc.* General notice that John Wythur, Jr., of Upton-by-Gloucester is under excommunication for contempt in not appearing for more than forty days to answer charges and has remained contumacious, that the secular arm has been invoked and he has been taken and delivered into the bp.'s custody until he is penitent and receives formal absolution.

215 *6 Feb. 1403, Worc.* Offer of indulgence of forty days to those who, invoking the grace of God and the merits and prayers of the Blessed Virgin
fol. 69r and of the confessors and patrons, Oswald and Wolfstan, and of all the

---

[9] Parish revenues were a necessity for clergy pursuing studies at university and prior to the Statue of Provisors many had received benefices by papal provision. Now at the Convocation at St. Paul's, 1399, scholars at Oxford and Cambridge petitioned, referring to the pious foundations at universities intended that clergy should have sufficient doctrine. They pointed to the lack of provisions, not to contest the statutes of 25 Edward III and 13 Richard II, but to argue that they did need a remedy (Reg. Arundel 1, fol. 53).

saints, and having confessed and being penitent, contribute of their goods to the repair of the king's road Wotton Way, commonly called Elbrugge Way by Glouc., or give aid in other ways, and ratifies all indulgences that have been granted or will be granted, properly, in this matter.

216 *9 Feb. 1403, Worc.* The same to the house or hosp. of St. Lawrence Cirencester, *mutatis in ea parte mutandis.*

217 *12 Feb. 1403, Hartlebury.* Similar letter for the maintenance and repair of the bridge called Manusfordbrugge in his dioc.

218 *10 Feb. 1403, Worc.* Lic. to Dns. John Judde, r.p.c. of All Saints, Worc. to be absent for two consecutive years, to put his ch. to farm with suitable persons and to receive the fruits, provided that the obsequies and cure of souls and charities are not neglected. A suitable proctor is to answer to the ordinaries and the rec. is to return to his ch. at the end of the two years and reside.

219 *27 Sept. 1402, Hillingdon.* Mand. to Mr. Wm. Forster, commissary general. Dns. John Asshton, r.p.c. of Coberley, has presented Dns. Robt. Swynford, p., to the chty. of Beauvale in the ch. of Coberley which is vacant and of his patronage as he says. He is to hold an inquiry how it is vacant and when the vacancy began, in what portions and of what rights it consists, its annual value and the duties attached to it, also whether its foundation and order require continued sworn residence or not, by what right and possession the one presenting acts and who last presented. He is to make inquiry also into the age, birth, life and conversation, orders and merits of the presentee, summoning the chap. if need be, and send the results by letters patent and close under his seal and the seals of those taking part in the inquiry together with their full names.

fol. 69v

220 *Undated, Hartlebury.* Richard Broun, a poor man, is under necessity of visiting the apostolic see and needs faculties to allow him to beg sustenance. Forty days indulgence to those who help him.[10] This privilege is for one year.

221 *2 Feb. 1403, Westminster.* Writ from King Henry to the bp. It refers to the Convocation at St. Paul's on 21 Oct. and the tenth and half tenth granted by the churchmen from ecclesiastical benefices customarily taxed — poor nunneries and hospitals excepted — the first half tenth payable at the

---

[10] 'qui de bonis a deo sibi collatis praefato Ricardo grata contulerint subsidia.'

Annunciation [25 Mar], the second at the Nativity of John the Baptist [24 June] and the third at the Purification [2 Feb.], this grant not to be made a precedent and no other levies to be made during that period. The king orders that the collectors be appointed and their names be sent to the Exchequer by 1 March.

222 *18 Feb. 1403, Hartlebury.* Mand. from the bp. to the a. & c. of Osney obtaining the p.c. of Bibury *in proprios usus.* The bp. refers to the royal writ concerning the tenth and half tenth and makes them collectors in the archdeaconry of Glouc., houses of the poor nuns of St. Mary Magdalen, Bristol, and the hosp. for poor lepers of St. Bartholomew, Glouc. excepted. They are to include the portion of the ch. of Bibury and any persons holding portions or pensions usually taxed or holding at farm. Sequestration may be applied to recalcitrants and ecclesiastical censures may be used, including excommunication. The names of any who remain obdurate more than forty days are to be sent in so that the secular arm may be invoked.

223 *18 Feb. 1403, Hartlebury.* Mand. under the same form to the p. & c. of St. Oswald, Glouc., to levy and collect the tenth and half tenth in the archdeaconry of Worc., excepting the poor nunneries of Whistones, Westwood, Cook Hill, Pinley and Wroxall and the hosps. for the poor of Sts. Wolfstan and Oswald, Worc. [city].

224 *18 Feb. 1403, Hartlebury.* Letter of the bp. to the Treasurer and barons of the Exchequer that he has made the a. & c. of Osney, who are obtaining the p.c. of Bibury, and the p. & c. of St. Oswald, Glouc., collectors of the tenth and half tenth in the archdeaconries of Glouc. and Worc., respectively, with the foregoing exceptions.

225 *1 Apr. 1403, Hartlebury.* Mand. to Mr. Wm. Forster, commissary general, and Rich. Wynchecombe, archdcn. of Glouc. The bp. quotes the recent Statute of 4 Henry IV that reaffirmed the earlier Statute of 15 Richard II concerning appropriation of chs. and endowment of vicges., and provided that it be put into execution and if any ch. had been appropriated by lic. of Richard or the present king since that fifteenth year contrary to that Statute such appropriation must be altered to conform with it before Easter next and if this is not done the appropriations and lic. are void except Haddenham ch. in the diocese of Ely.

The Statute of 15 Richard II is recited in part which noted the injury done to parishioners by appropriations and provided that in any future lic. to appropriate the diocesan must order that those appropriating and their successors pay and distribute a suitable sum of money annually from the fruits and profits of the ch. for relief of the par. poor.

The bp. then refers to current appropriations, that of the chs. of Himbleton and Stoke to the pr. and chap. of the cath. ch. of Worc. and of Eckington p.c. to the a. & c. of Pershore. He is concerned that the appropriating houses should not incur the penalties of the Statute in ignorance and that the chs. appropriated receive indemnification. He orders Forster and the archdcn. to go to these chs. with all speed, determine the annual value of their rents and emoluments and in what they consist, also what sums they individually amount to, the obligations of the vic. of Himbleton at the time and what will be needed to support him. They are to ascertain these things by diligent inquiry through reliable recs., vics. and more worthy (*valentiores*) parishioners by sworn evidence.

Cite the pr. and chap. the a. & c. to appear before him [the bp.] Maundy Thur. [12 Apr.]. In the case of the p. & c. this is for the providing of fitting portions and sustentation of the vics. who will be in Himbleton ch. The vicge. he means, *volente domino*, to set in order and also to require an adequate sum of money for distribution to the par. poor of Stoke according to Statute. The a. & c. are to come and hear his order for the sum to be distributed to the par. poor of Eckington ch. appropriated to their monas. and to do further in the foregoing matters what the tenor of the Statute requires and is reasonable. A report is to be made before Maundy Thur. as to what they have done and discovered.[11]

fol. 71v   **226**   *11 Apr. 1403, Worc.* Certification that Mr. Wm. Forster, commissary general, and Rich. Wynchecombe, archdcn. of Glouc. have reported the execution of the bp.'s orders. They have held an inquiry into the revenues, their annual value, nature and amounts, for the chs. of Himbleton, Stoke and Eckington and also the duties of the vic. of Himbleton who is to be supported. The inquiry was made through recs. and vics. and more worthy parishioners by sworn testimony as directed, and in the schedules annexed to their certification are the names of those taking part in the inquiry, and the details of the portions, emoluments and fruits and their value are given more fully. The pr. and chap. of Worc. and the a. & c. of Pershore have been cited to appear before the bp. in accord with his mand.

---

[11] For a discussion of the principles and procedures of an appropriation see Haines, *The Administration of the Diocese of Worcester*, pp. 140-167. See also Appendix 1.

227   *13 Apr. 1403, Worcester.* The bp. regulating the appropriation of the p.c. of Blessed Mary before-the-Abbey Gate to the conv. of St. Peter, Glouc., directed that the a. & c. provide a suitable portion of the fruits and revenues for the p.c. as follows.[12] The present vic. and his successors who from time to time are to be presented by the a. & c. and instituted by the bp. or his successors in the vicge. of the p.c. shall have, first, for their dwelling that manse with its appurtenances in which the vics. have been accustomed to live within the town of Glouc. from early times, maintained and repaired at the expense of the a. & c. as often as necessity calls for it. The vic. and his successors will receive for their support from the a. & c. each year £10 in legal money, in the monas., paid at the four principal terms of the year, beginning with Easter following the date of this settle-

fol. 72r   ment and they are to have nothing more from oblations or any other emoluments or revenues, for the vics. are not charged with other duties except the cure of souls of the parishioners and to serve the ch. and duly administer the sacraments or cause them to be administered. Therefore it is considered that the sum of £10 is sufficient and suitable because no other burden is required and the rest of the charges, ordinary and extraordinary, will be borne by the a. & c. and their successors along with the receiving and providing procurations for bp.'s officers and staff and those of their successors and finding sustentations for them, and any chplns. needed for serving the ch. and chpls. annexed to it, excepting the present vic., for whose support we have assigned a suitable portion. Future vics. after their presentation, both before the abt. and before the instituting offl., shall swear to render to the a. & c. and their successors or deputies all oblations, obventions, revenues and other emoluments pertaining to the ch. that come into their hands, faithfully and without any diminution whatever and will commit no fraud neither cause nor permit such but will prevent such by all

---

[12] The following rubric in a late fifteenth or early sixteenth century hand was added as a title to this section and was repeated at sections 228, 229, 230.

'Compositio est arbitrata inter abbatem et conventum sancti Petri Gloucestrie et vicarium ecclesie parochialis Sancte Marie ante portam ibidem.'

The memorandum begins as follows.

'Quorum interest noverint universi quod nos Ricardus permissione divina Wygorniensis episcopus de consensu expresso Religiosorum et virorum Abbatis et Conventus monasterii sancti Petri ville Gloucestrie nostre diocesis ecclesiam parochialem beate Marie ante portam Abbathie eiusdem ville in usus proprios obtinencium congruam porcionem de fructibus et obvencionibus dicte parochialis ecclesie Religiosis predictis et eorum monasterio appropriate canonice et unite limitamus taxamus et ... ordinamus quod vicarius ibidem qui nunc est et successores sui ... habebunt...'

means possible and if unable to prevent it will inform the a. & c. If the payment of any part of the £10 is in arrears at any term for eight days either in part or whole, twice the amount owing must be paid and all fruits and obventions of the ch. are to be sequestrated until the vic. is satisfied. Moreover, since it is reasonable and consonant with equity that those who enjoy the emoluments should accept and recognize the charge, it is ordered that the a. & c. distribute annually 26s. 8d. as alms to the parish poor, i.e. 13s. 4d. at All Saints and the same at Christmas, doing it in the p.c. This distribution is to be made in perpetuity and to none but the poor of the p.c. and in the place and at the terms stated. Consideration of the annual value of such a benefice has led us to limit this, taking note of the appropriate charges and alms from the revenues of the ch. that the said religious who are subject to the apostolic see pay each year. The terms of the grant follow. First: from the fruits and revenues of the ch. they pay the ps. and clks. serving in the chpl. of All Saints in the monas. twelve marks sterling. For wax and oil for the chpl., 16s. 8d. For bread for the ps. and clks. serving there twelve marks. For victuals, bread and clothes for the par. poor of the said ch. and of Holy Trinity, Glouc. sixteen marks. For the sick mks. and their nurses and the office of the infirmary and especially for the older mks. who are ill £10.

fol. 72v　These charges and alms and the distribution of the 26s. 8d. and all others laid down by these directions the bp. firmly commands to be observed inviolably every year, reserving to himself and successors full power if need be to add to or reduce them and to interpret obscurities if such there are.

Memorandum that the a. & c. declared that they had carefully considered the dispositions of the bp. and gave their full assent and affixed their common seal.[13]

228　*13 Apr. 1403, Worcester.* [*St. Peter's Conv. Glouc. obtains Holy Trinity.*] The bp. sets the following terms to which a. & c. agree. It is ordered that the present vic. and his successors be presented by the a. & c. and instituted by the bp. and his successors shall have, first, for their dwelling a suitable house within the town walls to be ordered and assigned to them by the abt., to be maintained and kept in proper repair at the expense of the a. & c. as often as necessary. They shall have from the a. & c. likewise for their support 12 marks legal money paid at the four principal

---

[13] 'Datum in domo nostra capitulari quartodecimo die mensis Aprilis anno domini suprascripto.'

terms beginning next Easter. They shall have nothing else from oblations or other emoluments from the ch. since the bp. is not burdening the vic. with other duties except the cure of souls and the serving of the vicge. or causing it to be served creditably and administering the sacraments and sacramentals. The bp. believes this sum of 12 marks a sufficient and fitting portion because the vicar is held to no other duty and the a. & c. and their successors will support the other charges ordinary and extraordinary along with those of providing a par. chpln. with the proper means of serving the chpl. of Blessed Mary of Graslone annexed to the aforesaid p.c., and receiving

fol. 73r   members of the bp.'s staff and providing their procurations. Future vicars, after being presented, shall swear before the abt. and the one instituting them that they will render to the a. & c. their successors or deputies all oblations, obventions, income and other emoluments pertaining to the ch. that come into their hands, intact without diminution, and will practice no fraud or procure such but will, as far as they can, prevent it, failing which they will inform the a. & c. If any payment of any part of the 12 marks to the vic. be delayed eight days the a. & c. must pay double the arrears and the revenues of the ch. are to be sequestrated until the vic. receives satisfaction. Furthermore, since it is reasonable and equitable that those who enjoy the emolument should accept and acknowledge the charge, it is ordered that the a. & c. distribute 13s. 4d. to the par. poor at Christmas every year in the p.c. This order is to be observed inviolably. Full power is reserved where necessary to add to the vicge. or reduce it and to interpret obscurities.

229   *13 Apr. 1403, Worcester.* [*Himbleton p.c. and Worc. cath.*] The bp. orders that a suitable portion be reserved for the present vic. and his successors who are to be presented by the pr. and chap. and instituted by himself or his successors. They are to have a hall with a room and a house for their cook and another house for a barn for storing their corn with a garden in the recy, and sixteen acres of arable land. For their support they are to receive from the pr. and chap. ten marks of legal money annually, paid in

fol. 73v   the cath. ch. at the four principal terms, i.e. Michaelmas, Christmas, Easter and the Nativity of John the Baptist, in equal portions, beginning the first term's payment at Michaelmas next. They will have nothing else from the oblations or other emoluments since they are charged with no other duties except the cure of souls and divine offices and the administering of the sacraments and sacramentals. The sum of ten marks along with the sixteen acres of arable land will be a sufficient portion for the support of the vic., it is considered, for he is held to no other burden and the pr. and chap. will support all the other charges ordinary and extraordinary together with receiving the bp.'s staff and paying their procurations. Individual vics. after presentation shall swear in the presence of the pr. and the one who institutes them that they will hand over all emoluments, will practise no fraud, etc. ... The pr. and chap. are to distribute 3s. 4d. to the par. poor each Christmas. The bp. reserves the right to add to or reduce the foregoing and to interpret obscurities.

fol. 74r **230** *13 Apr. 1403, Worcester.* [*Toddington p.c. and the monas. of Hailes.*] The vic. and his successors who will be presented by the a. & c. shall have a suitable manse not far from the ch. built in this first instance at the expense of the religious and completely constructed and afterwards maintained and repaired at the expense of the vic. as often as necessary. He shall have portions and tithes throughout the par. as follows: tithes of lambs, calves, pigs, geese, eggs, apples, milk, cheese, honey, flax, hemp, fallen wood, doves, vineyards, fisheries, also oblations made in the ch. or elsewhere in the par. The vic. shall have trentals and any unspecified goods given or bequeathed, the pence offered in memory of the dead and mortuary fees and all kinds of personal tithes of stipendiaries, artisans, merchants and from pastures and of increase of animals, and from arable lands and if they are changed into pasture, grazing of the cemetery and prunings of trees growing there. He shall have also a virgate of land lately belonging to the recy. of Toddington in Stanley Pont-large with an acre of meadow there. The vic. is to serve the ch. and chpl. of Stanley Pontlarge in masses as is customary or cause them to be served at his own charge and will attend to the cure of souls. The a. & c. will pay the repairs of the chancels and customary procurations and dues to archdeaconry and synod and all other charges ordinary and extraordinary. The bp. reserves the right to add to or reduce these terms and to interpret obscure points.

231 *13 Apr. 1403, Worc.*[14] Regulation of an appropriation by Bp. Tideman of Kidderminster p.c. to the pry. of Maiden Bradley. The bp. had reserved for himself and his successors power to allot a suitable portion from its revenues for the support of the vic. This had not been done, so Bp. Clifford proceeded to carry it out.

---

[14] See Appendix 8. For the ordinance of Bishop Tideman reciting canons and constitutions for appropriation and the details of that of Pucklechurch, see *Historical Manuscripts Commission. Calendar of MSS, Dean and Chapter of Wells*, 1:251. Also Lyndwood 3, 16, *De Decimis*, the detailed list of tithes etc. stipulated as standard for the province of Canterbury.

fol. 74v　The vic. presented by the p. & c. and canonically instituted shall have a good manse in the street called Halestrete with barn, stable, dovecote and another small house with a yard lying along another part of the street opposite the manse and a meadow called Smalemede with a croft adjacent and all tithes of hay and sheaves of every sowing between Stour and Dernford and the tithe of hay of the ville of Nethermitton and a croft annexed to the cemetery of the ch. called Colvercroft containing two acres, and three crofts which are called Dodlescroft by Whitmarsh. The vic. shall have all kinds of small tithes throughout the par. of calves, milk, cheese, apples, flax, hemp, onions, garlic, doves, pigs, geese, vineyards, fisheries, honey, eggs, hens, bees, grazing of pastures, of barley and of gardens and yards wherever sown and of mills in the par. and every kind of oblation in the ch. of Kidderminster and elsewhere in the par. and the obventions of wax and mortuary offerings where death occurred within the par. together with the grass growing in the cemetery and trimmings of the trees, also the offerings in Lent that are customarily entered in the lenten roll from old time. They shall have the tithes of lamb's wool and fallen wood anywhere in the par. except in the woods of the pr. of Maiden Bradley called Borlash and the parks of Trimley and Aymour.

The charges that the present vic. and his successors are to support are: first, to find a par. chpln. and a dcn. in Kidderminster ch. and another chpln. in the chpl. of Mitton, all to serve by provision of the vic., and the bread and wine for the communion of the parishioners at Easter and for the ps. as often as they shall celebrate, and processional tapers and incense and other necessary lights both for morning masses and other canonical hours celebrated daily in the choir, also a lamp burning before the high altar in Kidderminster ch. The vic. will repair dilapidations of the chancel there not in excess of 3s. 4d., he will pay procurations whenever diocesan and archdeacon visit and he will receive offls. and commissaries of the bp. and archdcn. honourably.

Further, the present vic. and his successors shall pay annual pensions of 13s. 4d. to the bp. of Worc. and to the pr. and chap. of the cath. ch. and of five marks to the p. & c. of Maiden Bradley, at the due and customary terms, and for service owed to the bp. 2s. and for Peter's pence 3s. 4d. and tithes and aids granted to the king or legates or apostolic nuncios or to the diocesan and expenses of procurations in convocations of the clergy when need be. Other charges, ordinary and extraordinary, if such occur, the p. & c. of Maiden Bradley will assume. Liberty to increase or reduce the foregoing terms if need be is reserved and also the right to interpret obscurities.

fol. 75r The bp. refers to the statute of 4 Henry IV regarding appropriations, in a measure penal. Deeming this statute to be consonant with works of piety, and in case someone has claimed that the right and title of the religious in the canonically appropriated ch. can be impugned because of delay in complying with it, and striving, as required, to follow out the statute within the time stipulated, the bp. orders the religious of the conv. to distribute ten shillings among the par. poor of Kidderminster at Christmas Eve and ten more at Embertide, on Ash Wednesday, each year in perpetuity, six trustworthy parishioners to be present to testify to the true discharge of this.

232 *13 Apr. 1403, Worcester. [The vicge. of St. Philip and St. James, Bristol.]* Bp. Clifford having examined the register of Henry Wakefield, bp. of Worc. [1375-1395], found as follows. The bp. appropriated the ch. to the monas. of Blessed Mary, Tewkesbury, and their pry. of St. James, Bristol, with the consent of the pr. and chap. of the cath. ch. of Worc. and of others whose consent was required. The perp. vic. was to have a suitable portion from the fruits and revenues for his support and the charges incumbent on him, and later this was set out in detail with the consent of the religious of the monas. and pry.

Hugh Hopere, the first presentee to the vicge. was to have a manse suited to his position built at the expense of the a. & c. and maintained afterward by himself and his successors. They were to receive annually from the a. & c., out of the fruits and revenues of the ch. twelve silver marks at Michaelmas and the Annunciation, in equal portions, at the hands of the pr. of the pry. or cell of St. James. The religious expressly agreed that whenever the
fol. 75v payment stopped the bp. or custodian of the spirituals or administrator of the spirituals, if the see was vacant, could compel them to pay by sequestrating the revenues of the ch.

The a. & c. and the pr. of St. James were to have all tithes, revenues and emoluments, and the obventions that came into the hands of the vic. which he was to pay to them without diminution. He was to serve the divine offices faithfully and attend to the cure of souls. Other charges ordinary and extraordinary the a. & c. of Tewkesbury and the pr. and pry. of St. James were to assume at their expense. Having considered carefully the emoluments of the ch. and deciding that this ordering was suitable, adequate and just, the bp. decreed that it stand permanently.[15] Dated at his manor at Bredon, 10 Oct. 1394.

---

[15] 'eam habere volumus et decernimus robur perpetue firmitatis'.

Bp. Clifford next referred to the statute of 4 Henry IV, which is quoted in full with its reference to that of 15 Richard II, and its direction that any appropriations not complying with terms of the latter must do so before Easter. There follows the recitation of the earlier statute of 15 Richard II. The bp. orders the a. & c. and the pr. of St. James to have regard to the statute, the indemnities it prescribed and the penalties, and distribute annually 6s. 8d. to the par. poor at Christmas to add to their sustenance which grant he considers to be suitable in view of the poverty of the par. ch. and the various other heavy charges to which the religious were obligated.

fol. 76r   **233**   *10 Apr. 1403, London.* The a. & c. of Winchcombe, OSB, having obtained the p.c. of Bledington by a canonical appropriation,[16] the bp. directs that a suitable portion of the revenues be provided for the perp. vic. in the following terms and for any other vic. whenever the benefice is vacant. The vics. shall have for their manse the place of the rec.'s manse that was assigned from former times along with the buildings on it, which buildings the vic. will keep in repair at his own expense and rebuild whenever necessary. From the beginning [of this vicge.] the buildings standing there have been repaired by the mks. and are handed over to the vic. The vic. shall have from the a. & c. ten marks legal money yearly at the four principal terms in equal portions, i.e. at the Nativity of St. John the Baptist 33s. 4d., at Michaelmas, Christmas and Easter the same, the first term's payment to be at the next Nativity of St. John the Baptist. The vic. shall have nothing else from the oblations or emoluments of the ch. since the portion is sufficient for his support and responsibilities. He will see to the cure of souls and serve in the ch. and administer the sacraments and sacramentals for the parishioners or cause them to be served. Other charges ordinary and extraordinary incumbent on the ch. shall not be put upon the vic. but the a. & c. shall carry them. Vicars at their institution shall swear on the holy gospels that they will faithfully give to the a. & c. all oblations, obventions, trentals and other offerings in memory of the dead without diminution. The a. & c. shall receive all other revenues and emoluments except those assigned above to the vic. nothwithstanding any opposition the present vic. may make.

fol. 76v   If there is any deficiency in the payment of any portion of the ten marks at any term for fifteen days the a. & c. must pay double the part in arrears and

---

[16] Boniface IX had allowed the abbot and convent of Winchcombe to appropriate Bledington parish church without making provision for a vicar but Clifford made them do so (Rose Graham, *V.C.H.*, Glouchestershire 2:20).

all fruits of the par. are to remain sequestrated until the vic. is satisfied about that double sum. The bp. reserves for himself and successors, with the consent of the a. & c. by authority of the Apostolic See, a pension of 3s. 4d. as indemnity for himself and his ch. on this appropriation to be paid annually at Michaelmas by them. In addition, the bp. orders, with the consent of the a. & c. that 6s. 8d. from the fruits of the ch. or a quartern of corn and another of barley be distributed among the par. poor at Lent each year. The right is reserved to alter and interpret the terms.

The a. & c. considered the foregoing carefully and gave their full assent, 10 Apr. 1403.[17]

fol. 77r **234** *2 July 1404, Hillingdon.* Certification by Mr. John Medeford, archdcn. of Berkshire, of an exch. between John Rolton, chpln. of the perp. chty. of La Stane, called Chapelwyke, Salisbury dioc., and Wm. Bateile, perp. vic. of p.c. of Budbrooke (pat.: d. & c. of the coll. ch. of Blessed Mary, Warwick). Letter to the archdcn. of Worc. to induct.

235 *12 July 1404, Hillingdon.* Exch. between Dns. Lawrence Staundene, perp. vic. of p.c. of Lewknor, Lincoln dioc. and Dns. Walter Nicole, r.p.c. of Haseley (pat.: p. & c. of Holy Sepulchre, Warwick). Letters of inst. Lawrence had mand. to induct to the archdcn. of Worc.

236 *18 July 1404, Hillingdon.* Admission and inst. of John de Bekynton, clk., as r.p.c. of Herforton (pat.: pr. and chap. of the cath. ch. of Worc.), vacant by the resignation of Dns. Wm. Gernon. Letters of inst. and induction to the archdcn. of Worc. or his offl.

fol. 77v **237** *20 July 1404, Hillingdon.* Exch. between Dns. John Graunger, perp. vic. of p.c. of Bisley (pat.: Walter Medeford, clk., holder of the first portion of Bisley p.c.) and Dns. John Smalrugge, r.p.c. of Huish, Salisbury dioc. Letters of inst. John Smalbrugge had mand. to induct to the archdcn. of Worc. or his offl.

238 *5 Aug. 1404, Hillingdon.* Admission and inst. of Dns. Rich. Sangere p., as r.p.c. of Charfield (pat.: Rich. Ruyhale and John Broun), vacant by the resignation of Dns. Robt. Bremhull. Letters of inst. and induction to the archdcn. of Glouc. or his offl.

[17] 'In quorum omnium testimonium sigillum nostrum commune presentibus duximus apponendum.'

239 *6 Aug. 1404, Hillingdon.* Admission and inst. of Dns. Walter Hatherley, p., as perp. vic. of p.c. of Frampton-on-Severn (pat.: p. & c. of Clifford, Hereford dioc.) vacant by the resignation of Dns. Wm. Morffe. Letters of inst. and induction to the archdcn. of Glouc. or his offl.

fol. 78r   **240** *13 Aug. 1404, Hillingdon.* Admission and inst. of the venerable father Mr. Thos. Merke, one time bp. of Carlisle, to the recy. of p.c. of Todenham (pat.: a. & c. of Westminster) vacant by the death of Dns. Thos. Fitzjon. Letters of inst. and induction to the archdcn. of Glouc. or his offl.·

241 *31 Aug. 1404, Alvechurch.* Appointment of John Hadham, br. of the hosp. of St. John the Baptist, Warwick, to be master or warden of the house. He acted on a submission of the brs. brought by Rich. Hukyns and John Hadham. This reported the death of John Lodebrok, last master; it referred to the long standing custom that they should elect one of the brs. when the office became vacant, and the right of the bp. to confirm or annul an election. The poverty of the house and the many burdens and the ex-

fol. 78v   penses attending an election were more than they could readily face so they were giving up the right to elect for this turn and asked him to make the appointment, promising to accept it. Dated 28 Aug. 1404.

The bp. accordingly appointed John Hadham master with cure and rule, with administration in spirituals and temporals, saving all his rights and customs and those of the cath. ch. of Worc. John Hadham had mand. to induct to the archdcn. of Worc. or his offl. or in their absence to the dn. of the coll. ch. of Warwick.

242 *14 Sept. 1404, Tewkesbury.* Certification by the custodian of spirituals of Hereford dioc., the see being vacant, of an exch. between Hugh Vaghan, r.p.c. of St. John the Baptist de Troye, Llandaff dioc., can. of Hereford and preby. of Hampton in the same, and Rich. Dyer, r.p.c. of St. Lawrence de Swindon. The certificate stated that he acted by authority of a commission of the bp. of Worc. in respect of the ch. of St. Lawrence, Swindon, and instituted Hugh. On the same day John Googh, *literatus*, Hugh's proctor, promised obedience and had letters of induction to the archdcn. of Glouc. or his offl. And on the same day the bp. at Pershore, by authority of a commission of Thos., bp. of Llandaff, admitted and instituted Rich. into the said ch. of St. John the Baptist, John Googh again as proctor promising obedience in Rich.'s name, and letters of induction went to the archdcn. of Llandaff or his offl.[18]

fol. 79r **243** *16 Sept. 1404, Gloucester.* Certification by the pr. of the cath. ch. of Bath of an exch. between Dns. Walter Eymer, perp. vic. of the prebendal ch. of Bitton (pat.: Robert Hallum, can. of Salisbury cath. and preby. of Bitton in that ch.) and Dns. Walter Harlyng, *alias* Wyot, r.p.c. of St. Michael's without-the-North Gate, Bath. Letter to induct to the archdcn. of Glouc. or his offl.

244 *23 Sept. 1404, Stanley Monkton.* Admission and inst. of Dns. Robt. Oppy, p., to the perp. vicge of p.c. of Bisley, vacant by the death of Dns. John Smalrugge (pat.: Walter Medeford, chancellor of Salisbury cath. and holder of the first portion of Bisley p.c.). Letters of inst. and induction to the archdcn. of Glouc. or his offl.

245 *23 Sept. 1404, Wotton-under-Edge.* Admission and inst. of Wm. Hasulton, clk., as master of the house of scholars of Wotton-under-Edge vacant by the resignation of the last master, John Stone, p. (pat.: Dns. Thos. Berkeley, lord of Berkeley). Letters of inst. and induction to the archdcn. of Glouc. or his offl.

fol. 79v **246** *19 Sept. 1404, Llanthony by Glouc.* Admission and inst. of Mr. John Bradeley, *alias* Wynchecombe, p., b. ll., as perp. vic. of p.c. of Sherborne, vacant by the death of Dns. Thos. Pece (pat.: a. & c. of Winchcombe OSB). Letters of inst. and induction to the archdcn. of Glouc. or his offl.

247 *27 Sept. 1404, Bristol.* Admission and inst. of John Binnyng., p., to the chty. of St. Michael of Winterbourne which Wm. Stoke lately obtained but became vacant by his acquiring another incompatible benefice (pat.: Thos. Bradstone, squire). Letters of inst. and induction to the archdcn. of Glouc. or his offl.

248 *29 Sept. 1404, Bristol.* Inst. of Adam Byrell, p., as perp. chpln. in one of two chtys. of St. Katherine in St. Stephen's ch., Bristol, the collation of which devolved to the bp. Letters of collation and induction to the dn. of Bristol and the rec. of St. Stephen's.

---

[18] The clerk made this marginal note: 'Memorandum quod dictus Wygorniensis Episcopus habuit inter cetera in commissione domini Landavensis Episcopi sibi facta de qua inferius fit mentio potestatem sufficientem ad recipiendam a Ricardo Dyer infrascripto canonicam obedienciam ac etiam ad eundem inducendum mandatum.'

fol. 80r   **249**   *3 Oct. 1404, Winchcombe.* Admission and inst. of Dns. Thos. Bayly, p., as perp. vic. of Tytherington (pat.: p. & c. of Llanthony by Glouc.). Letters of inst. and induction to the archdcn. of Glouc. or his offl.

250   *12 Oct. 1404, Alvechurch.* Exch. between Dns. Wm. Dalton, rec. of Normanton-on-Soar, York [dioc.] and Dns. John Claypoll, r.p.c. of Northferney (pat.: Lady Ann, countess of Stafford). Letters of inst. Wm. had mand. to induct to the archdcn. of Glouc. or his offl.

251   *12 Oct. 1404, Alvechurch.* Admission and inst. of Dns. John Hulot, p., to the perp. chty. in St. Katherine's chpl. of Compton which Dns. Philip Sandrys lately and last obtained but became vacant by his death (pat.: Edmund, bp. of Exeter). Letters of inst. and induction to the archdcn. of Glouc. or his offl.

fol. 80v   **252**   *17 Oct. 1404, Alvechurch.* Exchange between Dns. Robt. Wayte, r.p.c. of Clevelode (pat.: Dns. John Berkeley, kt.), and Dns. Wm. Etyndone, perp. vic. of p.c. of Wargrave, Salisbury dioc. Letters of inst. William had mand. to induct to the archdcn. of Worc. or his offl.

253   *31 Oct. 1404, Hartlebury.* Exch. between Dns. Wm. Palmere, r.p.c. of Birtsmorton (pat.: Rich. Ruyhale), and Dns. John Hoo, perp. vic. of p.c. of Ebrington (pat.: a. & c. of Biddlesden, O.Cist., Lincoln dioc.). Letters of inst. and induction, John, to the archdcn. of Worc., William, to the archdcn. of Glouc. or their offls.

254   *11 Nov. 1404, Hartlebury.* Admission and inst. of Dns. Thos. Hulle, p., to the recy. of p.c. of Oldberrow (pat.: a. & c. of Evesham, OSB). Letters of inst. and induction to the archdcn. of Worc. or his offl.

fol. 81r   **255**   *14 Nov. 1404, Offenham.* Admission and inst. of Dns. John Blakenhale, p., as perp. chpln. in the first chantry of Blessed Mary in the p.c. of St. Mary Magdalen, Tanworth, newly founded (pat.: the noble lady Rosie *alias* Rose Mountfort), he having sworn to observe the terms of the foundation. Letters of inst. and mand. to induct.

256   *14 Nov. 1404, Offenham.* Admission and inst. of Rich. Boys, p., as perp. chpln. to the second and newly founded chty. of Blessed Mary in the p.c. of St. Mary Magdelen, Tanworth (pat.: Rosie *alias* Rose Mountfort). Letters of inst. and induction.

257   *1 Dec. 1404, London.* Admission and inst. of Wm. Congesbury, clk., to St. Werburgh's p.c., Bristol, vacant by the death of Dns. John Molsam, in the person of John Sperey, notary public, as proctor (pat.: a. & c. of Keynsham). Letters of inst. and induction to the archdcn.

fol. 81v **258** *7 Dec. 1404, Hillingdon.* Admission and inst. of Dns. Rich. Bedhampton, p., to the perp. vicge. of p.c. of Lechlade, vacant by the death of Dns. Rich. Porter (pat.: the noble lady Elizabeth Juliers, countess of Kent). Letters of inst. and induction to Mr. Wm. Forster and the offl. of Worc.

259 *8 Dec. 1404, Hillingdon.* Admission and inst. of Dns. John Wybbe, p. to Areley p.c. (pat.: William Reede, r.p.c. of Martley, Worc. dioc.). Letters of inst. and induction to the archdcn.

260 *13 Dec. 1404, Hillingdon.* Exch. between Dns. Robt. Craumford, r.p.c. of Matheme and Dns. John Ely, holder of a portion in the ch. of Leigh commonly called Chokenhulle (pat.: a. & c. of Pershore, OSB, in each instance). Letters of inst. and induction to the archdcn. of Worc. or his offl.

fol. 82r **261** *15 Dec. 1404, Hillingdon.* Admission and inst. of Dns. Thos. Yocflete, p. to the perp. vicge. of p.c. of St. Nicholas, Bristol, vacant by the death of Dns. Nicholas Adam (pat.: a. & c. of St. Augustine's, Bristol). Letters of inst. and induction to the archdcn. of Glouc. or his offl.

262 *21 Dec. 1404, Hillingdon.* Admission and inst. of Dns. Hy. Sclatter, p., to the recy. of p.c. of Coln Rogers (pat.: a. & c. of St. Peter's Glouc.), Mr. Henry Foulere, b. ll., acting as proctor. Letters of inst. and induction to the archdcn. of Glouc. or his offl.

263 *2 Jan. 1405, Hillingdon.* Exch. between Dns. Roger Gerarde, r.p.c. of Drayton Basset, Coventry and Lichfield dioc., and Dns. John Mounford, r.p.c. of Church Lench (pat.: Dns. Wm. de Beauchamp, lord of Bergevenny). Letters of inst. Roger had mand. to induct to the archdcn. of Worc. or his offl.

264 *4 Jan. 1405, Hillingdon.* Admission and inst. of Dns. Thos. Bakere, p., as perpetual chpln. in the chty. in the chpl. of Holy Trinity, Worc., fol. 82v newly founded by Rich. Norton, a citizen of Worc. (pat.: Thos. Belne and Rich. Garscoigne, bailiffs of the city on nomination by Rich. Norton). Letters of inst. and induction to the archdcn. of Worc. or his offl.

265 *10 Jan. 1405, Hillingdon.* Exchange between Dns. John Palmer, perp. vic. of p.c. of Wheatenhurst (pat.: p. & c. of Bruton, OSA, Bath and

Wells dioc.) and Dns. John Cleydon, perp. vic. of p.c. of Whitfield, Lincoln dioc. Letters of inst. John Cleyton had mand. to induct to the archdcn. of Glouc. or his offl.

266 *25 Jan. 1405, London.* Report of certification by John de Maydenhith, dn. of Chich. and custodian of the spirituals of Winch. dioc., *sede vacante*, of an exch. between Hy. Mory, r.p.c. of Colmer, Winch. dioc. and Walter Fitzperees, r.p.c. of Winterbourne (pat.: Thos. de Braddeston). Letters to the archdcn. of Glouc. or his offl. to induct.

fol. 83r **267** *13 Feb. 1405, London.* Report of Certification by Hy., bp. of Bath and Wells, of an exch. between Rich. Benet, rec. of the chpl. with cure of Weyford, Bath and Wells dioc. and Wm. Chamberlayn, r.p.c. of Widford (pat.: Thos. de la More). Letter to the archdcn. of Glouc. or his offl. to induct.

268 *16 Feb. 1405, London.* Exh. between Dns. John Bekynton, r.p.c. of Herforton (pat.: pr. and chap. of the cath. ch. of Worc.) and Dns. Hy. Beset, perp. vic. of p.c. of Buckland, Salisbury dioc. Letters of inst. Hy. had mand. to induct to the archdcn. of Worc.

269 *8 Mar. 1405, London.* Exch. between Robt. Newby, perp. vic. of p.c. of Tetbury (pat.: a. & c. of Eynesham, OSB) and Rich. Colles, r.p.c. of Garsington, Lincoln dioc. Letters of inst. and mand. to induct, Robt. to the offl. of the archdcn. of Oxford, Rich. to the archdcn. of Glouc. or his offl.

fol. 83v **270** *10 Mar. 1405, London.* Report of certification by Mr. Nicholas Wykeham, archdcn. of Wiltshire in the ch. of Salisbury, of an exch. between John Moryene, r.p.c. of Condicote (pat.: King Henry) and Wm. Curteys chpln. or custodian of the chpl. of St. Nicholas of Grafton, Salisbury dioc. Letter to induct to the vic. of p.c. of Blockley.

271 *12 Mar. 1405, London.* Admission and inst. of Dns. Salomon Haywode perp. vic. of p.c. of Henbury-in-Saltmarsh, of the bp.'s collation. Letters of inst. and induction to Mr. Wm. Forster, offl. of Worc.

272 *13 Mar. 1405, London.* Admission and inst. of Dns. Thos. Staunton, p., as perp. vic. of the prebendal ch. of Bitton, vacant by the death of Dns. Walter Harlyng (pat.: Mr. Robt. Hallum, can. of Salisbury and preby. of Bitton preb.). Letters of inst. and induction to the archdcn. of Glouc. or his offl.

fol. 84r   **273**   *16 Mar. 1405, London.* Admission and inst. of John Laughton, clk., as r.p.c. of Suckley vacant by the resignation of John Bremore (pat.: King Henry). Letters of inst. and induction to the archdcn. of Worc. or his offl.

274   *16 Mar. 1405, London.* Exch. between Dns. Rich. Lovecok, perp. vic. of p.c. of Haselor (pat.: d. & c. of the coll. ch. of Blessed Mary, Warwick), and Dns. Wm. Elys, perp. chpln. of the chty. of St. Mary in Alcester p.c. (pat.: Thos. Molynton, baron of Wemme), Mr. John Pavy acting as proctor for both Wm. and Rich. Letters of inst. and mands. to induct to the archdcn. of Worc. or his offl.

275   *20 Mar. 1405, London.* Admission and inst. of Dns. Rich. Dene, p., as r.p.c. of Boxwell, vacant by the free resignation of Salomon Haywode (pat.: a. & c. of St. Peter's, Glouc., OSB). Letters of inst. and induction to the archdcn. of Glouc. or his offl.

fol. 84v   **276**   *31 Mar. 1405, London.* Admission and inst. of Dns. Robt. Clyveley, p., as r.p.c. of Flyford vacant by the death of Dns. Rich. Warde (pat.: John Dycleston and Margaret his wife). Letters of inst. and induction to the archdcn. of Worc. or his offl.

277   *4 Apr. 1405, St. Alban's.* Admission and inst. of Mr. John Oudeby, clk., to the cany. and preb. in the coll. ch. of Blessed Mary, Warwick, which Mr. Geoffrey Wyke lately obtained by the free resignation of Mr. Robt. Vomwell, perp. vic. of p.c. of St. Lawrence in Old Jewry, London, who acted as proctor for Mr. Geoffrey. (pat.: Dns. Rich. Beauchamp, earl of Warwick), John Skelton, clk., acting as proctor. Letters of inst. and induction to the dn. of the coll. ch. above.

278   *29 Apr. 1405, Hillingdon.* Admission and inst. of Dns. Thos. Welton, p., as r.p.c. of Rockhampton (pat.: King Henry). Letters of inst. and induction to the archdcn. of Glouc. or his offl.

279   *9 May 1405, London.* Exch. between Dns. John Hokere, r.p.c. of St. Michael's, Bristol (pat.: a. & c. of Blessed Mary, Tewkesbury), and Dns. John Stoy de Lonthorp, perp. vic. of Seaton, Exeter dioc. Letters of inst. John Stoy had mand. to induct to the archdcn. of Glouc. or his offl.

fol. 85r   **280**   *29 May 1405, London.* Admission and inst. of John Knyght, clk., as r.p.c. of Dumbleton, vacant by the death of Mr. John Arches (pat.: a. & c. of Blessed Mary, Abingdon, OSB), Salisbury dioc. Letters of inst. and induction to the archdcn. of Glouc. or his offl.

281 *10 June 1405, London.* Admission and inst. of Dns. Wm. Robynes, p., as perp. vic. of p.c. of Ettington vacant by the free resignation of Adam Kymberworth (pat.: p. & c. of Kenilworth, OSA, Coventry and Lichfield dioc., on nomination of Lady Beatrix Shirley who had custody of the lands of Dns. Hugh de Shirley, late lord of Ettington, kt., while his son and heir, Ralph, was a minor). Letters of inst. and induction to the archdcn. of Worc. or his offl.

282 *11 June 1405, London.* Exch. between Dns. John Tye, r.p.c. of Halford, of the bp.'s collation and dioc. and Dns. Stephen Doune, r.p.c. of Shawe, Salisbury dioc. Letters of inst. Stephen had mand. to induct to the archdcn. of Worc. or his offl.

fol. 85v **283** *12 June 1405, London.* Admission and inst. of Dns. Hugh Vrenshe, p., to the perp. chty. in the chpl. of Holy Trinity, Worc., vacant by the death of Dns. Thos. Baker (pat.: Thos. Belne and Rich. Garscuyne bailiffs of that city). Letters of inst. and induction to the archdcn. of Worc. or his offl.

284 *9 July 1405, Canterbury.* Admission and inst. of Dns. Walter Adam, p., as perp. vic. of p.c. of Down-Hatherley, vacant by the death of Dns. Robt. Joye (pat.: prioress and c. of Blessed Mary of Usk). Letters of inst. and induction to the archdcn. of Glouc. or his offl.

285 *12 July 1405, London.* Report of certification by Dns. Philip [Repington], bp. of Lincoln [1405-1419], of an exch. between John Ryder, r.p.c. of Uppingham, Lincoln dioc., and Mr. David Bredewell, dn. of the coll. ch. of Westbury of the bp.'s collation. Letters to Wm. Lane, master of St. Mark's hosp. [Billeswick], John Wyke, r.p.c. of p.c. of St. Stephen and Wm. Bryghtlamton, dn. of Bristol, to induct John Ryder.

fol. 86r **286** *12 July 1405, London.* Admission and inst. of Dns. Roger Pynnok, p., as r.p.c. of Fretherne (pat.: John Harsefeld and Thos. Alforde, recently r.p.c. of Coaley). Letters of inst. and induction to the archdcn. of Glouc. or his offl.

287 *15 July 1405, London.* Admission and inst. of Dns. Wm. Baker, p., as perp. vic. of p.c. of Kington, vacant by the death of Dns. John Shokbrugh (pat.: p. & c. of Blessed Mary of Kenilworth, OSA, Coventry and Lichfield dioc.). Letters of inst. and induction to the archdcn. of Worc. or his offl.

288 *29 July 1405, London.* Exch. between John Appulton, r.p.c. of Woolstone (pat.: pr. of Deerhurst, OSA (*sic*) and Rich. Reede, r.p.c. of Woldham, Roch. dioc., John was admitted to Woldham p.c. at the collation of Thos., abp. of Cant., primate of England and legate of the Apostolic See, the temporalities of the vacant see of Roch. being in his hands and the spiritual and ecclesiastical jurisdiction also. Letters of inst. Rich. had mand. to induct to the offl. of the archdcn. of Glouc.[19]

fol. 86v **289** *11 Aug. 1405, London.* Admission and inst. of Dns. John Wynbold, p., as r.p.c. of Alderley, vacant by the death of Dns. John Horel (pat.: Nicholas Chawsey, lord of Alderley). Letters of inst. and induction to the offl. of the archdcn. of Glouc.

290 *23 Sept. 1405, Oxford.* Report of certification by Philip, bp., Lincoln, of an exch. between Thos. Feryby, guardian or custodian of Wappenham p.c., Lincoln dioc., and Wm. Dalton, r.p.c. of Northferney. The commission by which Thos. was admitted to Northferney stated that he was presented by Lady Anne countess of Stafford and wife of Dns. Wm. Burgchier, kt., in his absence *in remotis* with the King. Letter to the offl. of the archdcn. of Glouc. to induct.

291 *23 Oct. 1405, London.* Admission and inst. of Dns. Rich. Cone, p., as r.p.c. of Arley, vacant by the death of Dns. John Webbe (pat.: D. Wm. Rede, r.p.c. of Martley, Worc. dioc.). Letters of inst. and induction to the archdcn. of Worc. or his offl.

292 *7 Nov. 1405, London.* Admission and inst. of Thos. Aldebury, clk., to the preb. in the coll. ch. of Warwick which Robt. Mile, clk., lately obtained but now is vacant by his death (pat.: Lady Margaret Beauchamp, countess of Warwick), John Ympey, *literatus*, acting as proctor. Letters of inst. and induction to the offl. of Worc.

fol. 87r **293** *11 Nov. 1405, London.* Exch. between John Loughton, r.p.c. of St. John the Baptist, Suckley (pat.: King Henry), and Nicholas Bateman, r.p.c. of Blessed Mary, Chigwell, London dioc. Letters of inst. Nicholas had mand. to induct to the archdcn. of Worc. or his offl.

294 *21 Nov. 1405, London.* Admission and inst. of John Welle, clk., as r.p.c. of Wotton-under-Edge, vacant by the death of Mr. Wm. Forster (pat.:

---

[19] From this point the official of the archdeacon of Gloucester received letters of induction that normally went to the archdeacon.

Thos., lord of Berkeley, kt.). Letters of inst. and induction to the offl. of the archdcn. of Glouc.

295 *24 Dec. 1405, London.* Exch. between Mr. Roger Smyth, r.p.c. of Yate (pat.: Wm. Beaumond, lord of Yate), and Hy. Gardyner, r. of Exminster, Exeter dioc., Mr. Robt. Raulyn, clk., acting as proctor for Roger. Letters of institution. Henry had mand. to induct to the offl. of the archdcn. of Glouc.

fol. 87v **296** *1 Feb. 1406, London.* Admission and inst. of Dns. Wm. Tybot, p., as perp. vic. of p.c. of Honington (pat.: p. & c. of Coventry cath.). Letters of inst. and induction to the archdcn. of Worc. or his offl.

297 *2 Feb. 1406, London.* Exch. between Dns. John Chaundeler, r.p.c. of Quenington, (pat.: Br. Walter Grendon, pr. of the hosp. of St. John of Jerusalem in England) and Dns. Walter Lambard, perp. vic. of the p.c. of St. Cleer, Exeter dioc. Letters of institution. Walter had mand. to induct to the offl. of the archdcn. of Glouc.

298 *4 Feb. 1406, London.* Admission and inst. of Dns. Roger Cotys de Cudlynton, p., to the perp. chty. of Thos. le White, son of Walter le White, in St. Stephen's p.c., Bristol, vacant by the death of Dns. Rich. Egger (pat.: John Wyke, r.p.c. of the same church). Letters of inst. and induction to the offl. of the archdcn. of Glouc.

299 *13 Feb. 1406, London.* Report of certification by the offl. of the prebendal jurisdiction of Ogbourne in the ch. of Salisbury of an exch. between Rich. Hobcok, r.p.c. of Stowell (pat.: John Harsefeld and Matthew

fol. 88r Clyfford) and Ingelraum Woderoue, perp. chpln. of the chpl. of St. Margaret of Shalbourne, Salisbury dioc., of the above mentioned offl.'s jurisdiction. Letter to the offl. of the archdcn. of Glouc. to induct.

300 *23 Feb. 1406, London.* Collation, it having devolved on the bp. for that turn, of Dns. Thos. Calle, pr., to the custodianship of the hosp. of Holy Trinity, Longbridge-by-Berkeley. The post was vacant by the free resignation of Thos. Lefey, p., proctor of Mr. Reginald Pony, the last custodian or master. Letters of collation and mand. to induct to the offl. of the archdcn. of Glouc. or Salamon Haywode perp. vic. of p.c. of Henbury-in-Saltmarsh.

301 *18 Mar. 1406, London.* Admission and inst. of Robt. Meysy, p., to the recy. of p.c. of Heythrop (pat.: a. & c. of St. Peter's, Glouc.). Letters of inst. and induction to the offl. of the archdcn. of Glouc.

fol. 88v **302** *18 Mar. 1406, London.* Exch. between Dns. Rich. de Armes, r.p.c. of Frampton-Cotterell (pat.: Wm. Beaumount) and Dns. Hy. Mory, r.p.c. of Winterbourne (pat.: Thos. Bradeston). Letters of inst. and induction to the offl. of the archdcn. of Glouc.

303 *18 Mar. 1406, London.* Admission and inst. of Dns. John Granger, p., to the perp. chty. of Blessed Mary in the cemetery of Bisley p.c., of the bp.'s collation.[20] Letters of inst. and induction to the offl. of the archdcn. of Glouc.

304 *19 Mar. 1406, London.* Admission and inst. of Dns. Wm. Stoke, p., as perp. vic. of p.c. of Standish (pat.: a. & c. of St. Peter's, Glouc.). Letters of inst. and induction to the offl. of the archdcn. of Glouc.

305 *19 Mar. 1406, London.* Admission and inst. of Dns. John Vaghan, p., to the perp. vicge. of p.c. of St. Nicholas, Bristol, vacant by the death of Dns. Thos. Yokflete (pat.: a. & c. of St. Augustine's, Bristol). Letters of inst. and induction to the offl. of the archdcn. of Glouc.

fol. 89r **306** *30 Mar. 1406, London.* Admission and inst. of Dns. John Machoun, p., to the recy. of p.c. of Newington (pat.: a. & c. of St. Peter's, Glouc.). Letters of inst. and induction to the offl. of the archdcn. of Glouc.

307 *5 Apr. 1406, London.* Exch. between Rich. Norreys, r.p.c. of Hampton Meysey[21] (pat.: Rich., lord of St. Maur) and John Cresset, r.p.c. of Hartlebury, of the bp.'s collation. Letters of inst., collation and induction, John, to the offl. of the archdcn. of Glouc. or in his absence the perp. vic. of p.c. of Fairford, Rich., to the perp. vic. of p.c. of Kidderminster and Dns. Thos. Crosse, p.

308 *15 Apr. 1406, London.* Admission and inst. of Wm., son of John de Helton, p., to the perp. chty. in the chpl. of St. Mary Alcester built beside St. Nicholas ch. (pat.: Thos. Molynton, lord of Wemme). Letters of inst. and induction to the archdcn. of Worc. or his offl.

309 *24 Apr. 1406, London.* Admission and inst. of John Whyn, p., as r.p.c. of Heyford (pat.: a. & c. of Evesham). Letters of inst. and induction to the offl. of the archdcn. of Glouc.

---

[20] 'ipsius patris collacionem iure sibi devoluto spectantem.'
[21] When Clifford became bishop of London he sent John Cresset as rector of Hampton Meysey to pay *communia servicia* to the papal Camera, 3,000 florins (*Obligationes et Solutiones*, tome 57, fols. 169v, 170).

310   *24 Apr. 1406, London.* Admission and inst. of Rich. Oversley, p., to the perp. chty. in St. Katherine's chpl., Compton which Dns. Lawrence Watty last obtained and is now vacant by his death (pat.: Edmund, bp. of Exeter, son and heir of the late Rich. de Stafford, kt.). Letters of inst. and induction to the offl. of the archdcn. of Glouc.

311   *1 May 1406, London.* Admission and inst. of John Salesbury, p., as perp. vic. of p.c. of Bledington (pat.: a. & c. of Winchcombe). Letters of inst. and induction to the offl. of the archdcn. of Glouc. or in his absence to Edmund, rec. of Icomb.

312   *2 May 1406, London.* Admission and inst. of John Houden, p., as r.p.c. of Cotes, the collation devolving to the bp. Letters of collation and induction to the offl. of the archdcn. of Glouc. and the chpln. of Cirencester p.c.

313   *12 May 1406, London.* Admission and inst. of Dns. Wm. Dene, p., as r.p.c. of St. Lawrence, Bristol, vacant by the free resignation of Dns. John Forster (pat.: Thos. Broke, kt.), Mr. Rich. Wassebourne, clk., acting as proctor. Letters of inst. and induction to the offl. of the archdcn. of Glouc.

314   *13 May 1406, London.* Exch. between Andrew Swynford, r.p.c. of Stowe St. Edward's (pat.: a. & c. of Evesham, OSB), and Nicholas Sherman, r.p.c. of Manston, Salisbury dioc. Letters of inst. Nicholas had mand. to induct to the offl. of the archdcn. of Glouc.

315   *17 May 1406, London.* Exch. between Henry Mory, r.p.c. of Frampton Cotterell (pat.: Wm. Beaumount) and John Bretforton, r.p.c. of Sudeley (pat.: Dns. John Dalyngrugg, kt.). Letters of inst. and induction to the offl. of the archdcn. of Glouc.

316   *28 May 1406, London.* Exch. between Thos. Nelet, r.p.c. of Dodington (pat.: a. & c. of St. Peter's, Glouc.) and John Pirye, perp. vic. of p.c. of Great Sodbury, Mr. John Swynerton, notary public, acting as proctor (pat.: Br. John Clyve, sacristan of the cath. ch. of Worc.). Letters of inst. and induction to the offl. of the archdcn. of Glouc.

317   *11 June 1406, London.* Admission and inst. of Edmund Normanton, p., as perp. vic. of p.c. of Compton Magna, vacant by the resignation of Dns. John Aldestre (pat.: a. & c. of Walden). Letters of inst. and induction to the archdcn. of Worc. or his offl.

318   *19 June 1406, London.* Admission and inst. of Thos. Stoke, p., as perp. vic. of p.c. of Holt, vacant by the death of Dns. Walter Nicole, the collation devolving to the bp. Letters of inst. and induction to the archdcn. of Worc. or his offl.

319 *22 June 1406, London.* Admission and inst. of Henry Spelly, p., as chpln. of the perp. chty. of Rich. White, St. Stephen's, Bristol, vacant by the death of Dns. John Olyver (pat.: John Barstaple, mayor of Bristol). Letters of inst. and induction to the offl. of the archdcn. of Glouc.

fol. 91r **320** *16 July 1406, London.* Admission and inst. of John Everdon, p., as r.p.c. of Kington (pat.: John Toky de Kyngton), vacant by the death of Dns. Wm. Adams, William Everdon, *literatus*, acting as proctor. Letters of inst. and induction to the archdcn. of Worc. or his offl.

321 *16 July 1406, London.* Royal writ *quod admittatis* of 12 July stating that the King had recovered presentation to Oddingley ch. in ct. against Edward Cherleton, kt., and Wm. Gereward, clk. The bp. admitted the king's presentee, John Bathe, clk. Letters of inst. and induction to Dns. John Bele, r.p.c. of St. Helen's Worc.

fol. 91v **322** *4 Aug. 1406, London.* Admission and inst. of Dns. Roger Parys, p., as perp., vic. of p.c. of Tetbury, vacant by the death of Dns. Rich. Colles (pat.: a. & c. of Eynsham, Lincoln dioc.), Andrew Neuport, clk., acting as proctor. Letters of inst. and induction to the offl. of the archdcn. of Glouc. and Dns. John Cuffe, p.

323 *21 Aug. 1406, Hillingdon.* Exch. between Lawrence Staunden, r.p.c. of Haseley (pat.: a. & c. of Holy Sepulchre, Warwick) and John Aynolph, r.p.c. of Bebington by Midhurst, Chich. dioc. Letters of inst. John had mand. to induct to the archdcn. of Worc.

324 *21 Aug. 1406, Hillingdon.* Admission and inst. of Dns. Philip Tylere, p., to the perp. vicge. of p.c. of Wenland (pat.: p. & c. of Little Malvern) on nomination of the rec. of Bredon, Thos. Knyght, clk., acting as proctor. Letters of inst. and induction to the r.p.c. of Bredon, or in his absence to the par. chpln. of that ch.

fol. 92r **325** *23 Aug. 1406, Hillingdon.* Admission and inst. of John Warlowe, clk., to p.c. of Dodington (pat.: a. & c. of St. Peter's, Glouc.). Letters of inst. and induction to the offl. of the archdcn. of Glouc.

326 *12 Sept. 1406, Hillingdon.* Admission and inst. of Dns. John Godard, p., to the perp. vicge. of p.c. of Coln St. Aldwyn (pat.: a. & c. of St. Peter's, Glouc.), Mr. Henry Foulere, clk., acting as proctor. Letters of inst. and induction to the offl. of the archdcn. of Glouc.

327 *28 Sept. 1406, London.* Inst of Dns. Rich. Clifford, p., r.p.c. of Cleeve, of bp.'s patronage, Dns. John Rydere, p., acting as proctor. Letters of collation, inst. and induction to Dns. Rich. Noreys, r.p.c. of Hartlebury.

fol. 92v **328** *30 Sept. 1406, London.* Admission and inst. of Dns. Stephen Brydsale, p. as perp. vic. of p.c. of Acton Turville, vacant by the death of Dns. Wm. Godefray (pat.: Geoffrey Crumpe, custodian of the chty. of Tormarton). Letters of inst. and induction to the offl. of the archdcn. of Glouc.

329 *2 Oct. 1406, London.* Report of certification by Philip, bp. of Lincoln, of an exch. between Dns. John Haywode, r.p.c. of Charlton-on-Otmoor, Lincoln dioc., and Thos. Willicotes, r. of Burton (pat.: a. & c., Evesham). Letters to the archdcn. [of Worc.].

330 *30 Sept. 1406, London.* Admission and inst. of Dns. John Coumber, p., as perp. vic. of p.c. of Stone-by-Chaddesley Corbett (pat.: d. & c. of the coll. ch. of Blessed Mary, Warwick). Letters of inst. and induction to the archdcn. of Worc. or his offl.

fol. 93r **331** *5 Nov. 1404, Hartlebury.*[22] Collation of Nicholas Herbury, clk., to the archdeaconry of Glouc. in the cath. ch. of Worc., vacant by the death of Mr. Rich. Wynchecombe. Letters of collation and inst., induction and installation to Br. John, pr. of the cath. ch. and Mr. Wm. Forster, offl. of Worc. and John Chiew, clk.

332 *3 Oct. 1406, London.* Report of certification by Philip, bp. of Lincoln; of an exch. between Dns. John Martyn, r.p.c. of North Scarle, Lincoln dioc., and Dns. John Neweton, r.p.c. of Bradley, Worc. dioc. John Martyn was presented to Bradley by King Henry by reason of the duchy of Lancaster holding the patronage. Letters of induction to Mr. John Pavy.

333 *14 Oct. 1406, London.* Exch. between Mr. Rich. Bruton, r.p.c. of Olveston (pat.: pr. and chap. of the cath. ch. of Bath), and Mr. Nicholas Danyel, chancellor of Wells cath. John Bay, *literatus*, acting as proctor. Mr.

fol. 93v Rich. Pittes, can. of Wells and vicar-general in spirituals while Hy., bp. of Bath and Wells was overseas. Letters of inst. Nicholas had mand. to induct to the offl. of the archdcn. of Glouc.

334 *16 Oct. 1406, London.* Report of certification by Philip, bp. of Lincoln of an exch. between Dns. Thos. Draper, r.p.c. of Rousham, Lincoln

---

[22] 'Anno domini millesimo quadringentesimo quarto'. See Calendar, # 253 and # 254.

dioc., and Dns. Wm. Bacon, vic. of Tanworth (pat.: p. & c. of the monas. of Blessed Mary the Virgin and St. Michael the Archangel of Maxstoke, Coventry and Lichfield dioc.), Edmund Langeford, clk., acting as proctor for Thos. Letters to the archdcn. of Worc. or his offl. to induct.

335 *13 Oct. 1406, London.* Admission and inst. of Nicholas Hambury, p., as perp. vic. of p.c. of Bromsgrove (pat.: pr. and chap. Worc. cath.). Letters of inst. and induction to the archdcn. of Worc. or his offl.

fol. 94r **336** *22 Oct. 1406, London.* Report of certification by Philip, bp. of Lincoln, of an exch. between Mr. Hy. de Ferers, can. and preby. of the fifth preb. in the coll. ch., of Blessed Mary, Leicester, Lincoln dioc., and Dns. Wm. Brigge, can. and preby. of the preb. which Dns. John Spellesbury lately obtained in the coll. ch. of Blessed Mary, Warwick (pat.: Rich., earl of Warwick), John Neweton, clk., acting as proctor for Hy. de Ferrers. Letters to Mr. John Pavy, commissary general of the bp. of Worc. to induct Hy.

337 *22 Oct. 1406, London.* Admission and inst. of John Berkeley, clk., as rec. or custodian of the free chpl. of Tockington, vacant by the death of John Pygot, Jr. (pat.: Dns. John de Berkeley, kt.). Letters of inst. and induction to the offl. of the archdcn. of Glouc. or in his absence to Dns. John, chpln. or custodian of the chty. in the chpl. of Over, Worc. dioc.

338 *24 Oct. 1406, London.* Report of certification by Philip, bp. of Lincoln of an exch. between Wm. Gunby, r.p.c. of Ridlington, Lincoln dioc. fol. 94v and Thos. Higgeley, r.p.c. of St. Nicholas, Worc. city, of the collation of the bp. of Worc. Letters to Mr. John Pavy, commissary general or in his absence to Dns. John Bele, r.p.c. of St. Helen's, Worc.

339 *25 Oct. 1406, London.* Report of certification by Philip, bp. of Lincoln of an exch. between John Ewer, vic. of p.c. of Kimble Magna, Lincoln dioc. and Robt. Dyere, perp. chpln. or custodian of the perp. chantry of Wortley (pat.: Thos., lord of Berkeley). Letters to the offl. of the archdcn. of Glouc. to induct John.

340 *25 Nov. 1406, London.* Admission and inst. of Mr. Thos. Wybbe, p., as r.p.c. of Belbroughton, vacant by the free resignation of Dns. Nicholas Hambury (pat.: Dns. John Cheyne, kt., John Knyghtley, John Kyrkeby, John Cole and Wm. Offechurch, lord of Forfeld). Dns. John Ryder, p., acting as proctor. Letters of inst. and induction to the archdcn. of Worc. or his offl.

341 *26 Nov. 1406, London.* Admission and inst. of John Clerk de Eburton, clk., as r.p.c. of Lasborough (pat.: John Grevell de Shesyncote). Letters of inst. and induction to the offl. of the archdcn. of Glouc.

342 *1 Dec. 1406, London.* Admission and inst. of Dns. Thos. Wryght, p., as r.p.c. of Wolverdington (pat.: John Botyler, lord of Wolverdington), vacant by the free resignation of Dns. Wm. Folkfull. Letters of inst. and induction to the archdcn. of Worc. or his offl.

343 *5 Jan. 1407, Hillingdon.* Admission and inst. of Dns. John Pole as perp. vic. of p.c. of Bisley vacant by the free resignation of Dns. Robt. Oppi (pat.: Walter Medford holder of the first portion of Bisley ch.). Letters of inst. and induction to the offl. of the archdcn. of Glouc.

344 *7 Jan. 1407, Hillingdon.* Admission and inst. of Hugh Swayn, p., as perp. vic. of p.c. of Nether Guiting vacant by the death of the last vicar (pat.: Br. Walter Grendon, pr., of the hosp. of St. John of Jerusalem in England). Letters of inst. and induction to the offl. of the archdcn. of Glouc.

345 *23 Jan. 1407, London.* Inst. of Dns. Robt. Craven, p., as r.p.c. of St. Nicholas, Worc., of the bp.'s collation. Letters of collation, inst., and induction to Dns. John [Bele], r.p.c. of St. Helen's, Worc.

346 *31 Jan. 1407, London.* Admission and inst. of John Hamond, p., as r.p.c. of Witley (pat.: Walter de Cokesey, squire). Letters of inst. and induction to the archdcn. of Worc. or his offl.

347 *5 Feb. 1407, London.* Admission and inst. of John Shawe, clk., as r.p.c. of St. John's Bristol (pat.: a. & c. of Tewkesbury). Letters for his induction to the offl. of the archdcn. of Glouc. or in his absence to the dn. of Bristol.

348 *15 Feb. 1407, London.* Admission and inst. of Wm. Bayly, clk., as r.p.c. of Notgrove, vacant by the free resignation of John Baroun (pat.: Dns. Rich. de Beauchamp earl of Warwick). Letters to the offl. of the archdcn. of Glouc. to induct.

349 *15 Feb. 1407, London.* Admission and inst. of Adam Merston, p., as r.p.c. of Compton Winiates vacant by the free resignation of Dns. Hugh Swon (pat.: Edmund Compton, lord of Compton Winiates). Letters of inst. and induction to the archdcn. of Worc. or his offl.

350 *15 Feb. 1407, London.* Exch. between Dns. John Gay, r.p.c. of
fol. 96v   Hazlebury, Salisbury dioc. (pat.: p. & c. of Bradenstoke), and Dns. John
Pole, perp. vic. of p.c. of Bisley (pat.: Walter Medeford, Bisley p.c.). Letters
of inst. John had mand. to the offl. of the archdcn. of Glouc. to induct.

351 *19 Feb. 1407, London.* Report of certification by Robt. [Mascall], bp.
of Hereford [1404-1416], of an exch. between Dns. Wm. Sowy, chpln. of
the perp. chty. of St. Leonard de Peryton, Hereford dioc., and Dns. John
Walkere, perp. vic. of p.c. of Cam (pat.: a. & c. of St. Peter's, Gloucester).
Letters to the offl. of the archdcn. of Glouc. to induct.

352 *3 Mar. 1407, London.* Admission and inst. of Mr. John Pedewell, inceptor in laws, as r.p.c. of Holy Trinity, Bristol (pat.: a. & c. of Tewkesbury), John Pedewell junior acting as proctor. Letters of inst. and induction
to the offl. of the archdcn. of Glouc.

fol. 97r   **353** *7 Mar. 1407, Hillingdon.* Admission and inst. of John Norton, clk.,
as perp. vic. of p.c. of Overbury (pat.: pr. and chap. of the cath. ch.,
Worc.). Letters of inst. and induction to the archdcn. of Worc. or his offl.

354 *7 Mar. 1407, Hillingdon.* Exch. between Thos. Wysebech, r.p.c. of
Hartfield, Chich. dioc., and Rich. Alkryngton, r.p.c. of Minchinhampton.
Thos. was presented by King Henry who held the alien pry. of Minchinhampton because of the war with France. Thos. Croxby, clk., was proctor
for Thos. Wysebech and Thos. Makerell, clk., for Rich. Alkrynton. Letters
of inst. Thos. had mand. to the offl. of the archdcn. of Glouc. to induct.

fol. 97v   **355** *14 Mar. 1407, Withington.* Admission and inst. of Dns. Hy. Payn,
p., as perp. vic. of p.c. of Badgeworth, vacant by the death of Dns. Hugh
Moyl (pat.: prioress and c. of Usk, Llandaff dioc.). Letters of inst. and induction to the offl. of the archdcn. of Glouc.

356 *4 Apr. 1407, Withington.* Admission and inst. of Dns. Anian Bar-
bour, p., to the perp. chty. of Newport in par. of Berkeley (pat.: Dns. Thos.
Berkeley). Letters of inst. and induction to the offl. of the archdcn. of
Glouc.

357 *4 Apr. 1407, Withington.* Admission and inst. of John Everton, clk.,
as perp. vic. of p.c. of Wolverley (pat.: pr. and chap. of the cath. ch.,
Worc.). Letters of inst. and induction to Dns. John Hambury, p., because
the archdcn. has no jurisdiction there.

fol. 98r   **358** *10 Apr. 1407, Withington.* Admission and inst. of Dns. Thos. Billey,
p., as perp. vic. of p.c. of Northleach, vacant by the free resignation of Dns.

Wm. Horseleye (pat.: a. & c. of St. Peter's, Glouc.). By order of the bp., with the agreement of the patrons, twelve marks sterling, were to be paid to Wm. Horseley at the four terms of the year in equal amounts to the end of his life, by assignment of Thos. Billey and his successors. Letters of inst. and induction to the offl. of the archdcn. of Glouc. or in his absence to Dns. Rich., chpln. of Northleach p.c.

359   *11 Apr. 1407, Withington.* Admission and inst. of Roger Mose, clk., as r.p.c. of Kington (pat.: Walter Younge de Somervyleaston and Margery his wife). Letters of inst. and induction to the archdcn. of Worc. or his offl.

360   *13 Apr. 1407, Withington.* Admission and inst. of Dns. Wm. Turnour, p., as r.p.c. of Overswell (pat.: a. & c. of Evesham). Letters to the offl. of the archdcn. of Glouc. to induct.

fol. 98 v   **361**   *23 May 1407, Blockley.* Letter received from Robt., bp. of Hereford, dated at London, 4 May. It stated that he had given to Dns. Thos. Staundon, clk., a canonry in his cath. ch. and the preb. of Inkberrow there which Mr. Hugh Holbache had lately obtained. The latter had resigned it because of an exch. with the vacant preb. of Timberscombe in the ch. of Wells which was also of the collation of the bp. of Hereford. Staundon had been duly instituted as a can. and preby. and had been assigned his stall in the choir and his place in the chap. Bp. Mascall now asked the bp. of Worc. to have him or his proctor inducted into bodily possession of his preb. [of Inkberrow]. Accordingly a letter was written to the r.p.c. of Alcester and vic. of p.c. of Inkberrow and also to the chpln. of that par. to this effect.

362   *26 May 1407, Blockley.* Admission and inst. of Wm. Paunteley, clk., as r.p.c. of Beverston, vacant by the death of John Pokulchurche (pat.: a. & c. of St. Peter's, Glouc.). Letters of inst. and induction to the offl. of the archdcn. of Glouc. or in his absence to the parochial chpln. of p.c. of Beverstone.

363   *2 June 1407, Tewkesbury.* Exch. between Dns. Stephen Doune, r.p.c. of Halford, of the bp.'s collation, and Dns. John Tymmes *alias* Tysho, fol. 99 r   r.p.c. of Oversley (pat.: Wm. Sloughtre *alias* Clench). Letters of inst. and induction, Stephen, to the offl. of the archdcn. of Glouc. and John, to the par. chpln. of Halford.

364   *30 June 1407, Alvechurch.* Exch. between Dns. Thos. Knyght, r.p.c. of Upton-on-Severn and Dns. Rich. Noreys, r.p.c. of Hartlebury, of the bp.'s collation. Letters of collation, inst. and induction, Rich. to John

Stokes and Dns. Thos. Chewe, parochial chpln. of Upton, above, and Thos., to Dns. Thos. Crosse, p., and par. chpln. of Hartlebury.

365 *8 July 1407, Alvechurch.* Admission and inst. of Dns. Hy. Leek, p., as r.p.c. of Beaudesert (pat.: Dns. Wm. de Beauchamp, lord of Bergevenny). Letters of inst. and induction to the archdcn. of Worc. or his offl.

fol. 99v **366** *10 July 1407, Alvechurch.* Admission and inst. of Dns. Thos. Crosse, p., as r.p.c. of St. Ewen's, Bristol (pat.: a. & c. of Tewkesbury). Letters of inst. and induction to the offl. of the archdcn. of Glouc.

367 *14 July 1407, Alvechurch.* Admission and inst. of Dns. John Hay, p., as r.p.c. of Flyford-by-Graffton, vacant by the death of Robt. [Clyveley] (pat.: Wm. Clopton lord of Clopton). Letters of inst. and induction to the archdcn. of Worc. or his offl.

368 *14 Sept. [erased].*

APPENDIX 1

Licence to reconcile a church after pollution

fol. 2v **6** Ricardus permissione divina Wygorniensis episcopus dilectis filiis rectori et parochianis ecclesie parochialis de Hambury iuxta Wyche nostre diocesis, salutem graciam et benedictionem. Ut a quocumque episcopo catholico Sedis Apostolice graciam et execucionem sui officii obtinente dictam ecclesiam sanguinis effusione pollutam reconsiliari facere valeatis eo non obstante quod infra nostram diocesem situatur. Dum tamen aliud canonicum non obsistat, liberam vobis et episcopo huius reconciliacionem huiusmodi facere volenti tenore presencium concedimus facultatem, salvis nobis procuracionibus in hac parte debitis et consuetis. In quorum testimonium sigillum nostrum fecimus hiis apponi. Datum in hospicio nostro London ... die mensis Decembris anno domini millesimo quadringentesimo primo et nostre translacionis anno primo.

APPENDIX 2

St Andrew's Church, Eastleach, Exchange

fol. 13r **46** Vicesimo quinto die dicti mensis Aprilis Anno domini supradicto prefatus Reverendus pater in hospicio suo London quandam permutacionem inter dominos Walterum Stonyng Rectorem ecclesie parochialis Sancti Andree de Estlech sue Wygorniensis diocesis et Robertum Bowyer Rectorem ecclesie de Tappelowe Lincolniensis diocesis expedivit prefatumque Robertum ad dictam ecclesiam de Estlech per religiosos viros abbatem et conventum monasterii de Tewkesbury dicte Wygorniensis diocesis eidem Reverendo patri presentatum dicte permutacionis obtentu admisit. Prefatumque Walterum Stonyng ad dictam ecclesiam de Tappelowe auctoritate commissionis venerabilis patris domini Henrici dei gracia Lincolniensis Episcopi dicto Reverendo patri in hac parte facte eciam admisit receptis primitus in hac parte resignacionibus utrobique. Idem Reverendus pater prefatum Robertum in prefata ecclesia de Estlech dictumque Walterum in dicta ecclesia Tappelowe canonice instituit rectores cum suis iuribus et pertinenciis universis inductione prefati Walteri in corporalem possessionem dicte ecclesie de Tappelowe et eius canonica obedientia dicto venerabili patri Episcopo Lincolniensi specialiter reservata, et habuerunt litteras institucionum, habuitque dictus Robertus litteras inductionis directas archidiacono Gloucestriensi ut est moris et iuravit obedienciam domino.

APPENDIX 3

COLLATION TO A PREBEND

fol. 17r The Prebend called Brianes Provendre in the collegiate church of Westbury.

Quartodecimo die mensis Julii predicto prefatus vicarius in spiritualibus apud London vigore cuiusdam spiritualis commissionis per Reverendum patrem dominum Ricardum dei gratia Episcopum Wygorniensem supradictum sibi facte: prebendam in ecclesia collegiata de Westbury Wygorniensis diocesis Brianes Provendre vulgariter nuncupatam per mortem domini Thome Butiller ultimi incumbentis eidem vacantem et ad collacionem dicti Reverendi patris pleno iure spectantem, Nicholo Herbury contulit ipsumque prebendarium instituit canonice in eadem cum suis iuribus et pertinenciis universis, episcopalibus iuribus et consuetudinibus ac ecclesie cathedralis Wygorniensis dignitate in omnibus semper salvis et habuit litteras collacionis ac ad inducendum quarum tenores inferius describuntur et dictus Nicholus iuravit obedienciam domino tunc ibidem. Tenor vero commissionis spe-

Commissio specialis cialis memorate sequitur sub hiis verbis. Ricardus permissione divina Wygorniensis Episcopus dilecto nobis in Christo magistro Gilberto de Stone ecclesie Herefordensis canonico vicario nostro in spiritualibus generali, salutem graciam et benedictionem; Ad conferendum vice et auctoritate nostris quodcumque beneficium ecclesiasticum nostrarum collacionis et diocesis sine cura vacans ad presens vel in proximo vacatur, dilecto nobis in Christo Nicholo Herbury, clerico consanguineo nostro cum suis iuribus et pertinenciis universis ipsumque in corporalem possessionem beneficii eiusdem inducendum inducive faciendum ceteraque omnia et singula exercendum et expediendum que in premissis et circa ea necessaria fierunt seu quomodolibet oportuna vobis plenam et liberam potestatem committimus per presentes quas sigillo fecimus communiri. Datum in hospicio nostro London sexto die mensis maii anno domini millesimo quadringentesimo secundo et nostre translacionis primo. Tenor quidem litterarum collacionis sequitur sub hac forma.

Collacio prebende Gilbertus de Stone ecclesie Herefordensis canonicus Reverendi in Christo patris et domini Ricardi dei gratia Wygorniensis Episcopi ipso Reverendo patre in remotis agente vicarius in spiritualibus generalis, dilecto nobis in Christo Nicholo Herbury clerico salutem in eo qui est omnium vera salus.

fol. 17v Prebendam in ecclesia collegiata de Westbury Wygorniensis diocesis Brianes Provendre vulgariter nuncupatam quam nuper obtinuit in eadem dominus Thomas Butiller per mortem eiusdem Thome vacantem et ad collacionem dicti Reverendi patris pleno iure spectantem tibi isto quartodecimo die mensis Julii anno domini millesimo quadringentesimo secundo auctoritate nobis in hac parte commissa conferimus teque prebendarium instituimus canonice in eadem cum suis iuribus et pertinenciis universis, episcopalibus iuribus et consuetudinibus ac ecclesie cathedralis Wygorniensis dignitate in omnibus semper salvis. In quorum testimonium sigillum officialitatis Wygorniensis quo utimur in officio presentibus apposuimus. Datum

'Cum mandatu London die et anno suprascriptis. Tenor insuper mandati ad inducendum sequitur
ad inducendum et est talis. Gilbertus etc. ut supra. Dilecto in Christo decano de Westbury Wygorniensis diocesis salutem in eo qui est omnium vera salus. Quia nos prebendam in ecclesia collegiata de Westbury predicta Brianes Provendre vulgariter nuncupatam quam nuper obtinuit in eadem dominus Thomas Butiller per mortem eiusdem Thome vacantem et ad collacionem dicti Reverendi patris pleno iure spectantem, dilecto nobis in Christo Nicholo Herbury clerico auctoritate dicti Reverendi patris nobis in hac parte commissa contulimus ipsumque prebendarium instituimus canonice in eadem vobis mandamus quatinus eundem Nicholum vel procuratorem suum eius nomine in corporale possessionem dicte prebende cum suis iuribus et pertinenciis universis per vos vel alium inducatis, stallum in choro et locum in capitulo eidem prebende conveniencia ab antiquo prefato Nicholo vel procuratori suo huius assignetis, certificantes nos oportuno tempore cum tenore presencium quid feceritis in premissis. Datum London sub sigillo officialitatis etc. ut supra die et anno domini suprascriptis.

APPENDIX 4

LICENCE FROM THE BISHOP OF LONDON FOR ORDINATIONS

fol. 25r   **108** Reverendo in Christo patri ac domino Ricardo Dei gracia Wygorniensi Episcopo Robertus permissione divina Londoniensis Episcopus salutem et fraternam in domino caritatem, ut in instante die sabbati quatuor temporum videlicet die decima septima presentis mensis Decembris in ecclesia nostra cathedrali sancti Pauli London seu alibi infra nostram civitatem vel diocesem ubicumque loco utique ad hoc honeste iuxta vestre paternitatis arbitrium limitando quibuscumque literatis primam tonsuram et aliis clericis ulteriores non sacros et sacros eis convenientes ordines quos non dum sunt assecuti conferre, dum tamen nullum in hac parte canonicum obsistat impedimentum, licite et libere valeatis paternitati vestre reverende tenore presencium specialem licenciam concedimus et committimus vices nostras. In cuius rei testimonium sigillum nostrum presentibus duximus apponendum. Datum in manerio nostro de Hadham die decima mensis Decembris anno domini millesimo quadringentesimo primo et nostre consecracionis anno vicesimo.

APPENDIX 5

COMMISSION OF BISHOP CLIFFORD TO THE BISHOP OF DUNKELD TO HOLD OR-
DINATIONS IN THE DIOCESE OF WORCESTER

fol. 42v **126** Venerabili in Christo patri ac domino Nicholo dei gracia Dunkeldensi
episcopo, Ricardus permissione divina Wygorniensis episcopus salutem et sinceram
in domino caritatem. Proponentes nuper in ecclesia conventuali Cirencestrensi
nostre diocesis die Sabbati quatuor tempora videlicet terciodecimo kalendarum Oc-
tobris anno domini infrascripto prout ex officii nostri debito tenebamur generales
ordines celebrare idemque propositum nostrum sicut moris est per totam nostram
diocesem debite fecimus publicare. Verum quia negociis regiis et aliis quibusdam
arduis prepediti dictis die et loco personaliter interesse commode non valemus ad
celebrandum ordines huius die et loco de quibus premittitur necnon ad ordinandum
hac vice dumtaxat tunc ibidem auctoritatem nostram quoscunque viros dicte nostre
diocesis literatos seu beneficiatos in eadem ordinari volentes ac alios per eorundem
diocesanos sufficienter dimissos sufficientes titulos et litteras dimissorias coram
nostris in ea parte examinatoribus exhibentes ac eisdem tam primam tonsuram
quam omnes alios ordines minores et sacros quos nondum assecuti sunt canonice
conferendum tamen etate natalibus literatura et moribus inveniantur ydonei
aliudque canonicum non obsistat, vestre paternitati reverende de cuius consciencie
puritate industria fiduciam in domino gerimus specialem liberam in domino
facultatem concedimus per presentes quas sigillo nostro fecimus communiri. Datum
in hospicio nostro London terciodecimo die mensis septembris anno domini
millesimo quadringentesimo quinto et nostre translacionis quinto.

APPENDIX 6

BISHOP CLIFFORD INSTRUCTS HIS COMMISSARY GENERAL TO EXAMINE AN ELECTION

fol. 58v **158** Ricardus etc. dilecto nobis in Christo magistro Willelmo Forster commissario nostro generali salutem gratiam et benedictionem. Presentato nobis electionis negocio de fratre Johanne Staunford canonico prioratus sancti Sepulcri
Warrewic nostre diocesis vacantis ut asseritur per mortem fratris Petri Warrewyk
nuper eiusdem loci prioris ibidem ut asseritur celebrato nobis ex parte confratrum
prioratus eiusdem extitit humiliter supplicatum quatinus in negocio electionis huius
iuxta iuris exigenciam procedere dignaremur et eundem electum ac huius electionis
negocium quatenus ad nos attinet expedire, verum quia dicte electionis expedi-

cionem quibusdam arduis prepediti ad presens personaliter intendere non valemus,
ad procedendum in huiusmodi electionis negocio ac ipsam examinandum et
plenarie discuciendum ac fine debito terminandum cum suis emergentibus in-
cidentibus dependentibus et connexis, vocatis primitus coelectoribus vel op-
positoribus si qui fuerint in specie ac aliis quorum interest in genere qui electioni
vel electo predictis se opponere voluerint necnon ad audiendum coelectores et op-
positores huius si qui fortassis appareant ad faciendum eisdem iusticie comple-
mentum et eciam ad recipiendum et examinandum in forma iuris testes instructores
et instrumenta coram vobis in hac parte legitime producendum et exhibendum
prefatamque electionem confirmandum vel infirmandum ceteraque omnia et singula
faciendum et expediendum que in premissis et ea tangentibus negocia fuerint seu
quomodolibet oportuna. Vobis de cuius consciencie puritate et industria fiduciam
in domino gerimus specialem tenore presencium vices nostras committimus cum
cohercionis cuiuslibet canonice potestate. De diebus vestre receptionis presencium
fol. 59r   ac confirmacionis seu infirmacionis electionis predicte necnon quid feceritis et fac-
tum fuerit in premissis nos de toto processu coram vobis in hac parte habendo lit-
teris vestris patentibus harum finem continentibus reddatis opportuno tempore
plenius cerciores. Datum in hospicio nostro London quinto die mensis novembris
anno domini millesimo quadringentesimo secundo et nostre translacionis secundo.

APPENDIX 7

Observing the Statute of Appropriations

fol. 71r   **225** Ricardus permissione divina Wygornien' Episcopus dilectis nobis in Christo
magistro Willelmo Forster clerico commissario nostro generali et Ricardo Wynchecombe Archdiacono nostro Gloucestrie salutem gratiam et benedictionem. Inter
cetera in parliamento excellentissimi in Christo principis et domini nostri Henrici
dei gratia Regis Anglie et Francie illustris quarti apud Westmonasterium anno regni
sui quarto celebrato statuta et salubriter ordinata unum speciale statutum inspeximus contineri cuius tenor talis est. Item ordeignez est et establiez que lestatut
de lappropriacions des esglises et lenduement des vicaries en ycelle fait lan quinzisme le Roy Richard second soit fermement tenuz et gardez et mis en due
execucion. Et si ascune esglise soit appropriez par la licence du dit Roy Richard ou
de Roy nostre seignur qore est puis le dit an quinzisme econtre le dit statut que soit
duement reformez selonc le fait de dit estatut parentre cy et le feste de pasque
prochein avenir. Et si tiel reformacion ne ce face deinz le temps susdit que les ap-
propriacions et licence ent faitz soient voidez et de tout repellez et annullez pur

toutz jours forspris lesglise de Hadynham en la diocise de Ely. Tenor vero statuti dicti Regis Ricardi secundi de quo supra fit mencio sequitur in hiis verbis. Item purce que plusours damages et diseases sont sovent evenuz et veignent deja en autre as parochiens de diverses lieux par les appropriacions des benefices des mesmes lieux accordez est le assentuz que chescune licence desore affaire ascune esglise parochiel soit expressement contenuz et compris que le diocesane del lieu en le appropriacion de tieux esglises ordeigne une covenable summe dargent destre paiez et distributz annuelment des fructz et profites des mesmes les esglises par ceux qaveront les ditz esglises en propre oeps pur lour successours as poures parochiens des ditz esglises en aide de lour viver et sustenance a toutz iours. Nos autem subditorum nostrorum quoruncumque et specialiter Religiosorum virorum prioris et capituli ecclesie nostre cathedralis Wygorniensis ecclesias de Humelton et Stoke prioris ac Abbatis et conventus monasterii de Pershore nostre diocesis ecclesiam parochialem de Ekyntone eiusdem nostre diocesis in usus proprios obtinencium indempnitati paterna solicitudine prospicere cupientes ac eisdem viris religiosis ne forsan penam dicti statuti ignoranter incurrant de oportuno in hac parte remedio providere vobis coniunctim et utrique vestrum divisim committimus et mandamus quatinus cum omni celeritate possibili ad dictas ecclesias personaliter accedentes de et super omnibus et singulis dictarum ecclesiarum de Humeltone Stoke et Ekyntone et eorum cuiuslibet redditibus, emolumentis et obvencionibus quibuscumque ac valore annuo eorundem et in quibus rebus consistit ac cuius valoris et ad quas summas singule eorundem particule se extendunt, una cum omnibus et singulis oneribus vicarius dicte ecclesie de Humelton qui pro tempore fuerit necessario supportandis per viros fidedignos Rectores et vicarios ac aliquos alios valentiores parochianos ecclesiarum predictarum inquirendorum noticiam verisimiliter obtinentes in forma testium iurandorum iuratos veram et diligentem faciatis inquisicionem, citantes eciam dictos Priorem et capitulum ac Abbatem et conventum quod die Jovis in cena domini proximo futuro in ecclesia nostra predicta si sua viderint interesse legitime compareant coram nobis dicti videlicet prior et capitulum ordinacionem nostram super congruis porcionibus limitandis pro sustentacione vicariorum qui pro tempore erunt in vicaria dicte ecclesie de Humeltone quam quidem vicariam volente domino tunc ibidem intendimus ordinare ac summam argenti competentem pauperibus parochianis ecclesie de Stoke predicte distribuendam iuxta formam statuti huius limitare necnon dicti Abbas et Conventus nostram limitacionem summe distribuende pauperibus parochianis ecclesie de Ekynton predicte eisdem Abbati et conventui et eorum monasterio appropriate et unite audituri et subituri ulteriusque facturi in premissis quod tenor dicti statuti exigit et consonum fuerit racioni. Et quid feceritis et inveneritis in premissis nos citra dictum diem Jovis reddatis seu reddat alter vestrum auctentico sub sigillo distinctius cerciores. Datum in castro nostro de Hertlebury | primo die mensis Aprilis Anno domini millesimo quadringentesimo tercio et nostre translacionis anno secundo.

fol. 71v

APPENDIX 8

Folio 74
BISHOP CLIFFORD REGULATES THE VICARAGE OF KIDDERMINSTER

fol. 74r **231** Universis sancte matris ecclesie filiis presentes litteras inspecturis Ricardus permissione divina Wygorniensis Episcopus: salutem in eo qui est omnium vera salus. Cum nuper bone memorie dominus Tidemannus predecessor noster immediatus ecclesiam parochialem de Kydermynstre nostre diocesis auctoritate sua ordinaria prioratui de Maydenbradley et Religiosis inibi domino famulantibus appropriaverit et unierit reservata sibi et successoribus suis libera potestate de fructibus et obvencionibus dicte parochialis ecclesie congruam porcionem pro sustentacione vicarii ibidem qui pro tempore fuerit et pro suis supportandis oneribus limitandi assignandi et eciam ordinandi nos congruam huiusmodi porcionem nondum assignatam seu quomodolibet ordinatam ipso terciodecimo die mensis Aprilis Anno domini millesimo quadringentesimo tercio ad perpetuam rei memoriam limitamus taxamus assignamus in hunc modum tenore presencium ordinamus. In primis quod
fol. 74v vicarius ibidem | qui nunc est et successores sui qui pro tempore erunt per eosdem priorem et conventum presentandi et auctoritate nostra seu successorum nostrorum instituendi canonice in vicariam parochialis ecclesie memorate habebit et habebunt pro more et habitacione sua unum mansum competens in vico vocato Halestrete cum horreo stabulo et columbari et una alia parva domo cum curtilagio adiacenti ex alia parte dicti vici videlicet ex opposito dicti mansi ac unum pratum vocatum Smalemede cum crofto adiacenti ac omnem decimam feni et garbarum cuiuscumque seminis inter Stouram et Derneforde et decimam feni villate de Nethermitton et unam croftam annexam cimiterio dicte ecclesie vocatam Colvercroft continentem duas acras terre et tres croftas que vocantur Dodlescroftes iuxta Whitemersh. Item dicti vicarii habebunt et percipient omnes et omnimodas decimas minutas ubicumque infra parochiam ecclesie de Kydermynstre predicte videlicet vitulorum, lactis, casei, pomorum, lini, canapi, separum, allei (*sic*), columbellorum, porcellorum, aucarum, vinariorum, piscacionum, mellis, ovorum, pullanorum, apum, pascuorum, pasturarum, necnon ortorum et gardinorum ac curtilagiorum quocumque semine seminentur ac molendinorum quorumcumque infra dictam parochiam ubilibet existencium omnes eciam et omnimodas oblaciones tam infra ecclesiam de Kydermynstre quam alibi infra parochiam eiusdem ecclesie provenientes ac obvenciones cere et mortuaria quecumque tam viva quam mortua infra parochiam antedictam una cum herbagio crescente in cimiterio ecclesie predicte et putacionibus arborum necnon obvenciones quadragesimales que in rotulo quadragesimali inscribi consueverunt ab antiquo ac eciam decimas agnorum, lane et silve cedue infra dictam parochiam ubicumque exceptis bosco prioris de Maydenbradeley vocato Borlash et parcis de Trympley et Aymour. Onera vero per vicarium qui nunc est et successores

suos ibidem qui pro tempore erunt suis successoribus temporibus imperpetuum supportanda sunt hec. Inprimis vicarius loci modernus et quilibet successorum suorum qui pro tempore fuerit inveniet unum capellanum parochialem et unum diaconum in ecclesia de Kydermynstre ac alium capellanum in capella de Mitton predicta qui quidem capellani et diaconus dictis ecclesie de Kydermynstre et capelle deservient sumptibus dicti vicarii laudabiliter in divinis ac panem et vinum tam pro communione parochianorum dictarum ecclesie et capelle in die pasche et eciam pro presbyteris inibi quocienscumque celebraturis et cereos processionales ac incensum et alia luminaria tam pro missis matutinis et aliis horis canonicis in choro cotidie celebrandis et dicendis necessaria et unam lampadem ardentem ante maius altare in dicta ecclesia de Kydermynstre et defectus cancelli eiusdem ecclesie quociens eiusdem reparacio tres solidos et quatuor denarios non excedit suis propriis sumptibus reparabit ac loci diocesanum et archidiaconum quociens visitaverint procurabit et procuraciones eorum exsolvet ac officiales et commissarios episcopi et archidiaconi honeste recipiet ut est moris. Preterea vicarius modernus et quilibet successorum suorum solvet episcopo Wygorniensi qui pro tempore fuerit annuam pensionem tresdecim solidorum et quatuor denariorum ac priori et capitulo ecclesie cathedralis Wygorniensis annuam pensionem tredecim solidorum et quatuor denariorum, ac priori et conventui de Maydenbradley annuam pensionem quinque marcarum annuatim terminis debitis et consuetis et pro servagio debito loci Episcopo duos solidos et pro denariis sancti Petri tres solidos et quatuor denarios ac decimas et subsidia domino nostro Regi seu legatis aut nunciis apostolicis seu loci diocesano concedendas seu concedenda ac expensas procuratorum in convocacionibus cleri quociens opus erit. Alia vero onera si qua fuerint ordinaria seu extraordinaria prior et conventus de Maydenbradley predicti subibunt. Plena et libera potestate dictam vicariam si oporteat augmentandi vel diminuendi necnon premissis si necesse fuerit addendi et ab eisdem detrahendi et obscura si que fuerint interpretandi seu declarandi nobis et successoribus nostris specialiter reservata, episcopalibus iuribus et consuetudinibus ac ecclesie nostre Cathedralis Wygorniensis dignitate in omnibus semper | salvis. Verum quia inter cetera in parliamento excellentissimi in Christo principis et domini nostri domini Henrici dei gracia Regis Anglie et Francie illustris apud Westmonasterium anno regni sui quarto celebrato statuta et salubriter ordinata unum statutum quodammodo penale inspeximus contineri, considerantes itaque statutum memoratum operibus pietatis consonum et conforme et quod dictis religionis aut eorum iuri seu titulo si quod vel quem in dicta ecclesia eis prout asserunt appropriata canonice et unita occasione execucionis retardate statuti predicti poterit derogari, nos eo libencius affectantes infra tempus superius limitatum idem statutum exequi ut tenemur tenore presencium ordinamus ut iidem religiosi inter pauperes parochianos ecclesie parochialis de Kydermynstre supradicte decem solidos argenti in vigilia natalis domini et alios decem solidos feria quarta in capite jeiunii annis singulis in perpetuum distribui faciant presentibus sex personis fidedignis eiusdem ecclesie de Kydermynstre parochianis qui de et super distribucionibus huius modi testimonium si oporteat perhibeant veritati. In quorum testimonium sigillum nostrum fecimus hiis apponi. Datum in palacio nostro Wygorniensi die et anno domini suprascriptis et nostre translacionis anno secundo.

APPENDIX 9

The first table of ordinations given in the Appendix merely indicates the numbers serving parish churches as rectors when they came up for ordination. Out of a total of 45, 11 were of Worcester diocese. One other clerk, John Gerlethorpe, was ordained to a vicarage. Of all the other men who appeared for ordination only four, seemingly, were ordained to title of their own patrimony, which may mean that the more prosperous classes produced few candidates for the priesthood.

The second table of ordinations that gives totals each time they were held represents appearances of candidates, not necessarily the actual number receiving orders. This is because many received the first tonsure and subdeacon's orders on the same day. Where such an individual received the further orders of deacon and priest from Bishop Clifford or the bishop of Dunkeld he represented three in the total. Of the total of 935 by this reckoning, 448 were of the diocese of Worcester. Of the 935, 99 received orders at the hands of the bishop of Dunkeld. Subtracting these from the total one has a figure of 836 ordinations by Clifford, of which 388 were of candidates from outside his own diocese.

Some explanation of this should be sought. There can be some degree of correlation of Clifford's ordinations of men from other sees with absences of their bishops or vacancies but not too much is explained in this way. Braybrook was Bishop of London when Clifford conferred orders on a goodly number of men of that diocese in his first two ordinations. No reason is given for Braybrook licensing him. One may conjecture that he had secular duties as a jurist trained in civil law. The next sizable group of London ordinands was in March 1405 when the see was vacant after Braybrook's death and sixteen men appeared. Roger Walden, although provided there in December 1404, was not at first accepted by the King and was installed only in the last week of June following, too late for ordinations in Ember Days, when Clifford ordained eleven more of the diocese. Bubwith, who, after Walden's death, was provided in May 1406, was not consecrated until 26 September,[1] after Ember Days, and the bishop of Worcester officiated for eight candidates of the London diocese that month.

The see of Bath and Wells, next to the diocese of Worcester, had an absentee bishop, Henry Bowet, continually engaged in diplomacy for the King. He was

---

[1] John Le Neve, *Fasti Ecclesiae Anglicanae, 1300-1541* (London, 1963), 5:2.

served by a suffragan, John Greenlaw, Bishop of Soltania, *in partibus*,[2] and few calls to ordain came to Clifford from that source. It was somewhat otherwise with Exeter, the diocese that provided most candidates from outside, eighty-seven all told. Their bishop was Edmund Stafford, a long time colleague of Clifford in the royal administration and a predecessor as Keeper of the Privy Seal. Stafford was chancellor during the first two years of Clifford's Worcester episcopate and gave up the seals of office in the winter of 1403-04.[3] It was during this period that Clifford's ordinations of men from Exeter diocese were most numerous, 64 out of 87. One infers that when associates were occupied with duties that made attention to ordinations inconvenient he was available as unofficial suffragan.

Table 1

Incumbent	Rectory	Dioc.	Acolyte	Subdeacon	Deacon	Priest
Aude, Thomas	St. Michael's Southampton	Winch.			14-3-05 t.b.s. 123	
Barton, Mr. John	Lamyat	Bath & Wells				21-5-07 t.b.s. 132
Bolter. Roger	Blackawton	Exeter	17-12-01 108	17-12-01 t.b.s. 108		10-3-03 t.b.s. 114
Bristowe, William	St. Peter-the-Little, York	York			16-3-07 t.b.s. 131	
Burgonn, John	St. Olaves, Exeter	Exeter	15-2-04 119	15-2-04 t.b.s. 119		
Burton, Thomas	Withy Brook	Coventry & Lichfield			18-9-06 t.e.s. 129	
Carsewell, John	St. Leonard's in St. Vedast Lane	London				17-12-01 s.d. 108

    [2] T. S. Holmes, *The Registers of Walter Giffard and of Henry Bowet*. The Somerset Record Society, 13 (London, 1899), xxiv.
    [3] *C. Pat. R. 1401-1405*, 375.

Incumbent	Rectory	Dioc.	Acolyte	Subdeacon	Deacon	Priest
Cergeaux John	St. Martin by-Looe	Exeter			14-3-05 d.o. 123	
Clayton, John	Croxby	Lincoln				10-4-06 t.b.s. 127
Compton, Richard	Sutton	Worc.			18-9-06 t.b.s. 128	18-12-06 t.b.s. 130
Coneway Owen	Llanmuair	Llandaff	17-12-01 108			
Congesbury, Mr. William	St. Werburgh's Bristol	Worc.				10-4-06 t.b.s. 127
Coryngham, John	Deene	Lincoln				15-2-04 t.b.s. 119
Elvestowe, John	Tarporley	Coventry & Lichfield				18-2-02 t.b.s. 109
Eton, Henry	Dodding-hurst	London		18-12-06 t.b.s. 129		
Fouler, Walter	Longwatton	Lincoln	18-12-06 130	18-12-06 t.b.s. 130		
Gabriell, Richard	Pyworthy	Exeter	18-12-06 129	18-12-06 t.e.s. 129		
Guillam Richard ap.	Bridell	St. David's				18-9-06 t.b.s. 128
Hereford, Thomas	Redmarton	Worc.		11-3-02 t.b.s. 110		

Incumbent	Rectory	Dioc.	Acolyte	Subdeacon	Deacon	Priest
Kerby, John	Oddington	Worc.		10-3-03 t.b.s. 114		14-4-03 t.b.s. 116
Kyrke, Richard atte	Widmerpool	York			18-2-02 t.b.s. 109	
Kyrkham, William	St. Matthew Ipswich	Norwich	18-9-06 t.e.s. 128	18-9-06 t.e.s. 128	18-12-06 t.e.s. 129	
Lucy, Nicholas	Stratton-by-Ciren-cester	Worc.			19-9-05 t.b.s. 126	18-12-06 t.b.s. 130
Malton, Mr. Thomas	Lydyard-Millicent	Salisbury				17-12-01 t.b.s. 108
Morton Mr. Thomas	Brinkley	Ely		18-2-02 t.b.s. 109		
Newport, Thomas	Pontvane	St. David's			16-3-07 t.b.s. 131	
Penne, John	Fleet	Lincoln				13-6-05 t.b.s. 125
Petche John	Comberton Magna	Worc.	23-12-02 113	23-12-02 t.b.s. 113	10-3-03 t.b.s. 114	31-3-03 t.b.s. 115
Pole, John	Cardynham	Exeter				10-3-03 t.b.s. 114
Pylton, William	Shifnal	Coventry & Lichfield			18-2-02 t.b.s. 109	11-3-02 t.b.s. 110
Shaw, John	St. John the Baptist, Bristol	Worc.		16-3-07 t.e.s. 131	21-5-07 t.e.s. 132	14-9-07 t.b.s. 133

Incumbent	Rectory	Dioc.	Acolyte	Subdeacon	Deacon	Priest
Skydmore Richard	Shillingford	Exeter		17-12-01 t.b.s. 108	18-2-02 t.b.s. 109	11-3-02 t.b.s. 110
Sloughtre, Mr. Thomas	Baunton	Worc.				18-2-02 t.b.s. 109
Smyth, Mr. Roger	Yate	Worc.		31-3-03 t.b.s. 115	14-4-03 t.b.s. 116	9-6-03 t.b.s. 117
Spridlyngton William	Springthorpe	Lincoln	15-2-04 119	15-2-04 t.b.s. 119		
Stoke, John	High Ongar	Lond.			14-3-05 t.b.s. 123	
Swyft, John	Ditcheat	Bath & Wells			17-12-01 t.b.s. 108	18-2-02 t.b.s. 109
Thoralby, John	Eccleston	Coventry & Lichfield			13-6-05 t.b.s. 125	
Walesby, John de	Walesby	Lincoln			13-6-05 t.b.s. 125	
Warlowe, John	Dodington	Worc.			18-12-06 t.b.s. 130	24-9-07 t.b.s. 133
Warre, Thomas	Lammana	Exeter				21-5-07 t.b.s. 132
Willicotes, Thomas	Burton	Worc.			22-12-03 t.e.s. 118	
Wylflete William	East Ham	London			14-3-05 t.b.s. 123	

Incumbent	Rectory	Dioc.	Acolyte	Subdeacon	Deacon	Priest
Wynwyk, William	Beeby	Lincoln	17-12-01 108	17-12-01 t.b.s. 108		
3enn, Philip ap Rees	Mounton	St. David's				29-3-04 t.b.s. 120
	Perpetual vicarage					
Gerlethorp John	Inkberrow	Worc.				31-3-03 t.b.s. 115

Table 2

Date Place Section	Totals	Bath & Wells	Canterbury	Carlisle	Chichester	Coventry & Lichfield	Durham	Ely	Exeter	Hereford	Lincoln	London	Norwich	Rochester	Salisbury	Winchester	Worcester	York	
17-12-01 London 108	84	5						1	9		7	40	1		4	10	1	6	
18-2-02 London 109	71	2	2			1		3	12		9	18	1	2	2	7	2	9	St. Asaph 1
11-3-02 London 110	30	2	1			1		1	9			2		1	3	3	3	2	Llandaff 1 St. David's 1
1-4-02 Eltham 111	1													1					
23-9-02 Hillingdon 112	7										1	1			1		4		
23-12-02 Hillingdon 113	22		1									3			5	4	6	2	Dublin 1

Date Place Section	Totals	Bath & Wells	Canterbury	Carlisle	Chichester	Coventry & Lichfield	Durham	Ely	Exeter	Hereford	Lincoln	London	Norwich	Rochester	Salisbury	Winchester	Worcester	York	
10-3-03 Llanthony 114	67				1	1			3	4	1					1	55		Ossory 1
31-3-03 Hartlebury 115	55					1			14		3	1			1		31	1	Dublin 1 Ossory 1 St. David's 1
14-4-03 Worcester 116	19					1			3	4	1						9		St. David's 1
9-6-03 Westminster 117	9								3		1	1					3	1	
22-12-03 Hillingdon 118	1																1		
15-2-04 London 119	25	2			1				11		5			1	1	2	2		
29-3-04 Hillingdon 120	4								1								2		St. David's 1
25-5-04 Hillingdon 121	15								1	1	1					6	6		
20-9-04 Llanthony 122	92	1							1	8					4		76		St. David's 1 No dioc. 1
14-3-05 London 123	47	1	2	2	2				2		7	16	1	3	1	2	6	1	No dioc. 1
18-4-05 Hillingdon 124	6			1					3			1						1	

Date Place Section	Totals	Bath & Wells	Canterbury	Carlisle	Chichester	Coventry & Lichfield	Durham	Ely	Exeter	Hereford	Lincoln	London	Norwich	Rochester	Salisbury	Winchester	Worcester	York	
13-6-05 London 125	36		1			2			2		5	11		2			12		St. David's 1
19-9-05* Cirencester 126	60		1	1				1	1	5	3				4		43		St. David's 1
10-4-06 London 127	4										1						3		
18-9-06 Hillingdon 128	39		3						2		8	8	1			4	7	4	St. David's 1 Llandaff 1
18-12-06 London 129	15					2			7			1	1		1		1	2	
18-12-06* Compton 130	64					2	1				3				1	1	56		
16-3-07 Withington 131	51	3			1				3		3				2		36	2	St. David's 1
21-5-07 Blockley 132	57	1							2		7				1		43	3	
24-9-07 Blockley 133	54	1				2					6				3		40	1	St. David's 1

* By the Bishop of Dunkeld.

APPENDIX 10

Institutions and Exchanges

The figures below are not precise because quite often the entry in the register is chapel or chantry', 'vicarage or chapel', 'chantry or hospital'. As nearly as possible this tabulation indicates the numbers of institutions and exchanges by categories of benefice.

	Institutions	*Exchanges*
Rectories	75	66
Vicarages	58	20
Chantries	19	4
Prebends	5	4
Chapels	3	1
Hospitals	2	1
House of Scholars	1	
Archdeaconry	1	
	164	96

The large number of exchanges may suggest clerical restlessness and too brief tenure of appointment. Among the few clergy who held more than two benefices in succession during Clifford's six year episcopate, only five gave one up in a year or less. Winterbournebradston church and chantry stand out in the exchange market several times and there could have been factors other than restlessness on the part of the incumbents. There is little in this register to show the clergy of this diocese as belonging to the 'choppe cherche' fraternity of fourteenth century complaint.

WORKS CITED

Baddelay, W. St. C. *Place-Names of Gloucestershire*. Gloucester, 1913.

Barron, Caroline. 'The Tyranny of Richard II', *Bull. Inst. Hist. Research* 41 (1968), 1-18.

Boyle, L. E. 'The Constitution *Cum ex eo* of Boniface VIII', *Mediaeval Studies* 24 (1962), 263-302.

Bracton, Henry de. *On the Laws and Customs of England*, transl. of *De Legibus et Consuetudinibus Angliae* by G. E. Woodbine, ed. S. E. Thorne. Cambridge, Mass., 1968, pp. 21-45.

Chaplais, Pierre. 'English Diplomatic Documents, 1377-99', in *The Reign of Richard II; Essays in Honour of May McKisack*, ed. F. R. DuBoulay and Caroline Barron. London, 1971.

Chew, H. M. *The English Ecclesiastical Tenants-in-Chief*. London, 1932.

Continuatio Eulogii, ed. F. S. Haydon, Rolls Series, 9. London, 1863.

Corpus Iuris Canonici, ed. A. Friedberg. 2 vols. Leipzig, 1879-1881.

Dugdale, Wm. *Monasticon Anglicanum*, 6 vols. in 8 parts. London, 1817-30.

Finke, Heinrich. *Acta Concilii Constanciensis*. Münster in W., 1923.

Grassi, J. L. 'Royal Clerks from the Archdiocese of York in the Fourteenth Century', *Northern History* 5 (1970), 12-33.

Guide to Worcestershire Records, 4th ed. Gloucester, 1964.

Haines, R. M. *The Administration of the Diocese of Worcester in the First Half of the Fourteenth Century*. London, 1965.

——. 'Education of English Clergy in the later Middle Ages', *Canadian Journal of History* 4 (1969), 1-22.

Hartridge, R. A. R. *A History of Vicarages in the Middle Ages*. Cambridge, 1930.

Historical Manuscripts Commission. *A Calendar of the Manuscripts of the Dean and Chapter of Wells*, ed. W. H. B. Bird. 2 vols. London, 1907.

Historical Manuscripts Commission, 9th Report. Report on the Manuscripts of the Dean and Chapter of St. Paul's, ed. H. S. Maxwell-Lyte. London, 1883-84, Appendix, part 1.

Holmes, T. S. *The Registers of Walter Giffard and of Henry Bowet*. The Somerset Record Society, 13. London, 1899.

Holtzmann, Walter, O. 'Die englische Heirat Pfalzgraf Ludwigs III', *Zeitschrift für die Geschichte des Oberrheins*, Neue Folge, 43 (1929-30), 1-38.

Howell, Margaret. *Regalian Right in Mediaeval England*. London, 1962.

Jacob, E. F. 'The Canterbury Convocation of 1406', in *Essays in Medieval History Presented to Bertie Wilkinson*, eds. T. A. Sandquist and M. R. Powicke. Toronto, 1969.

—— *Essays in the Conciliar Epoch.* 2nd ed. Manchester, 1953.

—— *Henry Chichele and Ecclesiastical Politics of his Age.* London, 1952.

—— *The Register of Henry Chichele, Archbishop of Canterbury, 1414-1443.* Oxford, 1938-47.

Junghanns, Hermann. *Zur Geschichte der englischen Kirchenpolitik von 1399 bis 1433.* Freiburg in B., 1915.

Kirby, J. L. *Henry IV of England.* London, 1970.

Knowles, David. *The Religious Orders in England.* Cambridge, 1955.

Le Neve, John. *Fasti Ecclesiae Anglicanae 1300-1541*, vol. 5, St. Paul's, London, comp. Joyce M. Horn. London, 1963.

Lenfant, J. *Histoire du Concile de Constance.* Amsterdam, 1714.

Logan, F. D. *Excommunication and the Secular Arm in Mediaeval England.* Toronto, 1968.

Lyndwood, Wm. *Provinciale (seu constitutiones Angliae)*, ed. H. Hall. Oxford, 1679.

Matthew, Gervase. *The Court of Richard II.* London, 1968.

Nicolas, N. *Proceedings and Ordinances of the Privy Council of England.* Record Commission. 7 vols. London, 1834-37.

Obligationes et solutiones, Archivio Segreto Vaticano, vol. 55.

Pantin, W. A. *Documents Illustrating the Activities of the General and Provincial Chapters of English Black Monks*, Camden Society, 3rd Series, vol. 54. London, 1937.

Perroy, Edouard. *Diplomatic Correspondence of Richard II.* Camden Society, 3rd Series, vol. 48. London, 1933.

Powicke, F. M. and C. R. Cheney, eds. *Councils and Synods with Other Documents Relating to the English Church.* Oxford, 1964.

Powicke, Maurice. *The Thirteenth Century.* Oxford, 1953.

Rotuli Scotiae in Turri Londinensi ... Asservati. Record Commission. 2 vols. London, 1819.

Royal and Historical Letters during the Reign of Henry the Fourth, ed. F. C. Hingeston. Rolls Series, 18. 2 vols. London, 1860.

Smith, A. H. *The Place-Names of Gloucestershire.* Cambridge, 1964.

Smith, W. E. L. *Episcopal Appointments and Patronage in the Reign of Edward II.* Chicago, 1938.

Tout, T. F. *Chapters in the Administrative History of Mediaeval England.* 6 vols. Manchester, 1920-33.

The Victoria History of London, vol. 1, ed. Wm. Page. London, 1909.

The Victoria History of the County of Worcester, eds. J. W. Willis-Bund and H. A. Doubleday. 4 vols. & Index. London, 1926.

Weske, D. B. *Convocation of Clergy*. London, 1937.

Wilkins, D. *Concilia Magnae Britanniae et Hiberniae*. 4 vols. London, 1737.

Willis-Bund, J. W., ed. *The Register of Bishop Godfrey Giffard*. Oxford, 1902.

—— ed. *The Register of the Diocese of Worcester during the Vacancy of the See* usually called *Registrum sede vacante*. Oxford, 1893-97.

Wylie, James. *History of England under Henry IV*. London, 1884-1898; reprinted 1969.

INDEX OF PERSONS AND PLACES

Note: Numbers in roman type refer to sections; italic numbers, to pages.

A

Abbey Dore (*Dora*), Cist. Abbey, *Heref.*, tit. of, 114.

Abingdon (*Abyndon*), Ben. Abbey, *Berks.*, a. & c. patrons, 280.
monks of, 133.

Absolon, Elias, 7u.

Acle, ch., *Norf.*, 205.

Acon, see St. Thomas of, also St. Nicholas.

Acton Turville (*Torvill, Turvyle*), vic., *Glos.*, 175, 328.

Adam:
Nicholas, vic., St. Nicholas, Bristol, 261.
Walter, p. vic., Down-Hatherley, *Glos.*, 284.

Admescote, *Worcs.*, 7n.

Adams, William, rec., Kington, *Worcs.*, 320.

Ahab, King, *34*.

Alberese, Gerard de, *28, 29.*

Albrighton (*Albryghton*), ch., *Worcs.*, 181.

Alcester (*Alcestre, Alyncestre*), ch., *Worcs.*, 37, 48, 210, 274, 308, 361.
rec., 361, vic., 310.
chpln., 361.
Mary Chapel, 274, 308.

Alcester, Ben. Abbey, *Worcs.*, a. & c. patrons, 35.
tit. of, 114-116, 128, 130, 131, 133.
John, abt. of, 148.
monks of, 121, 122, 123.

Aldebury, Thomas, clerk, preb., coll. ch. Warwick, 292.

Alder, Thomas, bp.'s gaoler, *28 n 64, 34.*

Alderley:
ch., *Glos.*, 289.
ld. of, *see* Chawsey.

Aldestre, John, p., vic., Compton Magna, *Glos.*, 317.

Aldryngton, Richard *alias* Colcomb, p., 176.

Aldsworth (*Aldesworth*), *Glos.*, 7*l*.

Aleyn, William, mr. & scholar, 17, fellow, Clare Hall, Cambridge, acol. & subdcn., 109.

Alford, Alforde, Thomas, p., rec., Strensham, *Worcs.*, 83, rec., Coaley, *Glos.*, 174, 200, 286.

Alkryngton, Richard, rec., Minchinhampton, *Glos.*, 354.

All Saints:
chantry in, Bristol, 184.
chapel, Gloucester, 227.
ch. Broad St. (*Bredstret*), London, 113.
college, Maidstone, *Kent*, tit. of, 128.
rec. of, Worcester, 26, 218.

Alphage, martyr, 26, 11.

Alta Anngre, *see* Ongar, High.

Alve, Robert, vic., Aston Cantlow, *Warw.*, 142.

Alvechurch (*Alvechurche*), episcopal manor, *Worcs.*, 26, 7, 7a, documents dated at, 168-173, 177, 241, 250-252, 364-367.

Anne, countess of Stafford, 250, 290, *see* Stafford.

Anngre, *see* Ongar, High.

Apostolic See, *22 n 40*, 130, 131, 133, 220, 233, 288.

Appellant, *see* Lords.

Appelton, Appulton, John, rec., Woolstone, *Glos.*, 288.

Arches, Mr. John, rec., Dumbleton, *Glos.*, 280.

Arderne, Elena de, 7g.

Arley (*Areley*), ch., *Warw.*, 142, 259, 291.

Armes, Richard de, rec., Frampton Cotterell, *Glos.*, 302.

Arrow (*Arewe, Arwe*), ch., *Warw.*, 187.
rec., of, 210.

Bristol (*Bristoll, Brystol*), *24*, documents dated at, 184, 247, 248, 257.
dn. of, 15, 248, 285, 347; *see* Brighlamton
churches and vicarages:
  All Saints, 184.
  Blessed Mary in-the-Market, 163.
  Holy Trinity, 352.
  St. Ewen (*Sanctus Audoenus*), 15, 177, 366.
  St. John the Baptist, 131-133, 347.
  St. Lawrence, 313.
  St. Michael, 73, 279, 304.
  St. Nicholas, 261, 305.
  St. Peter, 82, 94.
  St. Philip and St. James, 232.
  St. Stephen, 248, 285, 319.
  St. Werburgh, 41, 127, 257.
chantries in St. Stephen's: Richard le White, 319, Thomas le White, 298, St. Katherine, 248.
religious houses:
  St. Augustine, Aug. Abbey, *31*, 15.
  a. & c. patrons, 55, 261, 305.
  tit. of, 113, 115.
  abt. of, 148.
  cans. of, 122, 126.
  St. Bartholomew, hosp., 197.
  St. James, Ben. Pry., 232.
  St. Lawrence, hosp., tit. of, 109, 128.
  St. Mark, hosp., Billeswick, 285.
  tit. of, 110, 123, 126, 131.
  master of, 148.
  St. Mary Magdalen, hosp., 222.
  Carmelite friary, 122.
  Franciscan friary, 122.
Bristol, mayor of, *see* Stephenys, John.
Bristowe,
  Thomas, master, hosp. of the Holy Trinity, Longbridge, *Glos.*, 34.
  William, rec., St. Peter-the-Little, York, 131.
Broadwell (*Bradewell*), ch., *Glos.*, 84.
Brockhampton (*Brokhampton*), *Glos.*, 7d.
Broke, Thomas, knight, 7t, 313.
Bromlee, Richard, clerk, preb., B.V.M., Warwick, 79.
Brommyng, Richard, 7j.
Bromsgrove (*Bremesgrove*), vic., *Worcs.*, 335.

Broun:
  John, 238.
  Richard, 220.
Bruern (*Bruera*), Cist. Abbey, *Oxon.*
  tit. of, 110, 119, 132, 133.
  monks of, 131-133.
Bruet, Thomas, p., rec., Coaley, *Glos.*, 174.
Bruton, Aug. Pry., *Somerset*, p. & c.
  patrons, 265.
  tit. of, 119.
Bruton, Mr. Richard, rec., Olveston, *Glos.*, 333.
Bruttesmorton, *see* Birtsmorton.
Bryan, Brian, Reginald, bp. Worc., 142.
Bryd, John, vic., Marden, *Wilts.*, 186.
Brydsale, Stephen, p., vic., Acton Turville, *Glos.*, 328.
Brygge, John, escheator, *24 n 48*.
Bryghlampton, Bryghtlamton, Brightlampton, William, dn. of Bristol, 15, 285.
Bryghtwelton, Thomas, OSB, Winchcombe, 165.
Brystowe, William, rec., St. Peter-the-Little, York, 131.
Brytwodesberwe, *see* Brightwellsbarrow.
Bubwith, Nicholas, bp. London, 1 n 2, 129.
Bucke, John, p., vic. Paineswick, *Glos.*, 88.
Buckfast (*Bukfast, Bukfeste*), Cist. Abbey *Devon*, tit. of, 119.
Buckland (*Boclond*), vic., *Berks.*, 268.
Bucks, archdcn. of, *28 n 64*.
Budbrooke (*Budbrok*), vic., *Warw.*, 207, 234.
Budden, Richard, vic., Bradley, *Wilts.*, 202.
Burbach, Mr. John, p., rec., Hampton, *Worcs.*, 44, rec., Hampton Lucy, *Warw.*, 50.
Burden, *see* Burdon.
Burdet:
  Thomas, clerk, rec., Aston Cantlow, *Warw.*, 59, 106, 112.
  Thomas, knight, 187.
Burdon:
  Henry, donzel, 32.
  Lady Joan, 63.
  Robert, 7t.
Burford, vic., *Oxon.*, 192.
Burford, Walter, 7f.
Burgchier, William, knight, 290.
Burgess, Burgeys:

John, rec., St. Swithun's Worc., 12.

John, rec., Tholeweston, Salisbury dioc., 173.

Burgonn, John, rec., St. Olave's, Exeter, 119.

Burnell, Hugh, knight, ld. of Holgot-Weoly, 180.

Burnell's Inn, Oxford, 35.

Burton, ch., *Warw.*, 118, 211, 329, rec. of, 25, *see* Willicotes, Thomas.

Burton:
Thomas, rec., Withy Brook, *Warw.*, 129.
Thomas, b. ll., fellow, B.V.M., Winchester, Oxford, 131.
William, vic., Newbold Pacey, *Warw.*, 168.

Butiller, Thomas, preb., Westbury, *Glos.*, 65.

Butler's Marston (*Merston Botiler*), vic., *Warw.*, 35.

Buyhale, *see* Bywell.

Bybury, *see* Bibury.

Bylleswyk, *see* Billeswick, Bristol, St. Mark.

Byrell, Adam. chantry p., St. Stephen's, Bristol, 248.

Byshampton, *see* Bishampton.

Byslegh, *see* Bisley.

Bysshopesdon, *see* Bishopston.

Bytlesden, *see* Biddlesden.

Bytton, *see* Bitton.

Bywell (*Buyhale*), *Worcs.*, 7s.

C

Cade, Thomas, bp.'s bailiff, 28 n 64.

Calenders' Fraternity, Bristol, 184.

Call, Thomas, vic., choral, Wells, 108, 109.

Calle, Thomas, p. warden, hosp., Holy Trinity, Longbridge-by-Berkeley, 300.

Calne, Richard, OSA, Llanthony, acol., 136, dcn., 114, p., 122.

Calverhull, John, clerk, proctor, 96.

Cam (*Camme*), ch., *Glos.*, 351.

Cambridge, county, 14.

Cambridge:
Scholars at, 211n.
Clare Hall, tit. of, 109, 111.
St. Radegund, Ben. Pry., Ny., tit. of, 109.

Campden, Campedene, *see* Compton.

Canonsleigh (*Canonlegh*) Aug. Pry., *Devon*, tit. of, 108.

Cantelupe, Walter, bp. Worc., 142.

Canterbury:
documents dated at, 146, 284.
Thomas, abp., *17*, 1, 11, 123, 124, 142n, 148, 288; *see* Arundel.
appeals to, *22 n 40*, 142n, jurisdiction of, 113.
official of, 2.
St. Gregory, Aug. Pry., tit. of, 109, 123.

Cantock (*Cantok*), *Glos.*, 7t.

Cardynham (*Cardynan*), *Cornwall*, ch., 114.

Carlele, Thomas, provost, Queen's Hall, Oxford, 168.

Carlisle, bp. of, *see* Merke, Thomas.

Carmelite Order, *see* Index of Subjects, members of, *22 n 40*.

Carnarvon, sheriff of, *22 n 40*.

Carpenter, Richard, rec., Condicote (*Condycote*) *Glos.*, 193.

Carpynter, William, *see* Halford.

Carsewell, John, rec., St. Leonard in St. Vedast Lane, London, 108.

Carthusian order, *see* Index of Subjects.

Cassy, John, 7k.

Castleford (*Castelford*), ch., *Yorks.*, 196.

Caumpedene, *see* Compton.

Cauntelow, *see* Aston Cantlow.

Cavell, Robert, rec., Alcester, *Worcs.*, 37.

Cergeaux, John, rec., St. Martin-by-Looe, *Cornwall*, 123.

Chaddesley Corbett, *see* Stone.

Chadwick (*Chaddyswyche*) *Worcs.*, 2.

Chamberlain, Chamberlayn, Chaumberleyn, Chaumbreleyn:
John, rec., St. Michael's, Bristol, 73.
Richard, 194.
William, rec., Widford, *Glos.*, 226, 267.

Chambre, de la, Robt., 7a.

Chapelwick (*Chapelwyke*), chantry, *Berks.*, 234.

Chapman:
—, 7j.
Thomas, rec., Hampton Meysey, *Glos.*, 57.

Charfield (*Charefeld*), ch., *Glos.*, 238.

Charing, abp.'s manor, *Kent*, documents dated at, 11.

Charles VI, King of France, *17 n 19*.

Charles de, *see* Ralegh.

Charleton, Cherleton:
Edward, knight, 69, 321.
John, clerk, proctor, 59.

Hadham, John, warden, hosp. of St. John the Baptist, Warwick, 241.

Hagel, John, rec., Alderley, *Glos.*, 289.

Hailes (*Hayles*), Cist. Abbey, *Glos.*, a. & c. patrons, 97.
appropriation to, 230.
tit. of, 112, 113, 122, 125, 126, 128, 131, 132.
abt. of, 148.
monks of, 113, 114, 130-133.
collectors of half tenth, 139.

Halesowen (*Oweyn*), Premonst. Abbey, *Salop.* and *Worcs.*
a. & c. patrons, 42.
tit. of, 131-133.
abt. of, 148.
can. of, 132.

Halestrete, (street), *Worcs.*, 231.

Halford, *Warw.*, 18, ch., 282, 363, chpln. of, 363.

Halford, William, *alias* Carpynter, 18.

Haliwell (*Halywell*), Aug. Pry., Ny., *Middx.* tit. of, 108, 109, 123.

Halle, William, p., vic., Lower Swell, 95.

Halling (*Hallyng*), ch., *Glos.*, 61.

Hallow, chapel, *Worcs.*, 40.

Hallum, Mr. Robert, can., Salisbury and preb., vic., Bitton, 192, 243, 272.

Halywell, Thomas, rec., All Saints, Broad St., tit. of King Henry, 113.

Hambury:
John, p. 122, 357.
Nicholas, rec., Horton, *Glos.*, 68, vic., Bromsgrove, *Worcs.*, 335, rec., Belbroughton, *Worcs.*, 340.

Hamme, Roger de, 7j.

Hamond, John, p., rec., Witley, *Worcs.*, 346.

Hampton, *see* Shirehampton.

Hampton:
episcopal manor, *Worcs.*, 7o.
preb., Hereford cath., 242.
ch., *Worcs.*, 44

Hampton Episcopi, *see* Hampton Lucy.

Hampton-in-Arden, parish, *Warw.* Coventry and Lichfield dioc., 25 *n 51.*

Hampton Lucy (*Episcopi*), Bishop's Hampton, episcopal manor, documents dated at, 101.
ch., 50.
vic., 44.

Hampton Meysey (*Meisy, Meysy*), ch., *Glos.*, 57, 75, 307.

Hampton Monialium, *see* Minchinhampton.

Hanbury-by-Wick (*Hambury by Wyche, Hambury iuxta Wycham*), *Worcs.*, episcopal manor, 7.
documents dated at, 176.
ch., 6, 149, App. 1.

Harbury, *see* Herbury.

Harescomb, chapel or chantry, *Glos.*, 199.

Harewell, John, donzel, 22.

Harlyng, *alias* Wyot, Walter, rec., St. Michael-Without, Bath, 243, vic., Bitton, *Glos.*, 272.

Harnhill (*Harnhull*), ch., *Glos.*, 186.

Harsefeld, John, 200, 286, 299.

Hartfield (*Hertfeld*), ch., *Suss.*, 354.

Hartlebury (*Hertilbury, Hertlebury*), *Worcs.*, episcopal manor, 7, 7u.
documents dated at, *33*, 82, 84, 87-94, 142, 217, 220, 222-225, 253, 254, 264, 331.
ch., 105, 307, 364, rec. cf. 327.
chapel in bp.'s castle, ordinations, 25, 115.

Haselbury, *see* Hazlebury.

Haseley (*Haseleye*), ch., *Warw.*, 235, 323.

Haselor (*Haselore*), vic., *Warw.*, 274.

Haselton (*Hasulton*), ch., *Glos.*, 62.

Hasulton, William, clerk, master of scholars' house, Wotton-under-Edge, *Glos.*, 126, 130, 245.

Hatherley, vic., *see* Down-Hatherley.

Hatherley, Walter, p., vic., Frampton-on-Severn., *Glos.*, 239.

Havering (*Havryge*), ch., Linc. dioc., 179.

Haukyn, John, p., proctor, 76.

Hay, John, p., rec., Flyford-by-Grafton, *Worcs.*, 367.

Hayle, John, 7t.

Haym, Adam, 7j.

Haywode:
John, rec., Charlton-on-Otmoor, *Oxon.*, 329.
Salamon, Salomon, p., rec., Boxwell, *Glos.*, 100, 275, vic.
Henbury-in-Saltmarsh, *Glos.*, 271, 300.

Hazlebury (*Haselbury*), ch., *Wilts.*, 350.

Helton:
John de, 308.
William de, chantry p., 308.

Judde, John, rec., All Saints, Worcester, 218.

Juliers, Lady Elizabeth, countess of Kent, 258.

Jury, John, 18n.

K

Kalends Fraternity, *see* Calenders.

Katherine, prioress, Cook Hill, *Worcs.*, 37.

Kemp, Thomas, bp., Lond., *13 n 2.*

Kempley, Mr. Edmund, rec., Tortworth, *Glos.*, 74.

Kempsey (*Kemese, Kemensey, Kemysey*), episcopal manor, *Worcs.*, 7, 7r, 133a.

Kenilworth (*Kenileworth, Kenylworth*), Aug. Pry., *Warw.*, p. & c.
  patrons, 47, 60, 281, 187.
  cans. of, 133.

Kent, countess of, *see* Juliers.

Kent, John, 7t.

Kerby:
  John, m.a. rec., Oddington, *Glos.*, 81, 114-116.
  William, precentor, Yorkminster, 81.

Kerdyf, William, 7f.

Kereswell, *Worcs.*, 7r.

Keynesham, Keynsham, Aug. Abbey, *Somerset*, 14n, a. & c. patrons, 41, 257, tit. of, 108, 122, 131.

Kidderminster (*Kydermynstre*), vic., *Worcs.*, 76, 171, 231, vic., of, 231, 307, App. 8.

Kimble (*Kymbel*), Magna, vic., *Bucks.*, 339.

King, John, 2.

Kingley (*Kyngeley*), *Warw.*, 210.

Kingswood (*Kyngeswode*), Cist. Abbey, *Glos.*, 148.
  tit. of, 119, 129.
  abt. of, 148.
  monks of, 114, 121, 122, 126.

Kington (*Kyngton*), ch., *Worcs.*, 320, 359.
  vic., 18n, 287.
  dn. of, 161.

Kinsham (*Kylmesham*), *Worcs.*, 7h.

Kinwarton (*Kynwarton*), ch., *Warw.*, 37.

Kirkstead (*Kirkestede, Kyrkestede*), Cist. Abbey, *Lincs.*, tit. of, 108, 109.

Knossington (*Knossyngton, Knossynton*), ch., *Leics.*, 47.

Knowles, chapel, Hampton-in-Arden, *Warw.*, 25 n 51.

Knyght:
  Edmund, vic., Winterbourne-Monkton, *Wilts.*, 178.
  John, clerk, rec., Dumbleton, *Glos.*, 280.
  Thomas, p., rec., Upton-on-Severn, *Worcs.*, 43, 364, proctor, 324.

Knyghtley, John, 68, 340.

Kydermynstre, *see* Kidderminster.

Kydermystre, William, rec., St. Nicholas Acon, London, 64.

Kylmesham, *see* Kinsham.

Kymberworth, Adam, vic., Ettington, *Worcs.*, 281.

Kymbel, *see* Kimble.

Kynarton, John, rec., Knossington, *Leics.*, 47.

Kyng, Kynge, Kynges, John, vic., Butler's Marston, *Warw.*, 35, 116.

Kyngeley, *see* Kingley.

Kyngeley, William, rec., Arrow, *Warw.*, 210.

Kyngham, Thomas, rec., Oversley, *Glos.*, 104, rec., Shawe, *Berks.*, 183.

Kyngton, *see* Kington; *see* also Toky, John.

Kynwarton, *see* Kinwarton.

Kyrke, Richard atte, rec., Widmerpool, *Notts.*, 109.

Kyrkeby:
  John, 68, 340.
  Thomas de, p., vic., Sherbourne-by-Warwick, 77.

Kyrkham, William, rec., St. Matthew's, Ipswich, 128, 129.

L

Lacock (*Lacok*), Aug. Abbey, Ny., *Wilts.*, tit. of, 110, 115.

Lambard, Walter, vic. St. Cleer, *Cornwall*, 297.

Lammana (*Lamena*), ch., *Cornwall*, 132.

Lamyat (*Lameyate*), ch., *Somerset*, 132.

Lancastell, Thomas, examiner, proctor, 40, 48.

Lancaster, duchy of, 332.

Lancastre, Thomas, *see* Lancastell.

Lane, William, master, St. Mark's hosp., Bristol, [Billeswick], 148, 285.

Langdon (*Langedon*), Premonstratensian Pry., *Kent*, tit. of, 109, 110.

Langebrugge, *see* Longbridge.

INDEX OF ORDINATIONS

Sections 108-133

Note: Names can be located within the sections by acol., subdcn., etc., which follow in sequence for each section.

[1] Strassburg.

John, subdcn., 128.

Roger, p., 116.

Bengeworth, William, OSB, Malmesbury, acol. & subdcn., 126.

Bengrove, Robert, dcn., 109, p., 110.

Bergevenny, Thomas de, dcn., 110.

Berkyng, William, O. Cist., Stratford, dcn., 123.

Berly, John, OSA, B.V.M. Overy, Southwark, subdcn., 108.

Bermengeham, William, O. Premonst., Halesowen, acol., 132.

Bernard, John, subdcn., 108, dcn., 109.

Bernyn, William, p., 108.

Bernyngham, John, O. Carm., London, subdcn., 108.

Berwe, Robert, OSB, Tewkesbury, acol. & subdcn., 114.

Bery, William, subd., 125, dcn., 126.

Besford, Besseford, John, acol., 130, subdcn., 133.

Beterynge, Thomas, subdcn., 115, dcn., 116, p., 117.

Bever, Robert, OSB, St. Alban's, p., 109.

Bishampton, Byshampton, see Bailly, Nicholas.

Blakemore, William, p., 130.

Blanket, Walter, p., 122.

Blebury, John, OSB, Malmesbury, dcn., 122.

Blesard, John, subdcn., 125, dcn., 130, 131.

Blockeley, Blokkeley, Blokley, John, OSB, Chertsey, acol. & subdcn., 108, dcn., 109, p., 113.

John, OSB, Pershore, acol. & subdcn., 132, dcn., 133.

Bodyer, Budyer, Richard, OFM, Gloucester, acol., 114, subdcn., 122.

Boldrug, William, subdcn., 133.

Bolter, Roger, rec., Blackawton, Devon, acol. & subdcn., 108, p., 114.

Boneton, William, subdcn., 128, dcn., 130, p., 131.

William, subdcn., 119, p., 120.

Borngan, John, subdcn., 119.

Bosbury, John, OSB, Pershore, acol. & subdcn., 132, dcn., 133.

Bottal, Mr. Roger, b. ll., acol. & subdcn., 108, dcn., 109, p. 115.

Bounde, Thomas, acol., 129.

Bovet, Roger, dcn., 115.

Bragge, John, dcn., 119.

Braklee, John, p. 116.

Bremore, Mr. John, can., St. Paul's, acol. & subdcn., 123, dcn., 124, p., 125.

Brerely, William, fellow, Merton Hall, Oxford., subdcn., 114, dcn., 115, p., 116.

Brightwelton, Thomas, OSB, Winchcombe, p., 114.

Bristow, Bristowe, Brystowe, Geoffrey, OSB, Malmesbury, dcn., 122.

John, subdcn., 114, dcn., 115, p., 116.

John, OSA, Bristol, acol., 122, p., 126.

Roger, OSB, Tewkesbury, subdcn., 114.

Thomas, O. Carm., Bristol, p., 122.

Thomas, OSB, Malmesbury, acol. & subdcn., 126.

William, O. Cist., Kingswood, dcn., 114, p., 121.

William, rec., St. Peter-the-Little, York, dcn., 131.

Brok, Thomas, OSA, London, dcn., 115, p., 128.

Brokeman, Brokman, John, OSA, Leighs, acol. & subdcn., 123, dcn., 125.

Brugge, John, acol., 122, p., 126.

Richard, OSB, cath. ch., Worcester, dcn., 122, p., 126.

Richard, acol., 121, subdcn., 122.

Brys, Thomas, O. Carm., Newington, Kent, acol., 125.

Bryt, William, dcn., 109.

Budyer, Richard, see Bodyer.

Bullouk, John, dcn., 110.

Burdet, Thomas, acol., 112.

Burgonn, John, rec., St. Olave's, Exeter, acol. & subdcn., 119.

Burton, Mr. Robert, acol. & subdcn., 130.

Thomas, rec., Withy Brook, Warw., dcn., 129.

Thomas, b. ll., fellow, B.V.M. of Winchester, Oxford, dcn., 131.

Buryman, Peter, subdcn., 115, dcn., 117.

Bussh, John, OFM, St. Nicholas, Exeter, subd., 114.

Byshampton, see Bailly, Nicholas.

Bywell, John, subdcn., OSB. St. Albans, dcn., 123, p., 125.

Caleys, Richard, O. Carm., London, acol., 108, subdcn., 109.

---

[2] No surname given but to title of nuns of Cook Hill as before.

³ Memoranda include a third spelling 'Willicotes'.

INDEX OF SUBJECTS

Religious houses are arranged under their order and are found individually in the Index of Persons and Places.

A

Absence:
  from Convocation, 146, 147.
  of bp., *10, 22-26, 36*, 29, 30, 51, 52.
  permission for, 160, 162, 163, 218.
  for study, *32*, 5, 211.
Absolution, 210, 214.
Accounts, of sheriff of Glouc., 7.
Acres, 7, 229-231.
Admonition, *33 & n 93-95*, 1, 11.
Adviser, theological, *14, 22-23*.
Adultery, *33*.
Advowson, King's claim to recovery, 59, 321.
Aids:
  to apostolic See, *29*.
  to legates & nuncios, 231.
  to King, *29*, 231.
  from knight's fees, 7.
  charitable for bp., 29, 30, 149, 152-154.
  for Greek Emperor, *18 n 22*.
Alien Priories: *31 n 83*, 354.
  Deerhurst, *Glos.*, 102, 288.
  Minchinhampton, *Glos.*, 354.
Alliance, *25*.
Ambassador, *14*.
Alms:
  charitable, 11, 160.
  free, *28*, 7e, 142n.
Altar, 231.
Antipope, *25*.
Appeals, *22 n 40*, 142n, 153.
Appellant, Lords, *15*.
Apostolic See, 220, 227, 233. See also Court of Rome.
Appropriations: *37*, 142.
  Statute of, *31*, 225, 231, 232, App. 7.

bp.'s right to amend terms, 225-233.
of particular chs:
  Aston Cantlow, 141, 142.
  Bibury, 222, 224.
  Bledington, *233*.
  Blessed Mary before-the-Abbey Gate, Gloucester, 227.
  Cleeve, *31*.
  Eckington, 225, 226.
  Himbleton, *31*, 225, 226, 229.
  Holy Trinity, Gloucester, 228.
  Kidderminster, 231.
  Pucklechurch, *32 n 86*, 231n.
  Sts. Philip & James, Bristol, 232.
  Stoke, 225, 226.
  Toddington, 230.
  Weston-on-Avon, *34*.
  procedure, *32 n 86*, 225n 1.
Arches, court of, 2, 150.
  official of, 2.
Archdeaconry, *30*.
  Gloucester, 30, 61, 139, 152, 222, 331.
  Worcester, 29, 137, 138, 149, 152, 153, 169, 223.
Archives, 142.
Arrears, 227, 228, 233.
Augustinian order, Houses:
  Barlinch, Pry., *Somerset.*
  Berden, Pry., *Essex.*
  Bicester, Pry., *Oxon.*
  Bisham, Pry., *Berks.*
  Bodmin, Pry., *Cornwall.*
  Bradenstoke, Pry., *Wilts.*
  Bristol, Abbey.
  Bruton, Pry., *Somerset.*
  Canonsleigh, Pry., *Devon.*
  Canterbury, Pry.
  Christchurch, Pry., *Hants.*

J

Jubilee, *see* Indulgence.
Judges, *16*.
Jurisdiction:
  of church, *22*.
  of abp., Canterbury, 113.
  of bishops, *27, 28*.
  of archdcns., 61, 357.
  of see of Rochester, 288.
  of see of Worcester, 52.
  of religious houses, *27*.
Jury: *27 n 63*, 14n.
  of parishioners, 225, 226.
Justices, of King, 12-15.

K

Keeper of Privy Seal, *15-17, 32*.
Knights' Fees, 7.

L

Larceny, *22 n 41, 28*, 14n, 210.
Law, Canon, *19 n 28, 22, 27 n 60, n 63, 29
  n 69, 32 n 86, 34 n 101*, 33n, 70n, 150n,
  231n.
Law, of England, *22 n 40*, 59n.
Lay Fee, 142n.
Legates, 231.
Letters dimissory, 4, 21, 25, 26, 108-133,
  135, 144, 157, 159, 212.
Liber Albus, *16 n 18, 24 n 48, 26 n 56,
  n 57, n 58, 27 n 62, 28 n 66, 29 n 68,
  34*.
Liberty of bp., *27, 28*.
Licence:
  to be absent, 162, 163, 218; for study, 5,
    211.
  to elect bp., *19*.
  for private oratory, *32*, 3, 22, 23, 27.
  for pilgrimage, 28.
  for private mass, 164.
  to promote in orders, 134, 136.
  to appropriate, *34*, 225.
  to reconcile a church, 6.
  to ordain: from vicar in spirituals, Worc.,
    134, 136 from bp., Lond., 10, 108-
    110, 112, 113, 117-121, 129, 135.
    from Primate, London, *sede vacante*,
    123, 124.

from bp. Roch., 17, 111.
from official & custodian of spirituals,
  London, 125, 127-128.
Litanies, 11.
Literatus (knight or lay person with legal
  training), 48, 93, 175, 178, 242, 292,
  320, 333.
Loans, *31*.
Locum Tenens, 77, 123, 146, 195.
Lollards, *26*.

M

Magnate, *see* Tenant-*in-capite*.
Mandates:
  of bp., Worc.
    call to repentance, 11.
    to examine an election, 16, 158.
    disciplinary, 24, 161, 210.
    summons to Convention, 147, 149.
    to hold inquisition, 150, 219.
    to search records, 151.
    concerning charitable aid, 149, 152.
    to collectors of tenths, 222, 223.
    concerning appropriation, 225.
  of abp., Canterbury, for Convention,
    146.
Mandates to induct, 33, 45, 53-60, 62-68,
  71, 73, 75, 79, 82, 87, 93, 103-105,
  107, 142, 167, 173, 175, 178, 179, 181,
  183, 186, 188, 189, 192, 193, 195, 196,
  198, 202, 204, 205, 207, 235, 237,
  242n, 250, 252, 263, 265, 268, 269,
  274, 277, 279, 282, 288, 293, 295, 297,
  298, 300, 314, 323, 333, 350, 354.
Manors:
  of abp., Canterbury, 11, 146.
  of bp., Worc., *20, 23, 25-26, 31 n 82*, 7,
    18n, 232.
  of bp., London, *35*, 11, 146, App. 4.
  of laity, 22, 23, 176.
Manses, 150, 225, 227, 228-233.
Manumission, *34*.
Marriage:
  of Princess Blanche, *18, 20, 21, 24*, 51,
    52.
  of Princess Joan, 7.
  of Princess Philippa, *18*.
  treaties, *18*.
  suit (incomplete), 133a.
Martyrs, *see* Alphage & Becket.